Richard Herne Shepherd, George Chapman

The Comedies and Tragedies

Richard Herne Shepherd, George Chapman

The Comedies and Tragedies

ISBN/EAN: 9783744673808

Printed in Europe, USA, Canada, Australia, Japan

Cover: Foto ©Thomas Meinert / pixelio.de

More available books at **www.hansebooks.com**

CHAPMAN'S DRAMATIC WORKS.

1

THE COMEDIES AND TRAGE-
DIES OF GEORGE CHAPMAN
NOW FIRST COLLECTED WITH
ILLUSTRATIVE NOTES AND A
MEMOIR OF THE AUTHOR IN
THREE VOLUMES

VOLUME THE THIRD

LONDON
JOHN PEARSON YORK STREET COVENT GARDEN
1873

THE
Widdowes Teares

A
Comedie.

As it was often prefented in the blacke
and white Friers.

Written by
GEOR. CHAP.

LONDON,

Printed for *Iohn Browne*, and are to be fold at his fhop
in Fleet-ftreet in Saint *Dunftanes* Church-yard.
1 6 1 2.

To the right Vertuous and truly *noble Gentleman*, Mʳ Io. REED of Mitton, in the Countie of Glocefter Efquire.

SIR, *if any worke of this nature be worth the prefenting to Friends Worthie, and Noble; I prefume this, will not want much of that value.* Other Countrie men haue thought the like worthie of Dukes and Princes acceptations; Iniufti fdegnij; Il Pentamento Amorofe; Califthe, Paftor fido, &c. *(all being but plaies)* were all dedicate to Princes of Italie. And therefore only difcourfe to fhew my loue to your right vertuous and noble difpofition, This poor Comedie (of many defired to fee printed) I thought not vtterly vnworthie that affectionate defigne in me: Well knowing that your free iudgement weighs nothing by the Name, or Forme; or any vaine eftimation of the vulgar; but will accept acceptable matter, as well in Plaies; as in many leffe materialls, masking in more ferious Titles: And fo, till fome worke more worthie I can felect, and perfect, out of my other Studies, that may better expreffe me; and more fit the grauitie of your ripe inclination, I reft.

Yours at all parts moft truly affected.
GEO. CHAPMAN.

The Actors.

Tharsalio the wooer.
Lysander his brother.
Thir. Gouernour of Cyprus.
Lycas ser. to the widdow Countesse.
Argus, Gent. Vsher.
3. Lords suiters to Eudora the widdow Countesse.
Hyl. Nephew to Tharsalio, and Sonne to Lysander.
Captaine of the watch.
2. Souldiers.
Eudora the widdow Countesse.
Cynthia, wife to Lysander.
Sthenio.
Ianthe Gent. attending on Eudora.
Ero, waiting woman to Cynthia.

The VViddowes Teares.

A COMEDIE.

Actus Primi.

Sccena Prima.

THARSALIO *Solus, with a Glaſſe in his hand making readie.*

T

How blinde imperfect Goddeſſe, that delights
(Like a deepe-reaching Stateſman) to conuerſe
Only with Fooles : Iealous of knowing ſpirits ;
For feare their pierſing Iudgements might diſ-
    couer
Thy inward weakneſſe, and deſpiſe thy power ;
Contemne thee for a Goddeſſe ; Thou that lad'ſt

The Widdowes Teares.

Th'vnworthy Affe with gold; while worth and merit
Serue thee for nought; (weake Fortune) I renounce
Thy vaine dependance, and conuert my dutie
And facrifices of my fweeteft thoughts,
To a more Noble Deitie. Sole friend to worth,
And Patroneffe of all good Spirits, *Confidence,*
Shee be my Guide, and hers the praife of thefe
My worthie vndertakings.

Enter Lyfander with a Glaffe in his hand, Cyn-
thia, Hylus, Ero.

Lyfand. MOrrow Brother; Not readie yet?
Thar. No; I haue fomewhat of the Brother in me; I dare fay, your Wife is many times readie, and you not vp. Saue you fifter; how, are you enamoured of my prefence? how like you my afpect?
Cynth. Faith no worfe then I did laft weeke, the weather has nothing chang'd the graine of your complexion.
Thar. A firme proofe, 'tis in graine, and fo are not all complexions.
A good Souldiers face Sifter.
Cynth. Made to be worne vnder a Beuer.
Thar. I, and 'twould fhew well enough vnder a maske too.
Lyfand. So much for the face.
Thar. But is there no obiect in this fuite to whet your tongue vpon?
Lyfand. None, but Fortune fend you well to weare it: for fhee beft knowes how you got it.
Thar. Faith, 'tis the portion fhee beftowes vpon yonger Brothers, valour, and good clothes: Marry, if you aske how we come by this new fuite, I muft take time to anfwere it: for as the Ballad faies, in written Bookes I find it. Brother thefe are the bloffomes of fpirit: and I will haue it faid for my Fathers honour, that fome of his children were truly begotten.

A Comedie.   7

Lyſand. Not all?
Thar. Shall I tell you brother that I know will reioyce you? my former ſuites haue been all ſpenders, this ſhall be a ſpeeder.
Lyſand. A thing to bee heartily wiſht; but brother, take heede you be not gull'd, be not too forward.
Thar. 'T had beene well for me, if you had follow'd that counſaile: You were too forward when you ſtept into the world before me, and gull'd me of the Land, that my ſpirits and parts were indeede borne too.
Cynth. May we not haue the bleſſing to know the aime of your fortunes, what coaſt, for heauens loue?
Thar. Nay, tis a proiect of State: you may ſee the preparation; but the deſigne lies hidden in the breſts of the wife.
Lyſand. May we not know't?
Thar. Not vnleſſe you'le promiſe mee to laugh at it, for without your applauſe, Ile none.
Lyſand. The qualitie of it may bee ſuch as a laugh will not be ill beſtow'd vpon't; pray heauen I call not *Arſace* ſiſter.
Cynth. What? the Pandreſſe?
Thar. Know you (as who knowes not) the exquiſite Ladie of the Palace? The late Gouernours admired Widdow? The rich and haughtie Counteſſe *Eudora*? Were not ſhee a Iewell worth the wearing, if a man knew how to win her?
Lyſand. How's that? how's that?
Thar. Brother, there is a certaine Goddeſſe called *Confidence*, that carries a maine ſtroke in honourable preferments. Fortune waits vpon her; *Cupid* is at her becke; ſhee ſends them both of errands. This Deitie doth promiſe me much aſſiſtance in this buſineſſe.
Lyſand. But if this Deitie ſhould draw you vp in a basket to your Counteſſes window, and there let you hang for all the wits in the Towne to ſhoot at: how then?
Thar. If ſhee doe, let them ſhoote their bolts and

fpare not: I haue a little Bird in a Cage here that fings me better comfort. What fhould be the barre? you'le fay, I was Page to the Count her husband. What of that? I haue thereby one foote in her fauour alreadie; Shee has taken note of my fpirit, and furuaid my good parts, and the picture of them liues in her eie: which fleepe, I know, can not clofe, till fhee haue embrac't the fubftance.

Lyfand. All this fauors of the blinde Goddeffe you fpeake of.

Thar. Why fhould I defpaire, but that *Cupid* hath one dart in ftore for her great Ladifhip, as well as for any other huge Ladie, whom fhe hath made ftoope Gallant, to kiffe their worthie followers. In a word, I am affured of my fpeede. Such faire attempts led by a braue refolue, are euermore feconded by Fortune.

Cynth. But brother? haue I not heard you fay, your own eares haue been witneffe to her vowes, made folemnely to your late Lord; in memorie of him, to preferue till death, the vnftain'd honour of a Widdowes bed. If nothing elfe, yet that might coole your confidence.

Thar. Tufh fifter, fuppofe you fhould proteft with with folemne oath (as perhaps you haue done, if euer Heauen heares your praiers, that you may liue to fee my Brother nobly interred) to feede only vpon fifh, and not endure the touch of flefh, during the wretched Lent of your miferable life; would you beleeue it Brother?

Lyfand. I am therein moft confident.

Thar. Indeed, you had better beleeue it then trie it: but pray Sifter tell me, you are a woman: doe not you wiues nod your heads, and fmile one vpon an other when yee meete abroade?

Cynth. Smile? why fo?

Thar. As who fhould fay, are not we mad Wenches, that can lead our blind husbands thus by the nofes? do you not brag amongft your felues how grofly you abuse their honest credulities? how they adore you for Saints: and you beleeue it? while you adhorne their temples, and they beleeue it not? how you vow Widdow-hood in their life time, and they beleeue you, when euen in the sight of their breathlesse corse, ere they be fully cold, you ioine embraces with his Groome, or his Phisition, and perhaps his poisoner; or at least by the next Moone (if you can expect so long) solemnely plight new Hymineall bonds, with a wild, confident, vntamed Ruffine?

Lysand. As for example.

Thar. And make him the top of his house, and soueraign Lord of the Palace, as for example. Looke you Brother, this glasse is mine.

Lysand. What of that?

Thar. While I am with it, it takes impression from my face; but can I make it so mine, that it shall bee of no vse to any other? will it not doe his office to you or you: and as well to my Groome as to my selfe? Brother, Monopolies are cryed downe. Is it not madnes for me to beleeue, when I haue conquer'd that Fort of chastitie the great Countesse; that if another man of my making, and mettall, shall assault her: her eies and eares should lose their function, her other parts their vse, as if Nature had made her all in vaine, vnlesse I only had stumbl'd into her quarters.

Cynth. Brother: I feare mee in your trauaile, you haue drunck too much of that Italian aire, that hath infected the whole masse of your ingenuous Nature; dried vp in you all sap of generous disposition, poisond the very Essence of your soule, and so polluted your senses, that whatsoeuer enters there, takes from them contagion, and is to your fancie represented as foule and tainted, which in it selfe perhaps is spotlesse.

Thar. No sister, it hath refin'd my senses, and made mee see with cleare eies, and to iudge of obiects, as they truly are, not as they seeme, and through their maske to discerne the true face of thinges. It tells me how short liu'd Widdowes teares are, that their weeping

is in truth but laughing vnder a Maske, that they
mourne in their Gownes, and laugh in their Sleeues,
all which I beleeue as a Delphian Oracle: and am
resolu'd to burne in that faith, And in that resolution
doe I march to the great Ladie.

Lysand. You lose time Brother in discourse, by this
had you bore vp with the Ladie and clapt her aboord,
for I knowe your confidence will not dwell long in the
seruice.

Thar. No, I will performe it in the Conquerours stile.
Your way is, not to winne *Penelope* by suite, but by
surprise. The Castle's carried by a sodaine assault, that
would perhaps fit out a twelue-moneths siege. It would
bee a good breeding to my yong Nephew here, if
hee could procure a stand at the Palace, to see with
what alacritie Ile a-coast her Countesship, in what
garbe I will woo her, with what facilitie I will winne
her.

Lysand. It shall goe hard but weele heare your entertainement for your confidence sake.

Thar. And hauing wonne her Nephew; This sweet
face
Which all the Citie saies, is so like me,
Like me shall be preferr'd, for I will wed thee
To my great widdowes Daughter and sole Heire,
The louely sparke, the bright *Laodice.*

Lysand. A good pleasant dreame.

Thar. In this eie I see
That fire that shall in me inflame the Mother,
And that in this shall set on fire the Daughter.
It goes Sir in a bloud; beleeue me brother,
These destinies goe euer in a bloud.

Lysand. These diseases doe, brother, take heede of
them:
Fare you well; Take heede you be not baffeld.

Exeunt Lys. Cynth. Hyl. Ero. manet Thars.

Thar. Now thou that art the third blind Deitie
That gouernes earth in all her happinesse,
The life of all endowments, *Confidence;*

A Comedie.

Direct and prosper my intention.
Command thy seruant Deities, Loue and Fortune
To second my attempts for this great Ladie,
Whose Page I lately was; That shee, whose bord
I might not sit at, I may boord a bed
And vnder bring, who bore so high her head.   *Exit.*

Lysander, Lycus.

Lyc. 'Tis miraculous that you tell me Sir : he come to woo our Ladie Mistris for his wife?
Lys. 'Tis a phrensie he is possest with, and wil not be cur'd but by some violent remedie. And you shall fauour me so much to make me a spectator of the Scene. But is shee (say you) alreadie accessible for Suiters? I thought shee would haue stood so stifly on her Widdow vow, that shee would not endure the sight of a Suiter.
Lyc. Faith Sir, *Penelope* could not barre her gates against her woers, but shee will still be Mistris of her selfe. It is you know, a certaine Itch in femall bloud, they loue to be su'd to : but sheele hearken to no Suiters.
Lys. But by your leaue *Lycus, Penelope* is not so wise as her husband *Vlysses,* for he fearing the iawes of the *Syren,* stopt his eares with waxe against her voice. They that feare the Adders sting, will not come neare her hissing. Is any Suiter with her now?
Lyc. A Spartan Lord, dating himselfe our great Viceroies Kinsman, and two or three other of his Countrie Lords, as spots in his train. He comes armed with his Altitudes letters in grace of his person, with promise to make her a Duchesse if shee embrace the match. This is no meane attraction to her high thoughts; but yet shee disdaines him.
Lys. And how then shall my brother presume of acceptance? yet I hold it much more vnder her content-

ment, to marrie fuch a Naftie braggart, then vnder her honour to wed my brother : A Gentleman (though I fai't) more honourably defcended than that Lord: who perhaps, for all his Anceftrie would bee much troubled to name you the place where his Father was borne.

Lyc. Nay, I hold no comparifon betwixt your brother & him. And the Venerean difeafe, to which they fay, he has beene long wedded, fhall I hope firft rot him, ere fhee endure the fauour of his Sulphurous breath. Well, her Ladifhip is at hand; y'are beft take you to your ftand.

Lyf. Thankes good friend *Lycus.* *Exit.*

Enter Argus barehead, with whome another Vfher Lycus ioynes, going ouer the Stage. Hiarbas, and Pforabeus next, Rebus fingle before Eudora, Laodice, Sthenia bearing her traine, Ianthe following.

Reb. I Admire Madame, you can not loue whome the Viceroy loues.

Hiar. And one whofe veines fwell fo with his bloud, Madam, as they doe in his Lordfhip.

Pfo. A neare and deare Kinfman his Lordfhip is to his Altitude, the Viceroy; In care of whofe good fpeede here, I know his Altitude hath not flept a found fleepe fince his departure.

Eud. I thanke *Venus* I haue, euer fince he came.

Reb. You fleepe away your Honour, Madam, if you neglect me.

Hiar. Neglect your Lordfhip? that were a negligence no leffe than difloialtie.

Eud. I much doubt that Sir, It were rather a prefumption to take him, being of the bloud Viceroiall.

Reb. Not at all, being offered Madame.

Eud. But offered ware is not fo fweet you know. They are the graces of the Viceroy that woo me, not your Lordfhips, and I conceiue it fhould be neither

A Comedie. 13

Honor nor Pleafure to you, to be taken in for an other mans fauours.
Reb. Taken in Madam? you fpeake as I had no houfe to hide my head in.
Eud. I haue heard fo indeed, my Lord, vnleffe it be another mans.
Reb. You haue heard vntruth then; Thefe Lords can well witneffe I can want no houfes.
Hiar. Nor Palaces neither my Lord.
Pjo. Nor Courts neither.
Eud. Nor Temples I thinke neither; I beleeue wee fhall haue a God of him.

Enter Tharfalio.

Arg. See the bold fellow; whether will you Sir?
Thar. Away, all honour to you Madam?
Eud. How now bafe companion?
Thar. Bafe Madame: hees not bafe that fights as high as your lips.
Eud. And does that befeeme my feruant?
Thar. Your Court-feruant Madam.
Eud. One that waited on my boord?
Thar. That was only a preparation to my weight on your bed Madam.
Eud. How dar'ft thou come to me with fuch a thought?
Thar. Come to you Madam? I dare come to you at midnight, and bid defiance to the proudeft fpirit that haunts thefe your loued fhadowes; and would any way make terrible the acceffe of my loue to you.
Eud. Loue me? loue my dogge.
Thar. I am bound to that by the prouerb Madam.
Eud. Kennell without with him, intrude not here. What is it thou prefum'ft on?
Thar. On your iudgement Madam, to choofe a Man,

and not a Giant, as thefe are that come with Titles, and Authoritie, as they would conquer, or rauifh you. But I come to you with the liberall and ingenuous Graces, Loue, Youth, and Gentrie; which (in no more deform'd a perfon then my felfe) deferue any Princeffe.

Eud. In your fawcie opinion Sir, and firha too ; get gone ; and let this malipert humour returne thee no more, for afore heauen Ile haue thee toft in blanquets.

Thar. In blanquets Madam ? you muft adde your fheetes, and you muft be the Toffer.

Reb. Nay then Sir y'are as groffe as you are fawcie.

Thar. And all one Sir, for I am neither.

Reb. Thou art both.

Thar. Thou lieft ; keepe vp your fmiter Lord *Rebus*.

Hiar. Vfeft thou thus his Altitudes Cofen ?

Reb. The place thou know'ft protects thee.

Thar. Tie vp your valour then till an other place turne me loofe to you, you are the Lord (I take it) that wooed my great Miftris here with letters from his Altitude ; which while fhe was reading, your Lordfhip (to entertaine time) ftrodl'd and skal'd your fingers ; as you would fhew what an itching defire you had to get betwixt her fheetes.

Hiar. Slight, why does your Lordfhip endure him ?

Reb. The place, the place my Lord.

Thar. Be you his Attorney Sir.

Hiar. What would you doe Sir ?

Thar. Make thee leape out at window, at which thou cam'ft in : Whores-fonne bag-pipe Lords.

Eud. What rudeneffe is this ?

Thar. What tameneffe is it in you Madam, to fticke at the difcarding of fuch a fuiter ? A leane Lord, dub'd with the lard of others ? A difeafed Lord too, that opening certaine Magick Characters in an vnlawfull booke, vp-ftart as many aches in's bones, as there are ouches in's skinne. Send him (Miftris) to the Widdow your Tennant ; the vertuous Pandreffe *Arface*. I per-

A Comedie. 15

ceiue he has crownes in's Purfe, that make him proud
of a ftring; let her pluck the Goofe therefore, and her
maides dreffe him.
Pfo. Still my Lord fuffer him ?
Reb. The place Sir, beleeue it the place.
Thar. O good Lord *Rebus*; The place is neuer like
to be yours that you neede refpect it fo much.
Eud. Thou wrong'ft the noble Gentleman.
Thar. Noble Gentleman? A tumor, an impoftume hee
is Madam; a very hault-boy, a bag-pipe; in whom
there is nothing but winde, and that none of the fweeteft
neither.
Eud. Quitt the Houfe of him, by 'thead and Soul-
ders.
Thar. Thankes to your Honour Madame, and my
Lord Cofen the Viceroy fhall thanke you.
Reb. So fhall he indeede fir.
Lyc. Arg. Will you be gone fir ?
Thar. Away poore Fellowes.
Eud. What is he made of? or what Deuill fees your
childifh, and effeminate fpirits in him, that thus yee
fhun him ? Free vs of thy fight;
Be gone, or I proteft thy life fhall goe.
Thar. Yet fhall my Ghoft ftay ftill; and haunt thofe
beauties, and glories, that haue renderd it immortall.
But fince I fee your bloud runnes (for the time)
High, in that contradiction that fore-runs
Trueft agreements (like the Elements
Fighting before they generate;) and that Time
Muft be attended moft, in thinges moft worth;
I leaue your Honour freely; and commend
That life you threaten, when you pleafe, to be
Aduentur'd in your feruice; fo your Honour
Require it likewife.
Eud. Doe not come againe.
Thar. Ile come againe, beleeue it, and againe. *Exit.*
Eud. If he fhall dare to come againe, I charge you
fhut dores vpon him.
Arg. You muft fhut them (Madam)

To all men elfe then, if it pleafe your Honour,
For if that any enter, hele be one.
Eud. I hope, wife Sir, a Guard will keepe him out.
Arg. Afore Heauen, not a Guard (ant pleafe your Honour.)
Eud. Thou lieft bafe Affe; One man enforce a Guard?
Ile turne yee all away (by our Iles Goddeffe)
If he but fet a foote within my Gates.
Lurd. Your Honour fhall doe well to haue him poifon'd.
Hiar. Or begg'd of your Cofen the Viceroy. *Exit.*

Lyfander from his ftand.

Lyfand. This brauing wooer, hath the fucceffe expected; The fauour I obtain'd, made me witneffe to the fport; And let his Confidence bee fure, Ile giue it him home. The newes by this, is blowne through the foure quarters of the Cittie. Alas good Confidence: but the happineffe is he has a forehead of proofe; the ftaine fhall neuer ftick there whatfoeuer his reproch be.

Enter Tharfalio.

Lyfand. What? in difcourfe?
Thar. Hell and the Furies take this vile encounter,
Who would imagine this Saturnian Peacock
Could be fo barbarous to vfe a fpirit
Of my erection, with fuch lowe refpect?
Fore heauen it cuts my gall; but Ile diffemble it.
Lyfand. What? my noble Lord?
Thar. Well Sir, that may be yet, and meanes to be.
Lyfand. What meanes your Lordfhip then to hang

A Comedie.

that head that hath beene fo erected; it knocks Sir at your bofome to come in and hide it felfe.
Thar. Not a iot.
Lyfand. I hope by this time it needes feare no hornes.
Thar. Well Sir, but yet that bleffing runs not alwaies in a bloud.
Lyfand. What blanqueted? O the Gods? fpurn'd out by Groomes like a bafe Bifogno? thruft out by'th head and fhoulders?
Thar. You doe well Sir to take your pleafure of me, (I may turne tables with you ere long.)
Lyfand. What has thy wits fine engine taken cold? art ftuff't inth head? canft anfwere nothing?
Thar. Truth is, I like my entertainment the better that 'twas no better.
Lyfand. Now the Gods forbid that this opinion fhould run in a bloud.
Thar. Haue not you heard this principle, All thinges by ftrife engender?
Lyfand. Dogges and Cats doe.
Thar. And men and women too.
Lyfand. Well Brother, in earneft, you haue now fet your confidence to fchoole, from whence I hope't has brought home fuch a leffon as will inftruct his mafter neuer after to begin fuch attempts as end in laughter.
Thar. Well Sir, you leffon my Confidence ftill; I pray heauens your confidence haue not more fhallow ground (for that I know) then mine you reprehend fo.
Lyfand. My confidence? in what?
Thar. May be you truft too much.
Lyfand. Wherein?
Thar. In humane frailtie.
Lyfand. Why brother know you ought that may impeach my confidence, as this fucceffe may yours? hath your obferuation difcouered any fuch frailtie in my wife (for that is your aime I know) then let me know it.
Thar. Good, good. Nay Brother, I write no bookes

of Obſeruations, let your confidence beare out it ſelfe, as mine ſhall me.

Lyſand. That's ſcarce a Brothers ſpeech. If there be ought wherein your Brothers good might any way be queſtion'd can you conceale it from his boſome?

Thar. So, ſo. Nay my ſaying was but generall. I glanc't at no particular.

Lyſand. Then muſt I preſſe you further. You ſpake (as to your ſelfe, but yet I ouer-heard) as if you knew ſome diſpoſition of weakneſſe where I moſt had fixt my truſt. I challenge you to let me know what 'twas.

Thar. Brother? are you wiſe?

Lyſand. Why?

Thar. Be ignorant. Did you neuer heare of *Actæon*?

Lyſand. What then?

Thar. Curioſitie was his death. He could not be content to adore *Diana* in her Temple, but he muſt needes dogge her to her retir'd pleaſures, and ſee her in her nakedneſſe. Doe you enioy the ſole priuiledge of your wiues bed? haue you no pretie *Paris* for your Page? No yong *Adonis* to front you there?

Lyſand. I thinke none: I know not.

Thar. Know not ſtill Brother. Ignorance and credu-litie are your ſole meanes to obtaine that bleſſing. You ſee your greateſt Clerkes, your wiſeſt Politicians, are not that way fortunate: your learned Lawyers would loſe a dozen poore mens cauſes to gaine a leaſe ant, but for a Terme. Your Phiſition is ielous of his. Your Sages in generall, by ſeeing too much ouerſee that happineſſe. Only your block-headly Tradeſman; your honeſt meaning Cittizen; your not-headed Coun-trie Gentleman; your vnapprehending Stinckerd is bleſt with the ſole prerogatiue of his Wiues chamber. For which he is yet beholding, not to his ſtarres, but to his ignorance. For if he be wiſe, Brother, I muſt tell you the caſe alters.

How doe you reliſh theſe thinges Brother?

Lyſand. Paſſing ill.

A Comedie.

Thar. So do fick men folid meates : hearke you brother, are you not ielous ?
Lyfand. No : doe you know caufe to make me ?
Thar. Hold you there ; did your wife neuer fpice your broth with a dramme of fublimate ? hath fhee not yeelded vp the Fort of her Honour to a ftaring Soldado ? and (taking courage from her guilt) plaid open banckrout of all fhame, and runne the Countrie with him ? Then bleffe your Starres, bow your knees to *Iuno.* Looke where fhee appeares.

Enter Cynthia, Hylus.

Cynth. WE haue fought you long Sir, there's a Meffenger within, hath brought you letters from the Court, and defires your fpeech.
Lyfand. I can difcouer nothing in her lookes. Goe, Ile not be long.
Cynth. Sir, it is of weight the bearer faies : and befides, much haftens his departure. Honourable Brother ! crie mercie ! what, in a Conquerours ftile ? but come and ouercome ?
Thar. A frefh courfe.
Cynth. Alas you fee of how fleight mettall Widdowes vowes are made.
Thar. And that fhall you proue too ere long.
Cynth. Yet for the honour of our fexe, boaft not abroade this your eafie conqueft ; another might perhaps haue ftaid longer below ftaires, it but was your confidence, that furprif'd her loue.
Hyl. My vncle hath inftructed me how to accoaft an honorable Ladie ; to win her, not by fuite, but by furprife.
Thar. The Whelp and all.
Hyl. Good Vncle let not your neare Honours change your manners, bee not forgetfull of your promife to mee, touching your Ladies daughter *Laodice.* My

fancie runns fo vpon't, that I dreame euery night of her.

Thar. A good chicken, goe thy waies, thou haft done well ; eate bread with thy meate.

Cyn. Come Sir, will you in ?

Lyfand. Ile follow you.

Cynth. Ile not ftirre a foot without you. I can not fatisfie the meffengers impatience.

Lyf. He takes Thar. afide. Wil you not refolue me brother ?

Thar. Of what ?

Lyfander ftamps and goes out vext with Cynth. Hyl. Ero. So, there's venie for venie, I haue giuen't him 'ith fpeeding place for all his confidence. Well out of this perhaps there may bee moulded matter of more mirth, then my baffling. It fhall goe hard but Ile make my conftant fifter act as famous a Scene as *Virgil* did his Miftris; who caut'd all the Fire in Rome to faile fo that none could light a torch but at her nofe. Now forth: At this houfe dwells a vertuous Dame, fometimes of worthy Fame, now like a decai'd Merchant turn'd Broker, and retailes refufe commodities for vnthriftie Gallants. Her wit I muft imploy vpon this bufineffe to prepare my next encounter, but in fuch a fafhion as fhall make all fplit. Ho ? Madam *Arface*, pray heauen the Oifter-wiues haue not brought the newes of my woing hether amongft their ftale Pilcherds.

Enter Arface, Tomafin.

Arf. WHat ? my Lord of the Palace ?
Thar. Looke you.
Arf. Why, this was done like a beaten Souldier.
Thar. Hearke, I muft fpeake with you. I haue a fhare for you in this riche aduenture. You muft bee the Affe chardg'd with Crownes to make way to the Fort, and I the Conquerour to follow, and feife it. Seeft thou this iewell ?

A Comedie. 21

Arſ. Is't come to that? why *Tomaſin*.
Tom. Madam.
Arſ. Did not one of the Counteſſes Seruing-men tell vs that this Gentleman was ſped?
Tom. That he did, and how her honour grac't and entertained him in very familiar manner.
Arſ. And brought him downe ſtaires her ſelfe.
Tom. I forſooth, and commanded her men to beare him out of dores.
Thar. Slight, pelted with rotten egges?
Arſ. Nay more, that he had alreadie poſſeſt her ſheetes.
Tom. No indeede Miſtris, twas her blanquets.
Thar. Out you yong hedge-ſparrow, learne to tread afore you be fledge.   *He kicks her out*:
Well haue you done now Ladie.
Arſ. O my ſweet kilbuck.
Thar. You now, in your ſhallow pate, thinke this a diſgrace to mee; ſuch a diſgrace as is a batterd helmet on a ſouldiers head, it doubles his reſolution. Say, ſhall I vſe thee?
Arſ. Vſe me?
Thaa. O holy reformation! how art thou fallen downe from the vpper-bodies of the Church to the skirts of the Citie! honeſtie is ſtript out of his true ſub-ſtance into verball nicetie. Common ſinners ſtartle at common termes, and they that by whole mountaines ſwallow downe the deedes of darkneſſe; A poore mote of a familiar word, makes them turne vp the white o'th eie. Thou art the Ladies Tennant.
Arſ. For terme Sir.
Thar. A good induction, be ſucceſſefull for me, make me Lord of the Palace, and thou ſhalt hold thy Tene-ment to thee and thine eares for euer, in free ſmockage, as of the manner of Panderage, prouided alwaies.
Arſa. Nay if you take me vnprouided.
Thar. Prouided I ſay, that thou mak'ſt thy repaire to her preſently with a plot I will inſtruct thee in; and

for thy furer acceſſe to her greatneſſe, thou ſhalt preſent her, as from thy ſelfe with this iewell.
Arſa. So her old grudge, ſtand not betwixt her and me.
Thar. Feare not that.
Preſents are preſent cures for femall grudges,
Make bad, ſeeme good : alter the caſe with Iudges.
Exit.
Finis Actus Primi.

Actus Secundi.

Scœna Prima.

Lyſander, Tharſalio.

Lyſand. SO now we are our ſelues. Brother, that ill reliſht ſpeech you let ſlip from your tongue, hath taken ſo deepe hold of my thoughts, that they will neuer giue me reſt, till I be reſolu'd what 'twas you ſaid, you know, touching my wife.
Tharſ. Tuſh : I am wearie of this ſubiect, I ſaid not ſo.
Lyſ. By truth it ſelfe you did : I ouer-heard you. Come, it ſhall nothing moue me, whatſoeuer it be; pray thee vnfold briefly what you know.
Tharſ. Why briefly Brother. I know my ſiſter to be the wonder of the Earth ; and the Enuie of the Heauens. Vertuous, Loiall, and what not. Briefly, I know ſhee hath vow'd, that till death and after death, ſheele hold inuiolate her bonds to you, & that her black ſhal take no other hew ; all which I firmely beleeue. In briefe Brother, I know her to be a woman. But you know brother, I haue other yrons on th'anuile.
Exiturus.

A Comedie. 23

Lyſ. You ſhall not leaue mee ſo vnſatisfied; tell mee what tis you know.
Thar. Why Brother; if you be ſure of your wiues loialtie for terme of life: why ſhould you be curious to ſearch the Almanacks for after-times: whether ſome wandring *Æneas* ſhould enioy your reuerſion; or whether your true Turtle would ſit mourning on a wither'd branch, till *Atropos* cut her throat: Beware of curioſitie, for who can reſolue you? youle ſay perhaps her vow.
Lyſand. Perhaps I ſhall.
Thar. Tuſh, her ſelfe knowes not what ſhee ſhall doe, when ſhee is transform'd iuto a Widdow. You are now a ſober and ſtaid Gentleman. But if *Diana* for your curioſitie ſhould tranſlate you into a monckey: doe you know what gambolds you ſhould play? your only way to bee reſolu'd is to die and make triall of her.
Lyſand. A deare experiment, then I muſt riſe againe to bee reſolu'd.
Thar. You ſhall not neede. I can ſend you ſpeedier aduertiſement of her conſtancie, by the next Ripier that rides that way with Mackerell. And ſo I leaue you.   *Exit Thar.*
Lyſand. All the Furies in hell attend thee; has giuen me a
Bone to tire on with a peſtilence; ſlight know?
What can he know? what can his eie obſerue
More then mine owne, or the moſt pierſing ſight
That euer viewed her? by this light I thinke
Her priuat'ſt thought may dare the eie of heauen,
And challenge th' enuious world to witneſſe it.
I know him for a wild corrupted youth,
Whom prophane Ruffins, Squires to Bawds, & Strum-
  pets,
Drunkards, ſpeud out of Tauerns, into'th ſinkes
Of Tap-houſes, and Stewes, Reuolts from manhood;
Debaucht perdu's, haue by their companies
Turn'd Deuill like themſelues, and ſtuft his ſoule

With damn'd opinions, and vnhallowed thoughts
Of womanhood, of all humanitie,
Nay Deitie it felfe.

Enter Lycus.

Lyf. WElcome friend L*ycus*.
Lyc. Haue you met with your capricious brother?
Lyf. He parted hence but now.
Lyc. And has he yet refolu'd you of that point you brake with me about?
Lyf. Yes, he bids me die for further triall of her conftancie.
Lyc. That were a ftrange Phificke for a iealous patient; to cure his thirft with a draught of poifon. Faith Sir, difcharge your thoughts an't; thinke 'twas but a Buzz deuis'd by him to fet your braines a work, and diuert your eie from his difgrace. The world hath written your wife in higheft lines of honour'd Fame: her vertues fo admir'd in this Ile, as the report thereof founds in forraigne eares; and ftrangers oft arriuing here, (as fome rare fight) defire to view her prefence, thereby to compare the Picture with the originall. Nor thinke he can turne fo farre rebell to his bloud,
Or to the Truth it felfe to mifconceiue
Her fpotleffe loue and loialtie; perhaps
Oft hauing heard you hold her faith fo facred
As you being dead, no man might ftirre a fparke
Of vertuous loue, in way of fecond bonds;
As if you at your death fhould carrie with you
Both branch and roote of all affection.
T'may be, in that point hee's an Infidell,
And thinkes your confidence may ouer-weene.
Lyf. So thinke not I.
Lyc. Nor I : if euer any made it good.
I am refolu'd of all, fheele proue no changling.
Lyf. Well, I muft yet be further fatisfied;
And vent this humour by fome ftraine of wit,
Somewhat Ile doe; but what, I know not yet. *Exeunt.*

A Comedie.

Enter Sthenio, Ianthe.

Sthe. PAſſion of Virginitie, *Ianthe*, how ſhall we quit ourſelues of this Pandreſſe, that is ſo importunate to ſpeake with vs? Is ſhee knowne to be a Pandreſſe?

Ian. I, as well as we are knowne to be waiting women.

Sthe. A ſhrew take your compariſon.

Sthe. Lets cal out *Argus* that bold Aſſe that neuer weighs what he does or ſaies; but walkes and talkes like one in a ſleepe; to relate her attendance to my Ladie, and preſent her.

Ian. Who? ant pleaſe your Honour? None ſo fit to ſet on any dangerous exploit. Ho? *Argus*?

Enter Argus bare.

Arg. WHats the matter Wenches?

Seth. You muſt tell my Ladie here's a Gentlewoman call'd *Arſace*, her Honours Tennant, attends her, to impart important buſineſſe to her.

Arg. I will preſently. *Exit Arg.*

Iant. Well, ſhee has a welcome preſent, to beare out her vnwelcome preſence: and I neuer knew but a good gift would welcome a bad perſon to the pureſt. *Arſace*?

Enter Arſace.

Arſ. I Miſtris.

Sthe. Giue me your Preſent, Ile doe all I can, to make way both for it and your ſelfe.

Arſ. You ſhall binde me to your ſeruice Ladie.

Sthe. Stand vnſeene.

Enter Lyc. Eudora, Laodice, Reb, Hiar Pſor., comming after, Argus comming to Eudora.

Arg. HEre's a Gentle-woman (ant Pleaſe your Honour) one of your Tennants

Defires acceffe to you.
Eud. What Tennant? what's her name?
Arg. *Arface*, fhee faies Madam.
Eud. *Arface*? what the Bawde?
Arg. The Bawd Madam? *fhee ftrikes*, that's without my priuitie.
Eud. Out Affe, know'ft not thou the Pandreffe *Arface*?
Sth. Shee prefents your Honour with this Iewell?
Eud. This iewell? how came fhee by fuch a iewell? Shee has had great Cuftomers.
Arg. Shee had neede Madam, fhee fits at a great Rent.
Eud. Alas for your great Rent: Ile keepe her iewell, and keepe you her out, yee were beft: fpeake to me for a Pandreffe?
Arg. What fhall we doe?
Sthe. Goe to; Let vs alone. *Arface?*
Arf. I Ladie.
Sthe. You muft pardon vs, we can not obtaine your acceffe.
Arf. Miftris *Sthenio*, tell her Honour, if I get not acceffe to her, and that inftantly fhee's vndone.
Sthe. This is fome thing of importance. Madam, fhee fweares your Honour is vndone if fhe fpeake not with you inftantly.
Eud. Vndone?
Arf. Pray her for her Honours fake to giue mee inftant acceffe to her.
Sthe. Shee makes her bufineffe your Honour Madame, and entreates for the good of that, her inftant fpeech with you.
Eud. How comes my Honour in queftion? Bring her to mee.

Enter Arface.

Arf. OVr *Cypriane* Goddeffe faue your good Honor.
Eud. Stand you off I pray: How dare you Miftris

importune acceſſe to me thus, conſidering the laſt warning I gaue for your abſence ?
Arſ. Becauſe, Madam, I haue been mou'd by your Honours laſt moſt chaſt admonition, to leaue the offenſiue life I led before.
Eud. I ? haue you left it then ?
Arſ. I, I aſſure your Honour, vnleſſe it be for the pleaſure of two or three poore Ladies, that haue prodigall Knights to their husbands.
Eud. Out on thee Impudent.
Arſ. Alas Madam, wee would all bee glad to liue in our callings.
Eud. Is this the reform'd life thou talk'ſt on ?
Arſ. I beſeech your good Honour miſtake me not, I boaſt of nothing but my charitie, that's the worſt.
Eud. You get theſe iewels with charitie, no doubt. But whats the point in which my Honour ſtands endanger'd I pray ?
Arſ. In care of that Madam, I haue preſum'd to offend your chaſt eies with my preſence. Hearing it reported for truth and generally, that your Honor will take to husband a yong Gentleman of this Citie called *Tharſalio.*
Eud. I take him to husband ?
Arſ. If your Honour does, you are vtterly vndone, for hee's the moſt incontinent, and inſatiate Man of Women that euer Venvs bleſt with abilitie to pleaſe them.
Eud. Let him be the Deuill ; I abhorre his thought, and could I be inform'd particularly of any of theſe ſlanderers of mine Honour, he ſhould as dearely dare it, as any thing wherein his life were endanger'd.
Arſ. Madam, the report of it is ſo ſtrongly confident, that I feare the ſtrong deſtinie of marriage is at worke in it. But if it bee Madam : Let your Honours knowne vertue reſiſt and defie it for him : for not a hundred will ſerue his one turne. I proteſt to your Honour, When (Venvs pardon mee) I winckt at my

vnmaidenly exercife, I haue knowne nine in a Night made mad with his loue.

Eud. What tell'ft thou mee of his loue? I tell thee I abhorre him; and deftinie muft haue an other mould for my thoughts, then Nature or mine Honour, and a Witchcraft aboue both, to transforme mee to another fhape, as foone as to an other conceipt of him.

Arf. Then is your good Honour iuft as I pray for you, and good Madam, euen for your vertues fake, and comfort of all your Dignities, and Poffeffions; fixe your whole Woman-hood againft him. Hee will fo inchant you, as neuer man did woman: Nay a Goddeffe (fay his light hufwiues) is not worthie of his fweetneffe.

Eud. Goe to, be gone.

Arf. Deare Madam, your Honours moft perfect admonition haue brought mee to fuch a hate of thefe imperfections, that I could not but attend you with my dutie, and vrge his vnreafonable manhood to the fill.

Eud. Man-hood, quoth you?

Arf. Nay Beaftly-hood, I might fay, indeede Madam, but for fauing your Honour; Nine in a night faid I?

Eud. Goe to, no more.

Arf. No more Madame? that's enough one would thinke.

Eud. Well be gone I bid thee.

Arf. Alas Madam, your Honour is the chiefe of our Cittie, and to whom fhall I complaine of thefe inchaftities, (being your Ladifhips reform'd Tennant) but to you that are chafteft?

Eud. I pray thee goe thy waies, and let me fee this reformation you pretend continued.

Arf. I humbly thanke your good Honour, that was firft caufe of it.

Eud. Here's a complaint as ftrange as my Suiter.

Arf. I befeech your good Honour thinke vpon him, make him an example.

Eud. Yet againe ?
Arf. All my dutie to your Excellence. *Exit. Arf.*
Eud. Thefe forts of licentious perfons, when they are once reclaim'd, are moſt vehement againſt licence. But it is the courfe of the world to difpraife faults & ufe them; that fo we may vfe them the fafer. What might a wife Widdow refolue vpon this point now? Contentment is the end of all worldly beings: Befhrow her; would fhee had fpared her newes. *Exit.*
Reb. See if fhee take not a contrarie way to free her felfe of vs.
Hiar. Yon muſt complaine to his Altitude.
Pfor. All this for triall is; you muſt indure That will haue wiues, nought elfe, with them is fure.
Exit.

Tharfalio, Arface.

Thar. Haſt thou beene admitted then?
Arf. Admitted? I, into her heart, Ile able it; neuer was man fo prais'd with a difpraife; nor fo fpoken for in being rail'd on. Ile giue you my word; I haue fet her hart vpon as tickle a pin as the needle of a Diall; that will neuer let it reſt, till it be in the right pofition.
Thar. Why doſt thou imagine this?
Arf. Becaufe I faw *Cupid* fhoot in my wordes, and open his wounds in her lookes. Her bloud went and came of errands betwixt her face and her heart; and thefe changes I can tell you are fhrewd tell-tales.
Thar. Thou fpeak'ſt like a Doctriſſe in thy facultie; but howfoeuer, for all this foile, Ile retriue the game once againe, hee's a fhallow gamſter that for one difpleafing caſt giues vp fo faire a game for loſt.
Arf. Well, 'twas a villanous inuention of thine, and had a fwift operation, it tooke like fulphure. And yet this vertuous Counteffe hath to my eare fpun out many a tedious lecture of pure fifters thred agaiuſt concupifcence. But euer with fuch an affected zeale, as my

minde gaue me, fhee had a kinde of fecret titillation
to grace my poore houfe fometimes; but that fhee
fear'd a fpice of the Sciatica, which as you know euer
runs in the bloud.
Thar. And as you know, fokes into the bones. But
to fay truth, thefe angrie heates that breake out at the
lips of thefe ftreight lac't Ladies, are but as fymptoms
of a luftfull feuer that boiles within them. For wherefore rage wiues at their husbands fo, when they flie out,
for zeale againft the finne?
Arf. No, but becaufe they did not purge that finne.
Thar. Th'art a notable Syren, and I fweare to thee,
if I profper, not only to giue thee thy mannor-houfe
gratis, but to marrie thee to fome one Knight or other,
and burie thy trade in thy Ladifhip: Goe be gone.

Exit Arf.

Enter Lycus.

Thar. WHat newes *Lycus*? where's the Ladie?
Lyc. Retir'd into her Orchard.
Thar. A pregnant badge of loue, fhee's melancholy.
Lyc. 'Tis with the fight of her Spartane wooer. But
howfoeuer tis with her, you haue practis'd ftrangely vpon
your Brother.
Thar. Why fo?
Lyc. You had almoft lifted his wit off the hinges.
That fparke ieloufie falling into his drie melancholy
braine, had well neare fet the whole houfe on fire.
Thar. No matter, let it worke: I did but pay him
in's owne coine; Sfoot hee plied me with fuch a volley
of vnfeafon'd fcoffs, as would haue made Patience it
felfe turne Ruffine, attiring it felfe in wounds and
bloud: but is his humour better qualified then?
Lyc. Yes, but with a medicine ten parts more dangerous then the ficknefse: you know how ftrange his
dotage euer was on his wife; taking fpeciall glorie to
haue her loue and loialtie to him fo renowm'd abroad.
To whom fhee oftentimes hath vow'd conftancie after

life, till her owne death had brought forfooth, her widdow-troth to bed. This he ioi'd in ſtrangely, and was therein of infallible beliefe, till your ſurmiſe began to ſhake it; which hath loos'd it ſo, as now there's nought can ſettle it, but a triall, which hee's reſolu'd vpon.

Thar. As how man? as how?

Lyc. Hee is reſolu'd to follow your aduiſe, to die, and make triall of her ſtableneſſe, and you muſt lend your hand to it.

Thar. What to cut's throat?

Lyc. To forge a rumour of his death, to vphold it by circumſtance, maintaine a publike face of mourning, and all thinges appertaining.

Thar. I, but the meanes man: what time? what probabilitie.

Lyc. Nay, I thinke he has not lickt his Whelpe into full ſhape yet, but you ſhall ſhortly heare ant.

Thar. And when ſhall this ſtrange conception ſee light?

Lyc. Forthwith: there's nothing ſtaies him, but ſome odde buſineſſe of import, which hee muſt winde vp; leaſt perhaps his abſence by occaſion of his intended triall be prolonged aboue his aimes.

Thar. Thankes for this newes i' faith. This may perhaps proue happie to my Nephew. Truth is I loue my ſiſter well and muſt acknowledge her more then ordinarie vertues. But ſhee hath ſo poſſeſt my brothers heart with vowes, and diſauowings, ſeal'd with oathes of ſecond nuptialls; as in that confidence, hee hath inueſted her in all his ſtate, the ancient inheritance of our Familie: and left my Nephew and the reſt to hang vpon her pure deuotion; ſo as he dead, and ſhee matching (as I am reſolu'd ſhee will) with ſome yong Prodigall; what muſt enſue, but her poſt-iſſue beggerd, and our houſe alreadie ſinking, buried quick in ruin. But this triall may remoue it, and ſince tis come to this; marke but the iſſue *Lycus*, for all theſe ſolemne vowes, if I doe not make her proue in the handling as

weake as a wafer; fay I loft my time in trauaile. This
refolution then has fet his wits in ioynt againe, hee's
quiet.
Lyc. Yes, and talkes of you againe in the faireft
manner, liftens after your fpeede.
Thar. Nay hee's paffing kinde, but I am glad of this
triall for all that.
Lyc. Which he thinkes to be a flight beyond your
wing.
Thar. But hee will change that thought ere long.
My Bird you faw euen now, fings me good newes, and
makes hopefull fignes to me.
Lyc. Somewhat can I fay too, fince your meffengers
departure, her Ladifhip hath beene fomething alter'd,
more penfiue then before, and tooke occafion to queftion of you, what your addictions were? of what taft
your humor was? of what cut you wore your wit, and
all this in a kind of difdainefull fcorne.
Thar. Good Callenders *Lycus*. Well Ile pawne this
iewell with thee, my next encounter fhall quite alter
my brothers iudgement. Come lets in, he fhall commend it for a difcreet and honourable attempt.
 Mens iudgments fway on that fide fortune leanes,
 Thy wifhes fhall affift me:
Lyc. And my meanes. *Exeunt.*

Argus, Clinias, Sthenio, Ianthe.

Arg. I Muft confeffe I was ignorant, what'twas to
court a Ladie till now.
Sthe. And I pray you what is it now?
Arg. To court her I perceiue, is to woo her with letters from Court, for fo this Spartane Lords Court difcipline teacheth.
Sth. His Lordfhip hath procur'd a new Pacquet from
his Altitude.
Clin. If he bring no better ware then letters in's pacquet, I fhall greatly doubt of his good fpeede.

Ian. If his Lordſhip did but know how gracious his Aſpect is to my Ladie in this ſolitarie humour.
Clin. Well theſe retir'd walkes of hers are not vſuall; and bode ſome alteration in her thoughts. What may bee the cauſe *Sthenio.*
Sthe. Nay twould trouble *Argus* with his hundred eies to deſcrie the cauſe.
Ian. *Venus* keepe her vpright, that ſhee fall not from the ſtate of her honour; my feare is that ſome of theſe Serpentine ſuiters will tempt her from her conſtant vow of widdow-hood. If they doe, good night to our good daies.
Sthe. 'Twere a ſinne to ſuſpect her; I haue been witneſſe to ſo many of her fearfull proteſtations to our late Lord againſt that courſe; to her infinite oathes imprinted on his lips, and ſeal'd in his heart with ſuch imprecations to her bed, if euer it ſhould receiue a ſecond impreſſion; to her open and often deteſtations of that inceſtuous life (as ſhee term'd it) of widdowes marriages; as being but a kinde of lawfull adulterie; like vſurie, permitted by the law, not approu'd. That to wed a ſecond, was no better then to cuckold the firſt: That women ſhould entertaine wedlock as one bodie, as one life, beyond which there were no deſire, no thought, no repentance from it, no reſtitution to it. So as if the conſcience of her vowes ſhould not reſtraine her, yet the worlds ſhame to breake ſuch a conſtant reſolution, ſhould repreſſe any ſuch motion in her.
Arg. Well, for her vowes, they are gone to heauen with her husband, they binde not vpon earth: And as for Womens reſolutions, I muſt tell you, The Planets, & (as *Ptolomie* ſaies) the windes haue a great ſtroke in them. Truſt not my learning if her late ſtrangeneſſe, and exorbitant ſolitude, be not hatching ſome new Monſter.
Ian. Well applied *Argus*; Make your husbands Monſters.
Arg. I ſpoke of no husbands: but you Wenches haue

the pregnant wits, to turne Monsters into husbands, as you turne husbands into monsters.

Sthe. Well *Ianthe*, 'twere high time we made in, to part our Ladie and her Spartane wooer.

Ian. We shall appeare to her like the two fortunate Stars in a tempest, to saue the shipwrack of her patience.

Sthe. I, and to him to, I beleeue; For by this time he hath spent the last dramme of his newes.

Arg. That is, of his wit.

Sth. Iust good wittals. *Ian.* If not, & that my La: be not too deep in her new dumps, we shall heare from his Lordship; what such a Lord said of his wife the first night hee embrac't her: To what Gentleman such a Count was beholding for his fine children. What yong Ladie, such an old Count should marrie; what Reuells: what presentments are towards; and who penn'd the Pegmas; and so forth: and yet for all this, I know her harsh Suiter hath tir'd her to the vttermost scruple of her forbearance, and will doe more, vnlesse we two, like a paire of Sheres, cut a-sunder the thred of his discourse.

Sthe. Well then, lets in; But my masters, waite you on your charge at your perils, See that you guard her approch from any more intruders.

Ian. Excepting yong *Tharsalio*.

Sthe. True, excepting him indeede, for a guard of men is not able to keepe him out ant please your Honour.

Arg. O Wenches, that's the propertie of true valour, to promise like a Pigmey, and performe like a Giant. If he come, Ile bee sworne I doe my Ladies commandement vpon him.

Ian. What? beate him out?

Sthe. If hee should, *Tharsalio* would not take it ill at his handes, for he does but his Ladies commandement.

A Comedie.

Enter Tharſalio.

Arg. Well, by *Hercules* he comes not here.
Sthe. By *Venus* but hee does: or elſe ſhee hath heard my Ladies praiers, and ſent ſome gracious ſpirit in his likeneſſe to fright away that Spartane wooer, that hants her.
Thar. There ſtand her Sentinells.
Arg. Slight the Ghoſt appeares againe.
Thar. Saue yee my quondam fellowes in Armes; ſaue yee; my women.
Sthe. Your Women Sir?
Thar. 'Twill be ſo. What no courteſies? No preparation of grace? obſerue me I aduiſe you for your owne ſakes.
Ian. For your owne ſake, I aduiſe you to pack hence, left your impudent valour coſt you dearer then you thinke.
Clin. What ſenſeleſſe boldneſſe is this *Tharſalio*?
Arg. Well ſaid *Clinias*, talke to him.
Clin. I wonder that notwithſtanding the ſhame of your laſt entertainment, and threatnings of worſe; you would yet preſume to trouble this place againe.
Thar. Come y'are a widgine; Off with your hat Sir, acknowledge: forecaſt is better then labour. Are you ſquint ey'd? can you not ſee afore you. A little foreſight I can tell you might ſted you much as the Starres ſhine now.
Clin. 'Tis well ſir, tis not for nothing your brother is aſham'd on you. But Sir, you muſt know, wee are chardg'd to barre your entrance.
Thar. But Wifler, know you, that who ſo ſhall dare to execute that charge, Ile be his Executioner.
Arg. By *Ioue*, *Clinias*, me thinks, the Gentleman ſpeakes very honourably.
Thar. Well I ſee this houſe needes eformation, here's a fellow ſtands behind now, of a forwarder inſight then yee all. What place haſt thou?

Arg. What place you pleafe Sir.
Thar. Law you Sir. Here's a fellow to make a Gentleman Vfher Sir, I difcharge you of the place, and doe here inueft thee into his roome, Make much of thy haire, thy wit will fuit it rarely. And for the full poffeffion of thine office; Come, Vfher me to thy Ladie: and to keep thy hand fupple, take this from me.
Arg. No bribes Sir, ant pleafe your Worfhip.
Thar. Goe to, thou doft well; but pocket it for all that; it's no impaire to thee: the greateft doo't.
Arg. Sir, tis your loue only that I refpect, but finċe out of your loue you pleafe to beftow it vpon me, It were want of Courtfhip in mee to refufe it; Ile acquaint my Ladie with your comming.   *Exit . Arg.*
Thar. How fay by this? haue I not made a fit choife, that hath fo foone attain'd the deepeft myfterie of his profeffion: Good footh Wenches, a few courtfies had not beene caft away vpon your new Lord.
Sthe. Weele beleeue that, when our Ladie has a new Sonne of your getting.

Enter Argus, Eudora, Rebus, Hiar.
Pfor.

Eud. WHats the matter? whofe that, you fay, is come?
Arg. The bold Gentleman, ant pleafe your Honour.
Eud. Why thou flering Affe thou.
Arg. Ant pleafe your Honour.
Eud. Did not I forbid his approch by all the charge and dutie of thy feruice?
Thar. Madam, this fellow only is intelligent; for he truly vnderftood your command according to the ftile of the Court of *Venus*; that is, by contraries: when you forbid you bid.
Eud. By heauen Ile difcharge my houfe of yee all.
Thar. You fhall not neede Madame, for I haue al-

readie cafheer'd your officious Vfher here, and chos'd this for his Succeffor.

Eud. O incredible boldneffe!

Thar. Madam, I come not to command your loue with enforſt letters, nor to woo you with tedious ſtories of my Pedigree, as hee who drawes the thred of his defcent from *Ledas* Diſtaffe; when 'tis well knowne his Grandfire cried Coniskins in Sparta.

Reb. Whom meane you Sir?

Thar. Sir, I name none, but him who firſt ſhall name himſelfe.

Reb. The place Sir, I tell you ſtill; and this Goddeſſes faire prefence, or elſe my reply ſhould take a farre other forme vpon't.

Thar. If it ſhould Sir, I would make your Lordſhip an anſer.

Arg. Anſer's Latine for a Goofe, ant pleaſe your honor.

Eud. Well noted Gander; and what of that?

Arg. Nothing, ant pleaſe your Honor, but that he faid he would make his Lordſhip an anſwere.

Eud. Thus euery foole mocks my poore Suiter. Tell mee thou moſt frontleſſe of all men, did'ſt thou (when thou had'ſt meanes to note me beſt) euer obferue ſo bafe a temper in mee, as to giue any glance at ſtooping to my Vaſſall?

Thar. Your drudge Madam, to doe your drudgerie.

Eud. Or am I now ſo skant of worthie Suiters, that may aduance mine honour; aduance my eſtate; ſtrengthen my alliance (if I liſt to wed) that I muſt ſtoop to make my foot my head.

Thar. No but your ſide, to keepe you warme a bed. But Madame vouchfafe me your patience to that points ferious anſwere. Though I confeſſe to get higher place in your graces, I could wiſh my fortunes more honourable; my perſon more gratious; my minde more adorn'd with Noble and Heroicall vertues; yet Madame (that you thinke not your bloud difparadg'd by mixture with mine) daine to know this: howfoeuer

I once, only for your loue, difguis'd my felfe in the
feruice of your late Lord and mine; yet my defcent is
as honourable as the proudeſt of your Spartane at-
tempters; who by vnknown quills or conduits vnder
ground, drawes his Pedigree from *Lycurgus* his great
Toe, to the Viceroies little finger, and from thence
to his owne elbow, where it will neuer leaue itching.

Reb. Tis well Sir, prefume ſtill of the place.

Thar. Sfoot Madame, am I the firſt great perfonage
that hath ſtoopt to difguifes for loue? what thinke you
of our Countrie-man *Hercules*; that for loue put on
Omphales Apron, and fate fpinning amongſt her
Wenches, while his Miſtris wore his Lyons skin and
Lamb-skin'd him, if he did not his bufineffe.

Eud. Moſt fitly thou refembl'ſt thy felfe to that violent
outlaw, that claim'd all other mens poffeffions as his
owne by his meere valoure. For what leffe haſt thou
done? Come into my houfe, beate away thefe Honourable perfons?

Thar. That I will Madam. Hence ye Sparta-Vel-
uets.

Pfor. Hold, fhee did not meane fo.

Thar. Away I fay, or leaue your liues I proteſt here.

Hiar. Well Sir, his Altitude fhall know you.

Reb. Ile doe your errand Sir.

Exeunt.

Thar. Doe good Cofen Altitude; and beg the reuer-
fion of the next Ladie: for *Dido* has betrotht her loue
to me. By this faire hand Madam, a faire riddance
of this Calidonian Bore.

Eud. O moſt prodigious audacioufneffe!

Thar. True Madam; O fie vpon am, they are intollerable. And I can not but admire your fingular vertue
of patience, not common in your fexe; and muſt
therefore carrie with it fome rare indowment of other
Mafculine and Heroicall vertues. To heare a rude
Spartane court fo ingenuous a Ladie, with dull newes
from Athens, or the Vicerois court; how many dogs

A Comedie. 39

were ſpoil'd at the laſt Bull-baiting; what Ladies dub'd their husbands Knights, and ſo forth.

Eud. But haſt thou no ſhame? No ſenſe of what diſdain I ſhew'd thee in my laſt entertainement? chacing thee from my preſence, and charging thy dutie, not to attempt the like intruſion for thy life; and dar'ſt thou yet approch mee in this vnmannerly manner? No queſtion this deſperate boldneſſe can not chooſe but goe accompanied with other infinite rudeneſſes.

Thar. Good Madam, giue not the Child an vnfit name, terme it not boldnes, which the Sages call true confidence, founded on the moſt infallible Rocke of a womans conſtancie.

Eud. If ſhame can not reſtraine thee, tell mee yet if any brainleſſe foole would haue tempted the danger attending thy approch.

Thar. No Madam, that proues I am no Foole: Then had I been here a Foole, and a baſe low-ſprited Spartan, if for a Ladies froune, or a Lords threates, or for a Guard of Groomes, I ſhould haue ſhrunke in the wetting, and ſuffer'd ſuch a delicious flower to periſh in the ſtalke, or to be ſauadgely pluckt by a prophane finger. No Madam: Firſt let me be made a Subiect for diſgrace; let your remorſeleſſe Guard ſeaze on my deſpiſed bodie, bind me hand and foot, and hurle me into your Ladiſhips bed.

Eud. O Gods: I proteſt thou doſt more and more make me admire thee.

Thar. Madam, ignorance is the mother of admiration: know me better, and youle admire me leſſe.

Eud. What would'ſt thou haue mee know? what ſeekes thy comming? why doſt thou hant me thus?

Thar. Only Madam, that the *Ætna* of my̆ ſighes, and *Nilus* of my teares, pour'd forth in your preſence, might witneſſe to your Honor the hot and moiſt affection of my hart, and worke me ſome meaſure of fauour, from your ſweete tongue, or your ſweeter lips, or what elſe your good Ladiſhip ſhall eſteeme more conducible, to your diuine contentment.

Eud. Pen and Inck-horne I thanke thee. This you learn'd when you were a Seruing-man.

Thar. Madam, I am ſtill the ſame creature; and I will ſo tie my whole fortunes to that ſtile, as were it my happineſſe (as I know it will be) to mount into my Lords ſucceſſion, yet vow I neuer to aſſume other Title, or State, then your ſeruants: Not approching your boord, but bidden: Not preſſing to your bed, but your pleaſure ſhall be firſt known if you will command me any ſeruice.

Eud. Thy vowes are as vaine as a Ruffins othes; as common as the aire; and as cheape as the duſt. How many of the light huſwiues, thy Muſes, hath thy loue promiſt this feruice beſides, I pray thee?

Thar. Compare ſhadowes to bodies, Madam; Pictures to the life; and ſuch are they to you, in my valuation.

Eud. I ſee wordes will neuer free me of thy boldneſſe, and will therefore now vſe blowes; and thoſe of the mortalleſt enforcement. Let it ſuffice Sir, that all this time, and to this place, you enioy your ſafetie; keepe backe: No one foote follow mee further; for I proteſt to thee, the next threſhold paſt, lets paſſe a prepar'd Ambuſh to thy lateſt breath. *Exit. Eud.*

Thar. This for your Ambuſh, *He drawes.* Dare my loue with death?

Clin. Slight; follow ant pleaſe your Honour.

Arg. Not I by this light.

Clin. I hope Gentle-women you will.

Sthe. Not we Sir, we are no parters of fraies.

Clin. Faith nor Ile be any breaker of cuſtomes.

Exeunt.

Finis Actus Secundi.

A Comedie. 41

Actus Tertij.

Scœna Prima.

Enter Lyſander and Lycus booted.

Lyc. Would any heart of Adamant, for ſatisfaction of an vngrounded humour, racke a poore Ladies innocencie as you intend to doe. It was a ſtrange curioſitie in that Emperour, that ript his Mothers wombe to ſee the place he lay in.

Lyſ. Come do not lode me with volumes of perſwaſion; I am reſolu'd, if ſhee be gold ſhee may abide the taſt, lets away, I wonder where this wild brother is.

Enter Cynthia, Hylus, and Ero.

Cynth. Sir.
Lyſand. SI pray thee wife ſhew but thy ſelfe a woman; and be ſilent: queſtion no more the reaſon of my iourney, which our great Viceroies charge vrg'd in this letter doth enforce me to.

Cynth. Let me but ſee that letter, there is ſomthing in this preſaging bloud of mine, tells me this ſodaine iourney can portend no good, reſolue me ſweet, haue not I giuen you cauſe of diſcontent, by ſome miſpriſion, or want of fit obſeruance, let mee know that I may wreake my ſelfe vpon my ſelfe.

Lyſand. Come wife, our loue is now growne old and ſtaid,
And muſt not wanton it in tricks of Court,
Nor enterchang'd delights of melting louers;
Hanging on ſleeues, ſighing, loth to depart;
Theſe toies are paſt with vs; our true loues ſubſtance
Hath worne out all the ſhew, let it ſuffice,
I hold thee deare: and thinke ſome cauſe of weight

The Widdowes Teares.

With no excufe to be difpenft with all, Compells me from thy moft defired embraces; I ftay but for my Brother, came he not in laft night.

Hyl. For certaine no fir, which gaue vs caufe of wonder, what accident kept him abrode.

Cynth. Pray heauen it proue not fome wild refolution, bred in him by his fecond repulfe from the Counteffe.

Lyfand. Truft me I fomething feare it, this infatiate fpirit of afpiring, being fo dangerous and fatall; defire mounted on the wings of it, defcends not but headlong.

Hyl. Sir, fir, here's my Vncle. *Enter Tharf.*

Lyfand. What wrapt in careleffe cloake, face hid in hat vnbanded, thefe are the ditches brother, in which outraging colts plunge both themfelues and their riders.

Thar. Well, wee muft get out as well as wee may, if not, there's the making of a graue fau'd.

Cynth. That's defperately fpoken brother, had it not been happier the colt had beene better broken, and his rider not fallen in.

Thar. True fifter, but wee muft ride colts before wee can breake them, you know.

Lyfand. This is your blind Goddeffe *Confidence.*

Thar. Alas brother, our houfe is decaid, & my honeft ambition to reftore it, I hope be pardonable. My comfort is: the Poet that pens the ftorie will write ore my head *magnis tamen excidit aufis*; which in our natiue Idiome, lets you know, His mind was high, though Fortune was his Foe.

Lyfand. A good refolue brother, to out-ieft difgrace: come I had been on my iourney but for fome priuate fpeech with you: lets in.

Thar. Good brother ftay a little, helpe out this ragged colt out of the ditch.

Lyfand. How now.

Thar. Now I confeffe my ouerfight, this haue I purchas'd by my confidence.

Lyſand. I like you brother, 'tis the true Garb you know,
What wants in reall worth ſupply in ſhow.
Thar. In ſhow ? alas 'twas euen the thing it ſelfe,
I op't my counting houſe, and tooke away
Theſe ſimple fragments of my treaſurie,
Husband my Counteſſe cri'd take more, more yet,
Yet, I in haſt, to pay in part my debt,
And proue my ſelfe a husband of her ſtore,
Kiſt and came of; and this time tooke no more.
Cynth. But good brother.
Thar. Then were our honor'd ſpouſall rites perform'd,
Wee made all ſhort, and ſweet, and cloſe, and ſure.
Lyſand. Hee's wrap't.
Thar. Then did my Vſhers, and chiefe Seruants ſtoope,
Then made my women curtſies, and enuied
Their Ladies fortune : I was magnified.
Lyſand. Let him alone, this ſpirit will ſoone vaniſh.
Thar. Brother and ſiſter as I loue you, and am true ſeruant to *Venus*, all the premiſes are ſerious and true, and the concluſion is : the great Counteſſe is mine, the Palace is at your ſeruice, to which I inuite you all to ſolemnize my honour'd nuptialls.
Lyſand. Can this be credited !
Thar. Good brother doe not you enuie my fortunate atchieuement.
Lyſand. Nay I euer ſaid, the attempt was commendable.
Thar. Good.
Lyſand. If the iſſue were ſucceſſefull.
Thar. A good ſtate-concluſion, happie euents make good the worſt attempts. Here are your widdow-vowes ſiſter ; thus are yee all in your pure naturalls ; certaine morall diſguiſes of coineſſe, which the ignorant cal modeſtie, ye borrow of art to couer your buske points ; which a blunt and reſolute encounter, taken vnder a fortunate aſpect, eaſily diſarmes you off ;

and then alas what are you? poore naked finners,
God wot: weake paper walls thruft downe with a
finger; this is the way on't, boile their appetites to a
full height of luft; and then take them downe in the
nicke.

Cynth. Is there probabilitie in this; that a Ladie fo
great, fo vertuous, ftanding on fo high termes of
honour, fhould fo foone ftoope?

Thar. You would not wonder fifter, if you knew
the lure fhee ftoo'pt at: greatneffe? thinke you that
can curb affection; no, it whets it more; they haue
the full ftreame of bloud, to beare them: the fweet
gale of their fublim'd fpirits to driue them: the calme
of eafe to prepare them: the fun-fhine of fortune to
allure them: Greatneffe to waft them fafe through all
Rocks of infamie: when youth, wit, and perfon come
aboord once, tell me fifter, can you chufe but hoife
faile, and put forward to the maine?

Lyfand. But let me wonder at this frailtie yet; would
fhee in fo fhort time weare out his memorie, fo foon
wipe from her eies, nay, from her heart, whom I my-
felfe, and this whole Ile befides, ftill remember with
griefe, the impreffion of his loffe taking worthily fuch
roote in vs; howe thinke you Wife?

Cynth. I am afham'd ant, and abhorre to thinke,
So great and vow'd a patterne of our fexe,
Should take into her thoughts, nay to her bed,
(O ftaine to woman-hood) a fecond loue.

Lyc. In fo fhort time.

Cynth. In any time.

Lyfand. No wife.

Cynth. By *Iuno* no; fooner a lothfom Tode.

Thar. High words beleeue me, and I thinke fheele
keep them; next turne is yours Nephew; you fhall
now marrie my nobleft Ladie-Daughter; the firft marriage in *Paphos*; next my nuptialls fhall be yours;
thefe are ftrange occurrents brother, but pretie and
patheticall; if you fee mee in my chaire of Honour;
and my Counteffe in mine armes; you will then

beleeue, I hope, I am Lord of the Palace, then fhall you trie my great Ladies entertainement; fee your handes free'd of mee, and mine taking you to aduancement.

Lyfand. Well, all this rids not my bufineffe; wife you fhall bee there to partake the vnexpected honour of our Houfe. *Lycus,* and I will make it our recreation by the way, to thinke of your Reuells and Nuptiall fports; Brother my ftay hath beene for you; Wife pray thee bee gone, and foone prepare for the folemnitie, a Moneth returnes mee.

Cynth. Heauens guide your iourney.

Lyf. Fare-will.

Thar. Fare-well Nephew; profper in virilitie, but doe you heare; keepe your hand from your voice, I haue a part for you in our Hymeneall fhew.

Hyl. You fpeake too late for my voice, but Ile difcharge the part. *Exit Cyn. Hyl.*

Lyfand. Occurrents call yee them; foule fhame confound them all; that impregnable Fort of chaftitie and loyaltie, that amazement of the world, O yee Deities could nothing reftraine her? I tooke her fpirit to bee too haughtie for fuch a depreffion.

Thar. But who commonly more fhort heeld; then they that are high 'ith in-ftep.

Lyfand. Mee thinkes yet fhame fhould haue controul'd fo fodaine an appetite.

Thar. Tufh, fhame doth extinguifh luft as oile doth fire,
The bloud once het, fhame doth enflame the more,
What they before, by art diffembled moft
They act more freely; fhame once found is loft;
And to fay truth Brother; what fhame is due to't? or what congruence doth it carrie, that a yong Ladie, Gallant, Vigorous, full of Spirit, and Complexion; her appetite newe whetted with Nuptiall delights; to be confind to the fpeculation of a deaths head, or for the loffe of a husband, the world affording flefh enough, make the noone-tide of her yeares, the funne-fet of her pleafures.

Lyc. And yet there haue been fuch women.

Thar. Of the firſt ſtamp perhaps, when the mettal was purer then in thefe degenerate daies; of later yeares, much of that coine hath beene counterfait, and befides fo crackt and worne with vfe, that they are growne light, and indeede fit for nothing, but to be turn'd ouer in play.

Lyfand. Not all brother.

Thar. My matchleffe fifter only excepted : for fhee, you know is made of an other mettall, then that fhee borrow'd of her mother. But doe you brother fadly intend the purfuite of this triall ?

Lyfand. Irreuocably.

Thar. Its a high proiect : if it be once rais'd, the earth is too weake to beare fo waightie an accident, it cannot bee coniur'd downe againe, without an earthquake, therefore beleeue fhee will bee conftant.

Lyc. No, I will not.

Thar. Then beleeue fhee will not be conftant.

Lyfand. Neither, I will beleeue nothing but what triall enforces ; will you hold your promife for the gouerning of this proiect with skill, and fecrecie ?

Thar. If it muſt needes bee fo. But hearke you brother ; haue you no other Capricions in your head to intrap my fifter in her frailtie, but to proue the firmeneffe of her widdow vowes after your fuppos'd death.

Lyfand. None in the world.

Thar. Then here's my hand, Ile be as clofe, as my Ladies fhoe to her foote that pinches and pleafes her, and will beare on with the plot, till the veffell fplit againe.

Lyfand. Forge any death, fo you can force beliefe. Say I was poifon'd, drown'd.

Thar. Hang'd.

Lyfand. Any thing, fo you affift it with likely circumſtance, I neede not inſtruct you : that muſt bee your imploiment *Lycus*.

Lyc. Well Sir.

Thar. But brother you muſt ſet in to; to countenance truth out, a herſe there muſt be too; Its ſtrange to thinke how much the eie preuailes in ſuch impreſſions; I haue marckt a Widdow, that iuſt before was ſeene pleaſant enough, follow an emptie herſe, and weepe deuoutly.

Lyc. All thoſe thinges leaue to me.

Lyſan. But brother for the beſtowing of this herſe in the monument of our Familie, and the marſhalling of a Funerall.

Thar. Leaue that to my care, and if I doe not doe the mourner, as liuely as your Heire, and weepe as luſtily as your Widdow, ſay there's no vertue in Onions; that being done, Ile come to viſit the diſtreſt widdow; apply old ends of comfort to her griefe, but the burden of my ſong ſhall be to tell her wordes are but dead comforts; and therefore counſaile her to take a liuing comfort; that might Ferrit out the thought of her dead husband, and will come prepar'd with choiſe of ſuiters; either my Spartane Lord for grace at the Viceroies Court, or ſome great Lawyer that may ſoder vp her crackt eſtate, and ſo forth. But what would you ſay brother, if you ſhould finde her married at your arriuall.

Lyſand. By this hand ſplit her Weaſand.

Thar Well, forget not your wager, a ſtately chariot with foure braue Horſes of the Thracian breede, with all appurtenances. Ile prepare the like for you, if you proue Victor; but well remembred, where will you lurke the whiles?

Lyſand. Mewd vp cloſe, ſome ſhort daies iourney hence, *Lycus* ſhall know the place, write ſtill how all things paſſe, brother adiew; all ioy attend you.

Thar. Will you not ſtay our nuptiall now ſo neare.

Lyſand. I ſhould be like a man that heares a tale And heedes it not; one abſent from himſelfe, my wife ſhall attend the Counteſſe, and my Sonne.

Thar. Whom you ſhal here at your returne call me father, adiew: *Ioue* be your ſpeede.

My Nuptialls done, your Funeralls ſucceed. *Exeunt.*

Enter Argus barehead.

Arg. A Hall, a hall: who's without there? *Enter two or three with cuſhions.* Come on, y'are proper Groomes, are yee not? Slight I thinke y'are all Bridegroomes, yee take your pleaſures ſo. A companie of dormice. Their Honours are vpon comming, and the roome not readie. Ruſhes and ſeates inſtantly.

Thar. Now, alas fellow *Argus*, how thou art comberd with an office?

Arg. Perfume ſirrha, the roome's dampiſh.

Thar. Nay you may leaue that office to the Ladies, theyle perfume it ſufficiently.

Arg. Cry mercie Sir, here's a whole *Chorus* of *Syluans* at hand, cornetting, & tripping ath' toe, as the ground they troad on were too hot for their feete. The deuice is rare; and there's your yong Nephew too, he hangs in the clouds Deified with *Hymens* ſhape.

Thar. Is he perfect in's part? has not his tongue learn'd of the *Syluans* to trip ath' Toe?

Arg. Sir, beleeue it, he does it pretiouſly for accent and action, as if hee felt the part he plaid: hee rauiſhes all the yong Wenches in the Palace: Pray *Venus* my yong Ladie *Laodice* haue not ſome little prick of *Cupid* in her, ſhee's ſo diligent at's rehearſalls.

Thar. No force, ſo my next vowes be heard, that if *Cupid* haue prickt her, *Hymen* my cure her.

Arg. You meane your Nephew Sir that preſents *Hymen*.

Thar. Why ſo, I can ſpeake nothing but thou art with in me: fie of this wit of thine, 'twill be thy deſtruction. But howſoeuer you pleaſe to vnderſtand, *Hymen* ſend the boy no worſe fortune: And where's my Ladies honour?

Arg. At hand Sir, with your vnparagond ſiſter, pleaſe you take your chaire of Honour Sir?

Thar. Moſt ſeruiceable *Argus*, the Gods reward thy
ſeruice ; for I will not.

*Enter Eudora, leading Cynthia, Laodice, Sthenio,
Ianthe, Ero, with others
following.*

Eud. Come ſiſter, now we muſt exchange that name
For ſtranger Titles, let's diſpoſe our ſelues
To entertaine theſe *Syluane* Reuellers,
That come to grace our loued Nuptialls,
I'feare we muſt all turne Nymphs to night,
To ſide thoſe ſprightly wood-Gods in their dances ;
Can you doo't nimbly ſiſter? ſlight what aile you, are you not well?
Cynth. Yes Madam.
Eud. But your lookes, mee thinkes, are cloudie ;
ſuiting all the Sunne-ſhine of this cleare honour to
your husbands houſe.
Is there ought here that ſorts not with your liking?
Thar. Blame her not Miſtris, if her lookes ſhew care.
Excuſe the Merchants ſadneſſe that hath made
A doubtfull venture of his whole eſtate ;
His liuelyhood, his hopes, in one poore bottome,
To all encounters of the Sea and ſtormes.
Had you a husband that you lou'd as well,
Would you not take his abſent plight as ill?
Cauill at euery fancie? Not an obiect
That could preſent it ſelfe, but it would forge
Some vaine obiection, that did doubt his ſafetie ;
True loue is euer full of iealouſie.
Eud. Iealous? of what? of euery little iourney?
Meere fancie then is wanton ; and doth caſt
At thoſe ſleight dangers there, too doting glances ;
Miſgiuing mindes euer prouoke miſchances :
Shines not the Sunne in his way bright as here?
Is not the aire as good? what hazard doubt you?

D

Arg.   His horſe may ſtumble if it pleaſe your Honour ;
The raine may wet, the winde may blow on him ;
Many ſhrewd hazards watch poore trauailers.
Eud.   True, and the ſhrewdeſt thou haſt reckend vs,
Good fiſter, theſe cares fit yong married wiues.
Cynth.   Wiues ſhould be ſtil yong in their husbands loues.
Time beares no Sythe ſhould bear down them before him.
Our liues he may cut ſhort, but not our loues.
Thar.   Siſter be wife, and ſhip not in one Barke,
All your abilitie : if he miſcarrie,
Your well tried wifedome ſhould looke out for new.
Cynth.   I wiſh them happie windes that runne that courſe,
From me tis farre ; One Temple ſeal'd our troth.
One Tomb, one houre ſhall end, and ſhroud vs both.
Thar.   Well, y'are a *Phœnix*, there be that your cheere
Loue, with your husband be, your wifedome here.
Hearke, our ſports challenge it ; Sit deareſt Miſtris.
Eud.   Take your place worthieſt ſeruant.
Thar.   Serue me heauen.   *Muſique.*
As I my heauenly Miſtris, Sit rare fiſter.
Muſique : *Hymen* deſcends ; and ſixe *Syluanes* enter beneath, with Torches.
Arg.   A hall, a hall : let no more Citizens in there.
Laod.   O, Not my Coſen ſee ; but *Hymens* ſelfe.
Sthe.   He does become it moſt enflamingly.
Hym.   Haile honor'd Bridegroom, and his Princely bride
With the moſt fam'd for vertue, *Cynthia* ;
And this yong Ladie, bright *Laodice*,
One rich hope of this nobleſt Familie.
Sthe.   Hearke how he courts : he is enamour'd too.
Laod.   O grant it *Venus*, and be euer honour'd.
Hym.   In grace and loue of you, I *Hymen* ſearcht
The groues and thickets that embrace this Palace

A Comedie. 51

With this clear-flam'd, and good aboding Torch
For fummons of thefe frefh and flowrie *Syluans,*
To this faire prefence ; with their winding Haies,
Aƈtiue and Antique dances to delight
Your frolick eies, and helpe to celebrate
Thefe nobleft nuptialls ; which great Deftinie,
Ordain'd paft cuftome and all vulgar obieƈt
To be the readuancement of a houfe,
Noble and Princely, and reftore this Palace
To that name, that fixe hunderd Summers fince
Was in poffeffion of this Bridegroomes Ancetors,
The ancient and moft vertue-fam'd *Lyfandri.*
Syluans! the Courtfhips you make to your Dryads,
Vfe to this great Bride, and thefe other Dames,
And heighten with your fports, my nuptiall flames.
Laod. O would himfelfe defcend, and me command.
Sthe. Dance ; and his heart catch in an others hand.
   Syluans, take out the Bride and the reft : They dance,
      after which, and all fet in their places.
                  Hymen.
Hym. Now, what the Power and my Torches in-
   fluence
Hath in the bleffings of your Nuptiall ioyes
(Great Bride and Bridegroome) you fhall amply part
Betwixt your free loues, and forgoe it neuer.
Omn. Thankes to great *Hymen,* and faire *Syluanes*
   euer.   *Exeunt.*
           Finis Aƈtus Tertij.

Aƈtus Quarti.
Scœna Prima.

*Tharfalio, Lycus, with his Arme in a skarfe, a night
         cap on's head.*

Lyc.   ⎱ Hope Sir by this time.
Thar. I Put on man, by our felues.
Lyc.   ⎰ The edge of your confidence is well take

off; would you not bee content to with-draw your wager?

Thar. Faith fellow *Lycus*, if my wager were weakely built, this vnexpected accident might ſtagger it. For the truth is, this ſtrain is extraordinarie, to follow her husbands bodie into the Tombe, and there for his companie to burie her ſelfe quick: it's new and ſtirring, but for all this, Ile not deſpaire of my wager.

Lyc. Why Sir, can you thinke ſuch a paſſion diſ-ſembl'd?

Thar. All's one for that, What I thinke I thinke; In the meane time forget not to write to my Brother, how the plot hath ſucceeded, that the newes of his death hath taken; a funerall ſolemnitie perform'd, his ſup-pos'd Corſe beſtow'd in the monument of our Familie, thou and I horrible mourners: But aboue all that his intollerable vertuous Widow, for his loue, and (for her loue) *Ero* her hand-maid, are diſcended with his Corſe into the vault; there wipe their eies time out of minde, drinke nothing but their own teares, and by this time are almoſt dead with famine. There's a point will ſting it (for you ſay tis true) where left you him?

Lyc. At Dipolis Sir, ſome twentie miles hence.

Thar. He keepes cloſe.

Lyc. I ſir, by all meanes; skulks vnknowne vnder the name of a ſtrange Knight.

Thar. That may carrie him without diſcrying, for there's a number of ſtrange Knights abroad. You left him well.

Lyc. Well Sir, but for this iealous humour that hants him.

Thar. Well, this newes will abſolutely purge that humor. Write all, forget not to deſcribe her paſſion at thy diſcouerie of his ſlaughter: did ſhee performe it well for her husbands wager?

Lyc. Performe it, call you it? you may ieſt; men hunt Hares to death for their ſports, but the poore beaſts die in earneſt: you wager of her paſſions for

A Comedie. 53

your pleasure, but shee takes little pleasure in those earnest passions. I neuer saw such an extasie of sorrow, since I knew the name of sorrow. Her hands flew vp to her head like Furies, hid all her beauties in her discheuel'd haire, & wept as she would turne fountaine. I would you and her husband had beene behind the Arras but to haue heard her. I assure you Sir, I was so transported with the spectacle, that in despight of my discretion, I was forc't to turne woman, and beare a part with her. Humanitie broke loose from my heart, and stream'd through mine eies.

Thar. In prose, thou weptst. So haue I seen many a moist Auditor doe at a play; when the storie was but a meere fiction: And didst act the Nuntius well, would I had heard it: could'st thou dresse thy lookes in a mournefull habite?

Lyc. Not without preparation Sir; no more then my speech, twas a plaine acting of an enterlude to me, to pronounce the part.

Thar. As how for heauens sake?

Lyc. Phœbus addrest his Chariot towards the West To change his wearied Coursers, and so forth.

Thar. Nay on, and thou lou'st me.

Lyc. Lysander and my selfe beguild the way With enterchang'd discourse, but our chiefe Theame, Was of your dearest selfe, his honour'd wife; Your loue, your vertue, wondrous constancie.

Thar. Then was her Cu to whimper; on.

Lyc. When sodainly appear'd as far as sight A troope of horse, arm'd as we might descerne, With Iauelines, Speares, and such accoutrements. He doubted nought (As Innocencie euer Is free from doubting ill.)

Thar. There dropt a teare.

Lyc. My minde misgaue me. They might be mountaners. At their approch They vs'd no other language but their weapons, To tell vs what they were; *Lysander* drew, And bore him selfe *Achilles* like in fight,

And as a Mower fweepes off t'heads of Bents,
So did *Lyfanders* fword fhaue off the points
Of their affaulting lances.
His horfe at laft, fore hurt, fell vnder him;
I feeing I could not refcue, vs'd my fpurres
To flie away.
Thar. What from thy friend?
Lyc. I in a good quarrell, why not?
Thar. Good; I am anfwer'd.
Lyc. A lance purfued me, brought me back againe;
And with thefe wounds left me t'accompanie
Dying *Lyfander* : Then they rifl'd vs,
And left vs.
They gone; my breath not yet gone, gan to ftriue
And reuiue fenfe : I with my feeble ioynts
Crawl'd to *Lyfander*, ftirr'd him, and withall
He gafpt; cried *Cynthia !* and breath'd no more.
Thar. O then fhee howl'd out right.
Lyc. Paffengers came and in a Chariot brought vs
Streight to a Neighbour Towne; where I forthwith
Coffind my friend in leade; and fo conuaid him
To this fad place.
Thar. 'Twas well; and could not fhow but ftrangely.
Lyc. Well Sir, This tale pronounc't with terrour, fuited
with action clothed with fuch likely circumftance; My
wounds in fhew, her husbands herfe in fight, thinke
what effect it wrought: And if you doubt, let the fad
confequence of her retreat to his Tombe, bee your
wofull inftructer.
Thar. For all this, Ile not defpaire of my wager:
Thefe Grieues that found fo lowd, proue alwaies
    light,
True forrow euermore keepes out of fight.
This ftraine of mourning with Sepulcher, like an ouer-
doing Actor, affects grofly, and is indeede fo farre
forc't from the life, that it bewraies it felfe to be altogether artificiall.
To fet open a fhop of mourning! Tis palpable.
Truth the fubftance, hunts not after the fhadow of

popular Fame. Her officious oftentation of forrow condemnes her finceritie. When did euer woman mourne fo vnmeafurably, but fhee did diffemble ?

Lyc. O Gods! a paffion thus borne; thus apparell'd with teares, fighes, fwownings, and all the badges of true forrow, to be diffembl'd! by *Venus* I am forrie I euer fet foot in't. Could fhee, if fhee diffembl'd, thus dally with hunger, be deafe to the barking of her appetite, not hauing thefe foure daies relieu'd nature with one dramme of fuftenance.

Thar. For this does fhee looke to bee Deified, to haue Hymnes made of her, nay to her: The Tomb where fhe is to be no more reputed the ancient monument of our Familie the *Lyfandri*; but the new erected Altar of *Cynthia*: To which all the Paphian widdowes fhall after their husbands Funeralls, offer their wet muckinders, for monuments of the danger they haue paft, as Sea-men doe their wet garments at *Neptunes* Temple after a fhip wracke.

Lyc. Well, Ile apprehend you, at your pleafure: I for my part will fay; that if her faith bee as conftant as her loue is heartie, and vnaffected, her vertues may iuftly challenge a Deitie to enfhrine them.

Thar. I, there's an other point too. But one of thofe vertues is enough at once. All natures are not capable of all gifts. If the braine of the Weft, were in the heads of the learned; then might Parifh-Clerkes be common counfaile men, and Poets Aldermens deputies. My fifter may turne *Niobe* for loue; but till *Niobe* bee turn'd to a Marble, Ile not defpaire but fhee may proue a woman. Let the triall runne on, if fhee doe not out-runne it, Ile fay Poets are no Prophets, Prognofticators are but Mountibankes, & none tell true but wood-mongers. *Exit.*

Lyc. A fweet Gentleman you are. I meruaile what man ? what woman ? what name ? what action doth his tongue glide ouer, but it leaues a flime vpon't. Well, Ile prefently to Dipolis, where *Lyfander* ftaies; and will not fay but fhee may proue fraile: But this

Ile fay, If fhe fhould chance to breake, Her teares are
true, though womens truths are weake.   *Exit.*

*Enter Lyfander like a Souldier difguifde at all parts,
a halfe Pike, gorget. &c. he difcouers the Tombe,
lookes in and wonders, &c.*

O Miracle of nature! womens glorie;
  Mens fhame; and enuie of the Deities!
Yet muft thefe matchleffe creatures be fufpected;
Accus'd; condemn'd!
Now by th'immortall Gods,
They rather merit Altars, Sacrifice,
Then loue and courtfhip.
Yet fee the Queene of thefe lies here interred;
Tearing her haire, and drowned in her teares.
Which *Ioue* fhould turne to Chriftall; and a Mirrour
Make of them; wherein men may fee and wonder
At womens vertues. Shall fhee famifh then?
Will men (without diffwafions) fuffer thus
So bright an Ornament to earth, tomb'd quick.
In Earths darke bofome: Ho!
Who's in the Tombe there?
Ero. Who calls? whence are you?
Lyf. I am Souldier of the watch and muft enter.
Ero. Amongft the dead?
Lyf. Doe the dead fpeake? ope or Ile force it open.
Ero. What violence is this? what feeke you here
Where nought but death and her attendants dwell.
Lyf. What wretched foules are you that thus by night
lurke here amongft the dead?
Ero. Good Souldier doe not ftirre her,
Shee's weake, and quickly feiz'd with fwowning and
paffions, and with much trouble fhall we both recall
her fainting fpirits.
Fiue daies thus hath fhee wafted; and not once fea-
fon'd her Pallate with the taft of meate; her powers
of life are fpent; and what remaines of her famifht
fpirit, ferues not to breath but figh.

A Comedie. 57

Shee hath exil'd her eies from fleepe, or fight, and giuen them wholly vp to ceafeleffe teares ouer that ruthfull herfe of her deare Spoufe, flaine by Bantditos, Nobly borne *Lyfander*.

Lyfand. And hopes fhee with thefe heauie notes and cries to call him from the dead? in thefe fiue daies hath fhee but made him ftirre a finger or fetch one gafp of that forfaken life fhee mournes?
Come, honour'd Miftris; I admire your vertues;
But muft reproue this vaine exceffe of mone;
Rowfe your felfe Ladie, and looke vp from death,
Well faid, tis well; ftay by my hand and rife.
This Face hath beene maintain'd with better hufwiferie.

Cyn. What are you?
Lyf. Ladie, I am Sentinell,
Set in this hallowed place, to watch and guard
On forfait of my life, thefe monuments
From Rape, and fpoil'd of facrilegious handes
And faue the bodies, that without you fee
Of crucified offenders : that no friends
May beare them hence, to honour'd buriall.

Cyn. Thou feem'ft an honeft Souldier, pray thee then
Be as thou feem'ft; betake thee to thy charge
And leaue this place; adde not affliction
To the afflicted.

Lyf. You mifname the children.
For what you terme affliction now, in you
Is but felfe-humour; voluntarie Penance
Impos'd vpon your felfe : and you lament
As did the *Satyre* once, that ran affrighted
From that hornes found that he himfelfe had winded.
Which humor to abate, my counfaile tending your term'd affliction,
What I for Phificke giue, you take for poifon.
I tell you honour'd Miftris, thefe ingredients
Are wholefome, though perhaps they feeme vntoothfome.

Ero. This Souldier sure, is some decai'd pothecarie.
Lys. Deere Ghost be wise, and pittie your faire selfe
Thus, by your selfe vnnaturally afflicted:
Chide back, heart-breaking grones, clear vp those lamps,
Restore them to their first creation:
Windowes for light; not sluces made for teares.
Beate not the senselesse aire with needlesse cries,
Banefull to life, and bootlesse to the dead.
This is the Inne, where all *Deucalions* race
Sooner or later, must take vp their lodging;
No priuiledge can free vs from this prison;
No teares, no praiers, can redeeme from hence
A captiu'd soule; Make vse of what you see:
Let this affrighting spectacle of death
Teach you to nourish life.
Ero. Good heare him: this is a rare Souldier.
Lysand. Say that with abstinence you should vnlose
the knot of life: Suppose that in this Tombe for your
deare Spouse, you should entomb your selfe a liuing
Corse; Say that before your houre without due Summons from the Fates, you send your hastie soule to
hell: can your deare Spouse take notice of your faith
and constancie? Shall your deare Spouse reuiue to
giue you thankes?
Cynth. Idle discourser.
Lysan. No, your moanes are idle.
Goe to I say, be counsail'd; raise your selfe:
Enioy the fruits of life, there's viands for you,
Now, liue for a better husband.
No? will you none?
Ero. For loue of courtesie, good Mistris, eate,
Doe not reiect so kinde and sweet an offer,
Who knowes but this may be some *Mercurie*
Disguis'de, and sent from *Iuno* to relieue vs?
Did euer any lend vnwilling eares
To those that came with messages of life?
Cynth. I pray thee leaue thy Rhetorique.
Ero. By my soule; to speake plaine truth, I could

rather wifh t'employ my teeth then my tongue, fo your example would be my warrant.
Cynth. Thou haft my warrant.
Lyfand. Well then, eate my wench,
Let obftinacie ftarue.
Fall to.
Ero. Perfwade my Miftris firft.
Lyfand. Slight tell me Ladie,
Are you refolu'd to die? If that be fo,
Choofe not (for fhame) a bafe, and beggars death:
Die not for hunger, like a Spartane Ladie;
Fall valiantly vpon a fword, or drinke
Noble death, expell your griefe with poifon,
There 'tis, feize it.——Tufh you dare not die.
Come Wench thou haft not loft a husband;
Thou fhalt eate, th'art now within
The place where I command.
Ero. I proteft fir.
Lyf. Well faid; eate, and proteft, or Ile proteft
And doe thou eate; thou eat'ft againft thy will,
That's it thou would'ft fay.
Ero. It is.
Lyf. And vnder fuch a proteftation
Thou loft' thy Maiden-head.
For your owne fake good Ladie forget this husband,
Come you are now become a happy Widdow,
A bleffedneffe that many would be glad of.
That and your husbands Inuentorie together,
Will raife you vp husbands enow.
What thinke you of me?
Cynth. Trifler, purfue this wanton Theame no further;
Left (which I would be loth) your fpeech prouoke
Vnciuill language from me; I muft tell you,
One ioynt of him I loft, was much more worth
Then the rackt valew of thy entire bodie.
Ero. O know what ioynt fhee meanes.
Lyf. Well, I haue done.
And well done frailtie; proface, how lik'ft thou it.

Ero. Very toothsome Ingrediens surely sir,
Want but some lycor to incorporate them.
Lys. There tis, carouse.
Ero. I humbly thanke you Sir.
Lys. Hold pledge me now.
Ero. Tis the poison Sir,
That preserues life, I take it. *bibit Ancill.*
Lys. Doe so, take it.
Ero. Sighing has made me somthing short-winded.
Ile pledge y'at twice.
Lys. Tis well done; doe me right.
Ero. I pray sir, haue you beene a Pothecarie?
Lys. Marrie haue I wench; A womans Pothecarie.
Ero. Haue you good Ingredients?
I like your Bottle well. Good Mistris tast it.
Trie but the operation, twill fetch vp
The Roses in your cheekes againe.
Doctor *Verolles* bottles are not like it;
There's no *Guaicum* here, I can assure you.
Lys. This will doe well anone.
Ero. Now fie vpon't.
O I haue lost my tongue in this same lymbo.
The spring ants, spoil'd me thinkes; it goes not off
With the old twange.
Lys. Well said wench, oile it well; twill make it slide
  well.
Ero. Aristotle saies sir, in his Posterionds.
Lys. This wench is learned; And what saies he?
Ero. That when a man dies, the last thing that moues
is his heart, in a woman her tongue.
Lys. Right; and addes further, that you women are
a kind of spinners; if their legs be pluckt off, yet still
they'le wag them; so will you your tongues.
With what an easie change does this same weaknesse
Of women, slip from one extreame t' another?
All these attractions take no hold of her;
No not to take refection; 'T must not be thus.
Well said wench; Tickle that Helicon.
But shall we quit the field with this disgrace

A Comedie.   61

Giuen to our Oratorie? Both not gaine
So much ground of her as to make her eate?
Ero. Faith the trurh is fir: you are no fit Organe
For this bufineſſe;
Tis quite out of your Element:
Let vs alone, ſheele eate I haue no feare;
A womans tongue beſt fits a womans eare.
Ioue neuer did employ *Mercurie*,
But *Iris* for his Meſſenger to *Iuno*.
Lyf. Come, let me kiſſe thee wench; wilt vndertake
To make thy Miſtris eate?
Ero. It ſhall go hard Sir
But I will make her turne fleſh and bloud,
And learne to liue as other mortalls doe.
Lyf. Well ſaid: the morning haſts; next night expect me.
Ero. With more prouiſion good Sir.
Lyf. Very good.   *Exiturus.*
Ero. And bring more wine. *Shee ſhuts vp the Tomb.*
Lyf. What elſe; ſhalt haue enough:
O *Cynthia*, heire of her bright puritie,
Whoſe name thou doſt inherit; Thow diſdainſt
(Seuer'd from all concretion) to feede
Vpon the baſe foode of groſſe Elements.
Thou all art foule; All immortalitie.
Thou faſts for *Nectar* and *Ambroſia*,
Which till thou find'ſt, and eat'ſt aboue the ſtarres,
To all foode here thou bidd'ſt celeſtiall warrs.   *Exit.*
    Cynthia, Ero, the Tomb opening.
Ero. So; lets aire our dampiſh ſpirits, almoſt ſtifl'd in this groſe muddie Element.
Cyn. How ſweet a breath the calmneſſe of the night inſpires the aire withall?
Ero. Well ſaid; Now y'are your ſelfe: did not I tell you how ſweet an operation the Souldiers bottle had? And if there be ſuch vertue in the bottle; what is there in the Souldier? know, and acknowledge his worth when hee comes in any caſe Miſtris.
Cyn. So Maide.

Ero. Gods my patience? did you looke forsooth that *Iuno* should haue sent you meate from her owne Trencher, in reward of your widdowes teares? you might sit and sigh first till your heart-strings broke, Ile able't.
Cyn. I feare me thy lips haue gone so oft to the bottle, that thy tongue-strings are come broken home.
Ero. Faith the truth is, my tongue hath beene so long tied vp, that tis couer'd with rust, & I rub it against my pallat as wee doe suspected coines, to trie whether it bee currant or no. But now Mistris for an vpshot of this bottle; let's haue one carouse to the good speede of my old Master, and the good speede of my new.
Cyn. So Damzell.
Ero. You must pledge it, here's to it. Doe me right I pray.
Cyn. You say I must.
Ero. Must? what else?
Cyn. How excellent ill this humour suites our habite?
Ero. Go to Mistris, do not thinke but you and I shall haue good sport with this iest, when we are in priuate at home. I would to *Venus* we had some honest shift or other to get off withall; for Ile no more ant; Ile not turne Salt-peeter in this vault for neuer a mans companie liuing; much lesse for a womans. Sure I am the wonder's ouer, and 'twas only for that, that I endur'd this; and so a my conscience did you. Neuer denie it.
Cyn. Nay pray thee take it to thee.

Enter Lysander.

Cyn. Hearke I heare some footing neare vs.
Ero. Gods me 'tis the Souldier Mistris, by *Venus* if you fall to your late black *Santus* againe, Ile discouer you.
Lys. What's here? The maid hath certainly preuail'd with her; mee thinkes those cloudes that last

night couer'd her lookes are now difperft: Ile trie this further. Saue you Lady.

Ero. Honorable Souldier? y'are welcome; pleafe you ftep in fir?

Lyf. With all my heart fweet heart; by your patience Ladie; why this beares fome fhape of life yet. Damzell, th'aft performd a feruice of high reckoning, which cannot perifh vnrewarded.

Ero. Faith Sir, you are in the way to doe it once, if you haue the heart to hold on.

Cyn. Your bottle has poifond this wench fir.

Lyf. A wholfome poifon it is Ladie, if I may be iudge; of which fort here is one better bottle more.
  Wine is ordaind to raife fuch hearts as finke,
  Whom wofull ftarres diftemper; let him drinke.
I am moft glad I haue beene fome meane to this part of your recouerie, and will drinke to the reft of it.

Ero. Goe to Miftris, pray fimper no more; pledge the man of Warre here.

Cyn. Come y'are too rude.

Ero. Good.

Lyf. Good footh Ladie y'are honour'd in her feruice; I would haue you liue, and fhee would haue you liue freely; without which life is but death. To liue freely is to feaft our appetites freely; without which humanes are ftones; to the fatisfaction whereof I drinke Ladie.

Cyn. Ile pledge you Sir.

Ero. Said like a Miftris; and the Miftris of your felfe; pledge him in loue too: I fee hee loues you; Shee's filent, fhee confents fir.

Lyf. O happy ftarres. And now pardon Ladie; me thinks thefe are all of a peece.

Ero. Nay if you kiffe all of a peece wee fhall n'ere haue done: Well twas well offer'd, and as well taken.

Cyn. If the world fhould fee this.

Lyf. The world! fhould one fo rare as your felfe, refpect the vulgar world?

Cyn. The praife I haue had, I would continue.

Lyf. What of the vulgar? Who hates not the vulgar, deferues not loue of the vertuous. And to affect praife of that we defpife, how ridiculous it is?
Ero. Comfortable doctrine Miftris, edifie, edifie. Me thinkes euen thus it was when *Dido* And *Æneas* met in the Caue; And hearke Me thinks I heare fome of the hunters. *She shuts the tomb.*

Finis Actus Quarti.

Actus Quinti.

Scœna Prima.

Enter Tharfalio, Lycus.

Lyc. TIs fuch an obftinacie in you Sir, As neuer was conceipted, to runne on With an opinion againft all the world, And what your eies may witnes; to aduēture
The famifhment for griefe of fuch a woman
As all mens merits met in any one,
Could not deferue.
Thar. I muft confeffe it *Lycus*,
Weele therefore now preuent it if we may,
And that our curious triall hath not dwelt
Too long on this vnneceffarie hant:
Griefe, and all want of foode; not hauing wrouught
Too mortally on her diuine difpofure.
Lyc. I feare they haue, and fhee is paft our cure.
Thar. I muft confeffe with feare and fhame as much.
Lyc. And that fhee will not truft in any thing
What you perfwade her to.
Thar. Then thou fhalt haft
And call my brother from his fecret fhroude,
Where he appointed thee to come and tell him

A Comedie. 65

How all thinges haue succeeded.
Lyc. This is well.
If (as I say) the ill be not so growne,
That all help is denied her. But I feare
The matchlesse Deme is famisht. *Thar. looks into the*
Thar. Slight, whose here ? *tomb.*
A Souldier with my sister ? wipe, wipe, see
Kissing by *Ioue*; shee, as I lay tis shee.
Lyc. What ? is shee well Sir ?
Thar. O no, shee is famisht;
Shee's past our comfort, shee lies drawing on.
Lyc. The Gods forbid.
Thar. Looke thou, shee's drawing on.
How saist thou ?
Lyc. Drawing on ? Illustrious witchcrafts.
Thar. Lies shee not drawing on ?
Lyc. Shee drawes on fairely.
Our sister Sir ? This shee ? can this be shee ?
Thar. She, she, she, and none but she.
He dances & sings.
Shee only Queene of loue, and chastitie,
O chastitie; This women be.
Lyc. Slight tis prodigious. *Thar.* Horse, horse,
 horse,
Foure Chariot Horses of the Thracian breede,
Come, bring me brother. O the happiest euening,
That euer drew her vaile before the Sunne.
Who is't canst tell ?
Lyc. The Souldier Sir that watches
The bodies crucified in this hallow'd place.
Of which to lose one, it is death to him,
And yet the lustfull knaue is at his Venerie,
While one might steale one.
Thar. What a slaue was I
That held not out my windes strength constanly,
That shee would proue thus ? O incredible ?
A poore eight-pennie Souldier ? Shee that lately
Was at such height of interiection,
Stoope now to such a base coniunction ?

E

By heauen I wonder now I fee't in act,
My braine could euer dreame of fuch a thought.
And yet, tis true : Rare, pereles, is't not *Lycus* ?
Lyc. I know not what it is ; Nor what to fay.
Thar. O had I held out (villaine that I was,)
My bleffed confidence but one minute longer,
I fhould haue beene eternis'd. Gods my fortune,
What an vnfpeakable fweet fight it is ?
O eies Ile facrifice to your deare fenfe.
And confecrate a Phane to Confidence.
Lyc. But this you muft at no hand tell your brother.
Twill make him mad : For he that was before
So fcurg'd but only with bare iealoufie.
What would he be, if he fhould come to know it ?
Thar. He would be leffe mad : for your only way
To cleare his iealoufie, is to let him know it.
When knowledge comes fufpicion vanifhes.
The Sunne-beames breaking forth fwallow the mifts.
But as for you Sir Gallant : howfoeuer
Your banquet feemes fweet in your lycorous pallat,
It fhall be fure to turne gall in your maw.
Thy hand a little *Lycus* here without.
Lyc. To what ?
Thar. No bootie ferue you fir Soldado
But my poore fifter ? Come, lend me thy fhoulder,
Ile climbe the croffe ; it will be fuch a cooler
To my Venerean Gentlemans hot liuer,
When he fhall finde one of his crucified bodies
Stolne downe, and he to be forthwith made faft
In place thereof, for the figne
Of the loft Sentinell. Come glorifie
Firme Confidence in great Inconftancie.
And this beleeue (for all prou'd knowledge fweares)
He that beleeues in errour, neuer errs.   *Exeunt.*

The Tomb opens, Lyfander, Cynthia, Ero.

Lyf. Tis late ; I muft away.
Cyn. Not yet fweet loue.
Lyf. Tempt not my ftay, tis dangerous. The law is
ftrict, and not to bee difpenft with. If any Sentinell

A Comedie.   67

be too late in's watch, or that by his neglect one of the crucified bodies fhould be ftollen from the croffe, his life buyes it.
Cyn. A little ftay will not endanger them. The daies proclaimer has not yet giuen warning. The Cock yet has not beate his third alarme.
Lyf. What? fhall we euer dwell here amongft th' Antipodes? Shall I not enioy the honour of my fortune in publique? fit in *Lyfanders* chaire? Raigne in his wealth?
Cyn. Thou fhalt, thou fhalt; though my loue to thee Hath prou'd thus fodaine and for haft lept ouer The complement of wooing, Yet only for the worlds opinion.
Lyf. Marke that againe.
Cyn. I muft maintaine a forme in parting hence.
Lyf. Out vpon't, Opinion the blind Goddeffe of Fooles, Foe to the vertuous; and only friend to undeferuing perfons, contemne it. Thou know'ft thou haft done vertuoufly; thou haft ftrangly forrow'd for thy husband, follow'd him to death; further thou could'ft not, thou haft buried thy felfe quick. (O that 'twere true) fpent more teares ouer his carcafe, then would ferue a whole Citie of faddeft widdowes in a plague time; befides fighings, and fwownings, not to be credited.
Cyn. True, but thofe complements might haue their time for fafhion 'fake.
Lyf. Right, Opinion and Fafhion. Sfoot what call you time? t'haft wept thefe foure whole daies.
Ero. Nay berladie almoft fiue.
Lyf. Looke you there; nere vpon fiue whole daies.
Cyn. Well goe and fee; Returne, weele goe home.
Lyf. Hell be thy home, Huge Monfters damne yee, and your whole creation, O yee Gods; in the height of her mourning in a Tomb, within fight of fo many deaths! her husbands beleeu'd bodie in her eie. He dead, a few daies before; this mirrour of Nuptiall chaftitie; this Votreffe of widdow-conftancie: to

change her faith; exchange kisses, embraces, with a stranger; and but my shame with-stood, to giue the vtmost earnest of her loue, to an eight-pennie Sentinell: in effect, to prostitute her selfe vpon her husbands Coffin! Lust, impietie, hell, womanhood it selfe, adde if you can one step to this.

Enter Captaine with two or three Souldiers.

Cap. ONe of the crucified bodies taken downe!
Lys. Enough.   *(slincks away.)*
Cap. And the Sentinell not to be heard off?
1. No sir.
Cap. Make out; hast, search about for him; does none of you know him? nor his name?
2. Hee's but a stranger here of some foure daies standing; and we neuer set eie on him, but at setting the watch.
Cap. For whom serues he? you looke well to your watch masters.
1. For *Seigneur Stratio*, and whence he is, tis ignorant to vs; we are not correspondent for any, but our owne places.
Cap. Y'are eloquent. Abroad I say, let me haue him.   *Exeunt.*
This negligence will by the Gouernour be wholly cast on me, he hereby will suggest to the Viceroy, that the Citie guards are very caresly attended. He loues mee not I know; because of late I knew him but of meane condition; but now by fortunes iniudicious hand, guided by bribing Courtiers, hee is rais'd to this high seate of honour. Nor blushes he, to see him selfe aduanc't ouer the heads of ten times higher worths; but takes it all forsooth, to his merits; and lookes (as all vpstarts doe) for most huge obseruance. Well, my mind must stoope to his high place, and learne within it selfe to seuer him from that, and to adore the Authoritie the Goddesse, how euer borne by an vnworthie beast; and let the Beasts dull apprehension take the honour done to *Isis*, done to himselfe. I must sit

faſt, and bee ſure to giue no hold to theſe fault-hunting enemies. *Exit.*

Tomb opens, and Lyſander within lies along,
Cynthia and Ero.

Lyſ. Pray thee diſturbe me not; put out the lights.
Ero. Faith Ile take a nap againe.
Cyn. Thou ſhalt not reſt before I be reſolu'd
What happy winde hath driuen thee back to harbour?
Was it my loue?
Lyſ. No.
Cyn. Yet ſay ſo (ſweet) that with the thought thereof
I may enioy all that I wiſh in earth.
Lyſ. I am ſought for. A crucified body is ſtolne while I loiter'd here; and I muſt die for't.
Cyn. Die? All the Gods forbid; O this affright torments me ten parts more then the ſad loſſe of my deare husband.
Lyſ. (Damnation) I beleeue thee.
Cyn. Yet heare a womans wit,
Take counſaile of Neceſſitie and it
I haue a bodie here which once I lou'd
And honour'd aboue all; but that time's paſt.
Lyſ. It is, reuenge it heauen.
Cyn. That ſhall ſupply at ſo extrem a need the vacant Gibbet.
Lyſ. Canero. What? thy husbands bodie?
Cyn. What hurt is't, being dead it ſaue the liuing?
Lyſ. O heart hold in, check thy rebellious motion.
Cyn. Vexe not thy ſelfe deare loue, nor vſe delay.
Tempt not this danger, ſet thy handes to worke.
Lyſ. I can not doo't; my heart will not permit
My handes to execute a ſecond murther.
The truth is I am he that ſlew thy husband.
Cyn. The Gods forbid.
Lyſ. It was this hand that bath'd my reeking ſword
In his life bloud, while he cried out for mercie,
But I remorſeleſſe, panch't him, cut his throat,
He with his laſt breath crying, *Cynthia.*

The Widdowes Teares.

Cyn. O thou haſt told me newes that cleaues my heart,
Would I had neuer ſeene thee, or heard ſooner
This bloudie ſtorie; yet ſee, note my truth
Yet I muſt loue thee.
Lyſ. Out vpon the Monſter.
Goe, tell the Gouernour; Let me be brought
To die for that moſt famous villanie;
Not for this miching baſe tranſgreſſion
Of tenant negligence.
Cyn. I can not doo't.
Loue muſt ſalue any murther: Ile be iudge
Of thee deare loue, and theſe ſhall be thy paines
In ſteede of yron, to ſuffer theſe ſoft chaines.
Lyſ. O I am infinitely oblig'd.
Cyn. Ariſe I ſay, thou ſauer of my life.
Doe not with vaine-affrighting conſcience
Betray a life, that is not thine but mine:
Riſe and preſerue it. *Lyſ.* Ha? thy husbands bodie?
Hang't vp you ſay, in ſteede of that that's ſtolne;
Yet I his murtherer, is that your meaning?
Cyn. It is my Loue. *Lyſ.* Thy loue amazes me,
The point is yet how we ſhall get it thither,
Ha? Tie a halter about's necke, and dragge him to the Gallowes: ſhall I my loue?
Cyn. So you may doe indeede,
Or if your owne ſtrength will not ſerue, wee'le aide
Our handes to yours, and beare him to the place.
For heauens loue come, the night goes off apace.
Lyſ. All the infernall plagues dwell in thy ſoule;
Ile fetch a crow of yron to breake the coffin.
Cyn. Doe loue, be ſpeedie.
Lyſ. As I wiſh thy damnation. *Shut the Tomb.*
O I could teare my ſelfe into Atomes; off with this Antick, the ſhirt that *Hercules* wore for his wife, was not more banefull. Is't poſſible there ſhould be ſuch a latitude in the Sphere of this ſexe, to entertaine ſuch an extention of miſchiefe, and not turne Deuill. What is a woman? what are the worſt when the beſt are ſo

paſt naming? As men like this let them trie their wiues againe. Put women to the teſt; diſcouer them; paint them, paint them ten parts more then they doe themſelues, rather then looke on them as they are; Their wits are but painted that diſlike their painting. Thou fooliſh thirſter after idle ſecrets, And ill's abrode; looke home, and ſtore & choke thee;
There ſticks an Achelons horne of all, Copie enough. As much as Alizon of ſtreames receiues,
Or loftie Ilea ſhowes of ſhadie leaues.

Enter Tharſalio.

Who's that?

Thar. I wonder *Lycus* failes me. Nor can I heare whats become of him. Hee would not certaine ride to Dipolis to call my brother back, without my knowledge.

Lyſ. My brothers voice; what makes he here abouts ſo vntimely? Ile ſlip him. *Exiturus.*

Thar. Who goes there? *Lyſ.* A friend.

Thar. Deare friend, lets know you. A friend leaſt look't for but moſt welcome, and with many a long looke expected here.
What ſir vnbooted? haue you beene long arriu'd?

Lyſ. Not long, ſome two houres before night.

Thar. Well brother, y'haue the moſt rare, admirable, vnmatchable wife, that euer ſuffer'd for the ſinne of a husband. I cannot blame your confidence indeede now: 'tis built on ſuch infallible ground; *Lycus* I thinke be gone to call you to the reſcue of her life; why ſhee! O incomprehenſible!

Lyſan. I haue heard all related ſince my arriuall, weele meet to morrow.

Thar. What haſt brother? But was it related with what vntollerable paines, I and my Miſtris, her other friends, Matrones and Magiſtrates, labour'd her diuerſion from that courſe?

Lyſ. Yes, yes. *Thar.* What ſtreams of teares ſhe powr'd out; what treſſes of her haire ſhe tore! and

offer'd on your fuppos'd herfe! *Lyf.* I haue heard all.
Thar. But aboue all; how fince that time, her eies neuer harbour'd winck of flumber, thefe fixe daies; no nor tafted the leaft dramme of any fuftenance.
Lyf. How is that affurd? *Thar.* Not a fcruple.
Lyf. Are you fure there came no Souldier to her nor brought her victualls? *Thar.* Souldier? what Souldier?
Lyf. Why fome Souldier of the watch, that attends the executed bodies: well brother I am in haft; to morrow fhall fupply this nights defect of conference; Adieu. *Exit. Lyf.*
Thar. A Souldier? of the watch? bring her victualls? Goe to brother I haue you in the winde; hee's vnharneft of all his trauailing accoutrements. I came directly from's houfe, no word of him there; he knowes the whole relation; hee's paffionate: All collections fpeake he was the Souldier. What fhould be the riddle of this? that he is ftolne hether into a Souldiers difguife? he fhould haue ftaid at Dipolis to receiue news from vs. Whether he fufpected our relation; or had not patience to expect it, or whether that furious, frantique capricious Deuill iealoufie hath toft him hether on his hornes, I can not coniecture. But the cafe is cleare, hee's the Souldier. Sifter, looke to your fame, your chaftetie's vncouer'd. Are they here ftill? here beleeue it both moft wofully weeping ouer the bottle. *He knocks.*
Ero. Who's there. *Thar.* *Tharfalio*, open.
Ero. Alas Sir, tis no boote to vexe your fifter, and your felfe, fhe is defperate, & will not heare perfwafion, fhe's very weak.
Thar. Here's a true-bred chamber-maid. Alas, I am forrie for't; I haue brought her meat and Candian wine to ftrengthen her.
Ero. O the very naming an't, will driue her into a fwowne; good Sir forbeare.
Thar. Yet open fweet, that I may bleffe mine eies

A Comedie. 73

with fight of her faire fhrine; and of thy fweeteft felfe (her famous Pandreffe) open I fay. Sifter? you heare me well, paint not your Tomb without; wee know too well what rotten carcafes are lodg'd within; open I fay. *Ero* opens, and hee fees her head layd on the coffin, &c. Sifter I haue brought you tidings to wake you out of this fleeping mummerie.

Ero. Alas fhee's faint, and fpeech is painefull to her.

Thar. Well faid frubber, was there no Souldier here lately?

Ero. A Souldier? when?

Thar. This night, laft night, tother night; and I know not how many nights and daies. *Cyn.* Whofe there?

Ero. Your brother Miftris, that asks if there were not a fouldier here. *Cyn.* Here was no fouldier.

Ero. Yes Miftris I thinke here was fuch a one though you tooke no heede of him. *Thar.* Goe to fifter; did not you ioyne kiffes, embraces, and plight indeede with him, the vtmoft pledge of Nuptiall loue with him. Deni't, deni't; but firft heare me a fhort ftorie. The Souldier was your difguis'd husband, difpute it not. That you fee yonder, is but a fhadow, an emptie cheft containing nothing but aire. Stand not to gaze at it, tis true. This was a proiect of his owne contriuing to put your loialtie & conftant vowes to the teft; y'are warnd, be arm'd. *Exit.*

Ero. O fie a thefe perils. *Cyn.* O *Ero!* we are vndone.

Ero. Nay, you'd nere be warn'd; I euer wifht you to withftand the pufh of that Souldiers pike, and not enter him too deep into your bofom, but to keep facred your widowes vowes made to *Lyfander*. *Cyn.* Thou did'ft, thou did'ft.

Ero. Now you may fee th'euent. Well our fafetie lies in our fpeed: heele doe vs mifchiefe, if we preuent not his comming. Lets to your Mothers: and there cal out your mightieft friends to guard you from his furie. Let them begin the quarrell with him for practising this villanie on your sexe to intrappe your frailties.

Cyn. Nay I resolue to sit out one brunt more; to trie to what aime heele enforce his proiect: were he some other man, vnknowne to me; his violence might awe me; but knowing him as I doe, I feare him not. Do thou but second me, thy strength and mine shall master his best force, if he should proue outragious. Despaire they say makes cowardes turne couragious. Shut vp the Tomb. *Shut the Tomb.*

Enter one of the Souldiers sent out before to seeke the Sentinell.

1. All paines are lost in hunting out this Souldier; his fear (adding wings to his heeles) out-goes vs as farre as the fresh Hare the tir'd hounds. Who goes there?

Ent. 2 souldier another way

2. A friend. 1. O, your successe and mine touching this Sentinell, tells, I suppose, one tale; hee's farre enough I vndertake by this time. 2. I blame him not: the law's seuere (though iust and can not be dispenc'd.)

1. Why should the lawes of Paphos, with more rigour, then other Citie lawes pursue offenders? that not appeas'd with their liues forsait, exact a iustice of them after death? And if a Souldier in his watch forsooth. lose one of the dead bodies, he must die for't: It seems the State needed no souldiers when that was made a law. 2. So we may chide the fire for burning vs; or say the Bee's not good because she stings; Tis not the body the law respects, but the souldiers neglect; when the watch (the guard and safetie of the Citie) is left abandon'd to all hazards. But let him goe; and tell me if your newes sort with mine, for *Lycus*; apprehended they say, about *Lysanders* murther.

1. Tis true; hee's at the Captaines lodge vnder guard, and tis my charge in the morning to vnclose the leaden coffin, and discouer the bodie; The Captaine will assay an old conclusion often approu'd; that

A Comedie. 75

at the murtherers fight the bloud reuiues againe, and boiles a frefh; and euery wound has a condemning voice to crie out guiltie gainft the murtherer.

2. O world, if this be true; his deareft friend, his bed companion, whom of all his friends he cull'd out for his bofome!

1. Tufh man, in this topfie turuy world, friendfhip and bofom kindnes, are but made couers for mifchief, meanes to compaffe il. Near-allied truft, is but a bridge for trefon. The prefumptions crie loud againft him; his anfweres found difiointed; croffe-legd tripping vp one another. He names a Town whether he brought *Lyfander* murther'd by Mountainers, thats falfe, fome of the dwellers haue been here, and all difclaim it. Befides, the wounds he bears in fhow, are fuch as fhrews clofely giue their husbands, that neuer bleede, and finde to be counterfait.

2. O that iade falfhood is neuer found of all; but halts of one legge ftill. Truth pace is all vpright: found euery where.
And like a die, fets euer on a fquare.
And how is *Lycus* his bearing in this condition?

1. Faith (as the manner of fuch defperate offenders is till it come to the point) careleffe, & confident, laughing at all that feeme to pittie him. But leaue it to th'euent. Night fellow Souldier, youle not meet me in the morning at the Tomb, and lend me your hand to the vnrigging of *Lyfanders* herfe.

2. I care not if I do, to view heauens power in this vnbottomd feller.

Bloud, though it fleepe a time, yet neuer dies.
The Gods on murtherers fixe reuengefull eies.
Exeunt.

Lyfander folus with a crow of yron, and a halter which he laies downe and puts on his difguife againe.

COme my borrow'd difguife, let me once more
Be reconcild to thee, my truftieft friend;
Thou that in trueft fhape haft let me fee

That which my truer felfe hath hid from me,
Helpe me to take reuenge on a difguife,
Ten times more falfe and counterfait then thou.
Thou, falfe in fhow, haft been moft true to me;
The feeming true; hath prou'd more falfe then her.
Affift me to behold this act of luft,
Note with a Scene of ftrange impietie.
Her husbands murtherd corfe! O more then horror!
Ile not beleeue't vntri'd; If fhee but lift
A hand to act it; by the fates her braines flie out,
Since fhee has madded me; let her beware my hornes.
For though by goring her, no hope be fhowne
To cure my felfe, yet Ile not bleede alone. *He knocks.*
Ero. Who knocks? *Lyf.* The fouldier; open.
fhe opês & he enters
See fweet, here are the engines that muft doo't,
Which with much feare of my difcouerie
I haue at laft procur'd.
Shall we about this worke? I feare the morne
Will ouer-take's; my ftay hath been prolong'd
With hunting obfcure nookes for thefe emploiments,
The night prepares away; Come, art refolu'd.
Cyn. I, you fhall finde me conftant.
Lyf. I, fo I haue, moft prodigioufly conftant,
Here's a rare halter to hugge him with.
Ero. Better you and I ioyne our handes and beare
him thether, you take his head.
Cyn. I, for that was alwaies heauier then's whole
  bodie befides
Lyf. You can tell beft that loded it.
Ero. Ile be at the feet; I am able to beare againft
you I warrant you.
Lyf. Haft thou prepar'd weake nature to digeft
A fight fo much diftaftfull; haft fer'd thy heart
I bleede not at the bloudie fpectacle?
Haft arm'd thy fearefull eies againft th'affront
Of fuch a direfull obiect?
Thy murther'd husband ghaftly ftaring on thee;

A Comedie. 77

His wounds gaping to affright thee; his bodie foild with
Gore? fore heauen my heart fhruggs at it.
Cyn. So does not mine,
Loue's refolute; and ftands not to confult
With pettie terrour; but in full carrier
Runnes blind-fold through an Armie of mifdoubts,
And interpofing feares; perhaps Ile weepe
Or fo, make a forc't face and laugh againe.
Lyf. O moft valiant loue!
I was thinking with my felfe as I came; how if this
Brake to light; his bodie knowne;
(As many notes might make it) would it not fixe
Vpon thy fame, an vnremoued Brand
Of fhame, and hate; they that in former times
Ador'd thy vertue; would they not abhorre
Thy lotheft memorie?   *Cyn.*   All this I know,
But yet my loue to thee
Swallowes all this; or whatfoeuer doubts
Can come againft it.
Shame's but a feather ballanc't with thy loue.
Lyf. Neither feare nor fhame? you are fteele toth'
Proofe (but I fhall yron you): Come then lets to worke.
Alas poore Corps how many martyrdomes
Muft thou endure? mangl'd by me a villaine,
And now expos'd to foule fhame of the Gibbet?
Fore, pietie, there is fomewhat in me ftriues
Againft the deede, my very arme relents
To ftrike a ftroke fo inhumane,
To wound a hallow'd herfe? fuppofe twere mine,
Would not my Ghoft ftart vp and flie vpon thee?
Cyn. No, I'de mall it down againe with this.
                    She fnatches vp the crow.
Lyf. How now?   *He catches at her throat.*
Cyn. Nay, then Ile affay my ftrength; a Souldier and afraid of a dead man? A foft-r'ode milk-fop? come Ile doot my felfe.
Lyf. And I looke on? giue me the yron.

Cyn.   No, Ile not lofe the glorie ant. This hand, &c.
Lyf.   Pray thee fweet, let it not bee faid the fauage
act was thine; deliuer me the engine.
Cyn.   Content your felfe, tis in a fitter hand.
Lyf.   Wilt thou firft? art not thou the moft.
Cyn.   Ill-deftin'd wife of a transform'd monfter;
Who to affure him felfe of what he knew,
Hath loft the fhape of man.   *Lyf.*   Ha? croffe-
     capers?
Cyn.   Poore Souldiers cafe; doe not we know you
     Sir?
But I haue giuen thee what thou cam'ft to feeke.
Goe *Satyre*, runne affrighted with the noife
Of that harfh founding horne thy felfe haft blowne,
Farewell; I leaue thee there my Husbands Corps,
Make much of that.   *Exit. cum Er.*
Lyf.   What haue I done? O let me lie and grieue,
and fpeake no more.

*Captaine, Lycus with a guard of three or foure
Souldiers.*

Cap.   BRring him away; you muft haue patience
Sir: If you can fay ought to quit you of
thofe prefumptions that lie heauie on you, you fhall
be heard. If not, tis not your braues, nor your affec-
ting lookes can carrie it.
We muft acquite our duties.
Lyc.   Y'are Captaine ath' watch Sir.
Cap.   You take me right.
Lyc.   So were you beft doe mee; fee your prefumptions bee ftrong; or be affured that fhall proue a deare
prefumption, to brand me with the murther of my
friend. But you haue beene fuborn'd by fome clofe
villaine to defame me.
Cap.   Twill not be fo put off friend *Lycus*, I could
wifh your foule as free from taint of this foule fact; as
mine from any fuch vnworthy practife.
Lyc.   Conduct mee to the Gouernour him felfe; to
confront before him your fhallow accufations.

A Comedie. 79

Cap. Firſt Sir, Ile beare you to *Lyſanders* Tombe, to confront the murther'd body; and ſee what euidence the wounds will yeeld againſt you.

Lyc. Y'are wife Captaine. But if the bodie ſhould chance not to ſpeake; If the wounds ſhould bee tongue-tied Captaine; where's then your euidence Captaine? will you not be laught at for an officious Captaine?

Cap. Y'are gallant Sir.

Lyc. Your Captainſhip commands my ſeruice no further.

Cap. Well Sir, perhaps I may, if this concluſion take not; weele trie what operation lies in torture, to pull confeſſion from you.

Lyc. Say you ſo Captaine? but hearke you Captaine, Might it not concurre with the qualitie of your office, ere this matter grow to the height of a more threatning danger; to winck a little at a by-ſlip, or ſo?

Cap. How's that?

Lyc. To ſend a man abroad vnder guard of one of your fillieſt ſhack-rags; that he may beate the knaue, and run's way. I meane this on good termes Captaine; Ile be thankfull.

Cap. Ile thinke ont hereafter. Meane time I haue other emploiment for you.

Lyc. Your place is worthily repleniſht Captaine. My dutie Sir; Hearke Captaine, there's a mutinie in your Armie; Ile go raiſe the Gouernour.   *Exiturus.*

Cap. No haſt Sir; heele ſoone be here without your ſummons.

Souldiers thruſt vp Lyſander from the Tomb.

1. Bring forth the Knight ath' Tomb; haue we met with you Sir?   *Lyſ.* Pray thee ſouldier vſe thine office with better temper.   2. Come conuay him to the Lord Gouernour.

Firſt afore the Captaine Sir. Haue the heauens nought elſe to doe, but to ſtand ſtill, and turne all their malignant
Aſpects vpon one man?

2. Captaine here's the Sentinell wee fought for; hee's some new preſt Souldier, for none of vs know him.
Cap. Where found you him?
1. My truant was mich't Sir into a blind corner of the Tomb.
Cap. Well ſaid, guard him ſafe, but for the Corps.
1. For the Corps Sir? bare miſpriſion, there's no bodie, nothing. A meere blandation, a *deceptio viſus*. Vnleſſe this ſouldier for hunger haue eate vp *Lyſanders* bodie.
Lyc. Why, I could haue told you this before Captaine; The body was borne away peece-meale by deuout Ladies of *Venus* order, for the man died one of *Venus* Martys. And yet I heard ſince 'twas ſeene whole ath' other ſide the downes vpon a Coleſtafe betwixt two huntſmen, to feede their dogges withall. Which was a miracle Captaine.
Cap. Miſchiefe in this act hath a deepe bottom; and requires more time to ſound it. But you Sir, it ſeemes, are a Souldier of the neweſt ſtamp. Know you what tis to forſake your ſtand? There's one of the bodies in your charge ſtolne away; how anſwere you that? See here comes the Gouernour.

Enter a Guard bare after the Gouernour: Tharſalio, Argus, Clinias, before Eudora, Cynthia, Laodice, Sthenio, Ianthe, Ero, &c.

Guard. Stand aſide there.
Cap. Roome for a ſtrange Gouernour. The perfect draught of a moſt braineleſſe, imperious vpſtart. O deſert! where wert thou, when this woodden dagger was guilded ouer with the Title of Gouernour?
Guard. Peace Maſters; heare my Lord.
Thar. All wiſedome be ſilent; Now ſpeakes Authoritie.
Gouer. I am come in perſon to diſcharge Iuſtice.
Thar. Of his office.

A Comedie.   81

Gouer. The caufe you fhall know hereafter; and it is this. A villaine, whofe very fight I abhorre; where is he? Let mee fee him.
Cap. Is't *Lycus* you meane my Lord?
Gouer. Goe to firrha y'are too malipert; I haue heard of your Sentinells efcape; looke too't.
Cap. My Lord, this is the Sentinell you fpeake of.
Gouer. How now Sir? what time a day ift?
Arg. I can not fhew you precifely, ant pleafe your Honour.
Gouer. What? fhall we haue replications? Reioinders?
Thar. Such a creature, Foole is, when hee beftrides the back of Authoritie.
Gouer. Sirrha, ftand you forth. It is fuppofed thou haft committed a moft inconuenient murther vpon the body of *Lyfander.*
Lyc. My good Lord, I haue not.
Gouer. Peace varlet; doft chop with me? I fay it is imagined thou haft murther'd *Lyfander.* How it will be prou'd I know not. Thou fhalt therefore prefently bee had to execution, as iuftice in fuch cafes requireth. Souldiers take him away: bring forth the Sentinell.
Lyb. Your Lordfhip will firft let my defence be heard.
Gouer. Sirrha; Ile no fending nor prouing. For my part I am fatisfied, it is fo: thats enough for thee. I had euer a Sympathy in my minde againft him.
Let him be had away.
Thar. A moft excellent apprehenfion. Hee's able yee fee to iudge of a caufe at firft fight, and heare but two parties. Here's a fecond *Solon.*
Eud. Heare him my Lord; prefumptions oftentimes, (Though likely grounded) reach not to the truth.
And Truth is oft abus'd by likelyhood.
Let him be heard my Lord.
Gouer. Madam, content your felfe. I will doe iuftice; I will not heare him. Your late Lord, was

F

my Honourable Predeceſſour: But your Ladiſhip muſt pardon me. In matters of iuſtice I am blinde.

Thar. Thats true.

Gouer. I know no perſons. If a Court fauourite write to mee in a caſe of iuſtice: I will pocket his letter, and proceede. If a Suiter in a caſe of iuſtice thruſts a bribe into my hand, I will pocket his bribe, and proceede. Therefore Madam, ſet your heart at reſt: I am ſeated in the Throne of iuſtice; and I will doe iuſtice; I will not heare him.

Eud. Not heare him my Lord?

Gouer. No my Ladie: and moreouer put you in mind, in whoſe preſence you ſtand; if you Parrat to me long; goe to.

Thar. Nay the Vice muſt ſnap his Authoritie at all he meetes, how ſhalt elſe be knowne what part he plaies?

Gouer. Your husband was a Noble Gentleman, but Alas hee came ſhort, hee was no Stateſman. Hee has left a foule Citie behinde him.

Thar. I, and I can tell you twill trouble his Lordſhip and all his Honorable aſſiſtants of Scauingers to ſweepe it cleane.

Gouer. It's full of vices, and great ones too.

Thar. And thou none of the meaneſt.

Gouer. But Ile turne all topſie turuie; and ſet vp a new diſcipline amongſt you. Ile cut of all periſht members.

Thar. Thats the Surgeons office.

Gouer. Caſt out theſe rotten ſtinking carcaſes for infecting the whole Citie.

Arg. Rotten they may be, but their wenches vſe to pepper them; and their Surgeons to perboile them; and that preſerues them from ſtinking, ant pleaſe your Honour.

Gouer. Peace Sirrha, peace; and yet tis well ſaid too. A good pregnant fellow yfaith. But to proceede. I will ſpew drunkenneſſe out ath' Citie.

Thar. Into th' Countrie.

A Comedie. 83

Gouer. Shifters fhall cheate and flerue ; And no man fhall doe good but where there is no neede. Braggarts fhall liue at the head ; and the tumult that hant Tauernes. Affes fhall beare good qualities, and wife men fhall vfe them. I will whip lecherie out ath' Citie, there fhall be no more Cuckolds. They that heretofore were errand Cornutos, fhall now bee honeft fhop-keepers, and iuftice fhall take place. I will hunt ieloufie out of my Dominion.

Thar. Doe heare Brother ?

Gouer. It fhall be the only note of loue to the husband, to loue the wife : And none fhall be more kindly welcome to him then he that cuckolds him.

Thar. Beleeue it a wholfome reformation.

Gouer. Ile haue no more Beggers. Fooles fhall haue wealth, and the learned fhall liue by their wits. Ile haue no more Banckrouts. They that owe money fhall pay it at their beft leifure : And the reft fhall make a vertue of imprifonment; and their wiues fhall helpe to pay their debts. Ile haue all yong widdowes fpaded for marrying againe. For the old and wither'd, they fhall be confifcate to vnthriftie Gallants, and decai'd Knights. If they bee poore they fhall bee burnt to make fope afhes, or giuen to Surgeons Hall, to bee ftampt to falue for the French mefells. To conclude, I will Cart pride out ath' Towne.

Arg. Ant pleafe your Honour Pride ant be nere fo beggarly will looke for a Coch.

Gouer. Well faid a mine Honour. A good fignificant fellow yfaith : What is he ? he talkes much ; does he follow your Ladifhip ?

Arg. No ant pleafe your Honour, I goe before her.

Gouer. A good vndertaking prefence ; A well-promifing forehead, your Gentleman Vfher Madam ?

Eud. Yours if you pleafe my Lord.

Gouer. Borne ith' Citie ?

Arg. I ant pleafe your Honour, but begot ith' Court.

Gouer. Treffellegg'd ?

Arg. I, ant pleafe your Honour.

Gouer. The better, it beares a bredth; makes roome a both fides. Might I not fee his pace? *Argus ftalkes.*
Arg. Yes ant pleafe your Honour.
Gouer. Tis well, tis very well. Giue me thy hand: Madame I will accept this propertie at your hand, and wil weare it thredbare for your fake. Fall in there, firrha. And for the matter of *Lycus* Madam, I muft tell you, you are fhallow: there's a State point in't? hearke you: The Viceroy has giuen him, and wee muft vphold correfpondence. Hee muft walke; fay one man goes wrongfully out ath' world, there are hundreds to one come wrongfully into th' world.
Eud. Your Lordfhip will giue me but a word in priuate.
Thar. Come brother; we know you well: what meanes this habite? why ftaid you not at Dipolis as you refolu'd, to take aduertifement for vs of your wiues bearing?
Lyc. O brother, this iealous phrenfie has borne mee headlong to ruine.
Tnar. Go to, be comforted; vncafe your felfe; and difcharge your friend.
Gouer. Is that *Lyfander* fay you? And is all his ftorie true?
Berladie Madam this iealoufie will coft him deare: he vndertooke the perfon of a Souldier; and as a Souldier muft haue iuftice. Madam, his Altitude in this cafe can not difpence. *Lycus,* this Souldier hath acquited you.
Thar. And that acquitall Ile for him requite; the body loft, is by this time reftor'd to his place.
Soul. It is my Lord.
Thar. Thefe are State points, in which your Lordfhips time has not yet train'd your Lordfhip; pleafe your Lordfhip to grace a Nuptiall we haue now in hand.

Hylus and Laodice ftand together.
Twixt this yong Ladie and this Gentleman.
Your Lordfhip there fhall heare the ample ftorie.

And how the Affe wrapt in a Lyons skin
Fearefully rord; but his large eares appeard
And made him laught at, that before was feard.
Gouer. Ile goe with you. For my part, I am at a non plus.

Eudora whifpers with Cynthia.

Thar. Come brother; Thanke the Counteffe: fhee hath fwet to make your peace. Sifter giue me your hand.
 So; Brother let your lips compound the ftrife,
And thinke you haue the only conftant Wife.

Exeunt.

FINIS.

THE MEMORABLE MASKE

of the two Honorable Houſes or Inns of
Court; the Middle Temple, and
Lyncolns Inne.

As it was performd before the King, at
White-Hall on Shroue Munday at night;
being the 15. of February. 1613.

At the Princely celebration of the moſt Royall
Nuptialls of the Palſgraue, *and his thrice gratious*
Princeſſe Elizabeth. &c.

With a deſcription of their whole ſhow; in the manner
of their march on horſe-backe to the Court from
the Maiſter of the Rolls his houſe: with all
their right Noble conſorts, and moſt
ſhowfull attendants.

Inuented, and faſhioned, with the ground, and
ſpeciall ſtructure of the whole worke,

By our Kingdomes moſt Artfull and Ingenious
Architect, INNIGO IONES.

Supplied, Aplied, Digested, and written,
By GEO: CHAPMAN.

AT LONDON,

Printed by *G. Eld,* for *George Norton* and are to be
ſould at his ſhoppe neere Temple-bar.

TO THE MOST NO-
ble, and conſtant Combiner of Honor,
and Vertue, Sir EDWARD PHILIPS,
Knight, M.ʳ of the Rolls.

His Noble and Magnificent perform-
ance, renewing the ancient ſpirit, and
Honor of the Innes of Court; being
eſpecially furthered and followed by
your most laborious and honored
endeuors, (for his Maieſties ſeruice;
and honour of the all-grace-deſeruing Nuptialls,
of the thrice gracious Princeſſe Elizabeth, his
Highneſs daughter) deſerues eſpecially to be in this
ſort conſecrate, to your worthy memory and honor.
Honor hauing neuer her faire hand more freely
and nobly giuen to Riches (being a fit particle of
this Inuention) then by yours, at this Nuptiall
ſolemnity. To which aſsisted, and memorable
ceremony; the ioin'd hand and industry, of the
worthely honour'd Knight, Sir H. Hubberd, his
Maieſties Atturny generall, deſeruing, in good
part a ioint memory with yours, I haue ſubmitted
it freely to his noble acceptance. The poore paines
I added to this Royall ſeruice, being wholly choſen,
and commanded by your most constant, and free

The Epistle Dedicatorie.

fauour; I hope will now appeare nothing neglectiue of their expected duties. Hearty wil, and care enough, I am assured was employ'd in me; and the onely ingenuous will, being first and principall step to vertue; I beseech you let it stand for the performing vertue it selfe. In which addition of your euer-honour'd fauours, you shall euer binde all my future seruice to your most wished Commandement.

God send you long health, and your Vertues will endue you with honor enough,

By your free merits euer vow'd honorer,

and most vnfainedly affectioned,

GEO. CHAPMAN.

THE MASKE OF THE

Gentlemen of the two combin'd houfes,

or Inns of Court, the Middle-Temple,

and Lincolns Inne.

T the houfe of the moſt worthely honour'd preferrer and gracer of all honorable Actions, and vertues, (fir *Edward Philips* Knight, Maſter of the Rolls) al the Performers and their Afsiſtents made their *Rendes vous*, prepar'd to their performance, and thus ſet forth.

Fiftie Gentlemen, richly attirde, and as gallantly mounted, with Foot-men perticularly attending, made the noble vant-guarde of theſe Nuptiall forces. Next (a fit diſtance obſeru'd betweene them) marcht a mock-Maske of Baboons, attir'd like fantaſticall Trauailers, in Neapolitane ſutes, and great ruffes, all horſt with Aſſes; and dwarfe Palfries, with yellow foot-cloathes, and caſting Cockle-demois about, in courteſie, by way of lardges; Torches boarn on either hand of them;

lighting their state as ridiculously, as the rest Nobly. After them were sorted two Carrs Triumphall, adornd with great Maske heads, Festones, scroules, and antick leaues, euery part inricht with siluer and golde. These were through-varied with different inuention, and in them aduanc't, the choice Musitions of our Kingdome, sixe in each; attir'd like Virginean Priests, by whom the Sun is there ador'd; and therfore called the Phœbades. Their Robes were tuckt vp before; strange Hoods of feathers, and scallops about their neckes, and on their heads turbants, stucke with feuerall colour'd feathers, spotted with wings of Flies, of extraordinary bignesse; like those of their countrie: And about them march't two ranks of Torches. Then rode the chiefe Maskers, in Indian habits, all of a resemblance: the ground cloath of siluer, richly embroidered, with golden Sunns, and about euery Sunne, ran a traile of gold, imitating Indian worke: their bases of the same stuffe and work, but betwixt euery pane of embroidery, went a row of white Estridge feathers, mingled with sprigs of golde plate; vnder their breasts, they woare bawdricks of golde, embroidered high with with purle, and about their neckes, Ruffes of feathers, spangled with pearle and siluer. On their heads high sprig'd-feathers, compast in Coronets, like the Virginian Princes they presented. Betwixt euery set of feathers, and about their browes, in the vnder-part of their Coronets, shin'd Sunnes of golde plate, sprinkled with pearle; from whence sprung rayes of the like plate, that mixing with the motion of the feathers, shew'd exceedingly delightfull, and gracious. Their legges were adorn'd, with close long white silke stockings: curiously embroidered with golde to the Midde-legge.

And ouer these (being on horse backe) they drew greaues or buskins embrodered with gould, & enterlac't with rewes of fethers; Altogether estrangfull, and *Indian* like.

In their Hands (set in seuerall postures as they rode)

they brandiſht cane darts of the fineſt gould. Their vizerds of oliue collour; but pleaſingly viſag'd: their hayre, blacke and lardge, wauing downe to their ſhoulders.

Their Horſe, for rich ſhow, equalld the Maskers them-ſelues; all their capariſons being enchac't with ſunnes of Gould and Ornamentall Iewells. To euery one of which, was tackt a Scarffing of Siluer; that ran ſinuouſely in workes ouer the whole capariſon, euen to the daſeling of the admiring ſpectators.

Their heads, no leſſe gracefully and properly deckt with the like light skarffing that hung about their eares wantonly dangling.

Euery one of theſe horſe, had two Moores, attir'd like *Indian* ſlaues, that for ſtate ſided them; with ſwelling wreaths of gould, and watſhed on their heads, which aroſe in all to the number of a hundred.

The Torch-bearers habits were likewiſe of the *Indian* garb, but more ſtrauagant then thoſe of the Maskers; all ſhowfully garniſht with feueral-hewd fethers. The humble variety whereof, ſtucke off the more amplie, the Maskers high beauties, ſhining in the habits of themſelues; and reflected in their kinde, a new and delightfully-varied radiance on the beholders.

All theſe ſuſtaind torches of *Virgine* wax, whoſe ſtaues were great canes al ouer gilded; And theſe (as the reſt) had euery Man his Moore, attending his horſe.

The Maskers, riding ſingle; had euery Masker, his Torch-bearer mounted before him.

The laſt Charriot, which was moſt of all adornd; had his whole frame fill'd with moulded worke; mixt all with paintings, and glittering ſcarffings of ſiluer; ouer which was caſt a Canopie of golde, boarne vp with antick figures, and all compos'd *a la Groteſca*. Before this in the ſeate of it, as the Chariotere; was aduanc't a ſtrange perſon, and as ſtrangely habited, half French, halfe Swizz; his name *Capriccio*; wearing on his head a paire of golden Bellowes, a guilt ſpurre in one hand, and with the other mannaging the reignes of the fowre Horses that drewe it.

On a seate of the same Chariot, a little more eleuate, sate *Eunomia*, the Virgine Priest of the Goddesse *Honor*, together with *Phemis*, her Herald: The habite of her Priest, was a Robe of white silke, gathered about the necke; a pentacle of siluered stuffe about her shoulders, hanging foldedly downe, both before and behind.

A vestall vaile on her head of Tiffany, strip't with siluer, hanging with a trayne, to the earth.

The Herrald was attyr'd in an Antique Curace of siluer stuffe, with labells at thewings and basses; a short gowne of gould stuffe; with wide sleeues, cut in panes: A wreath of gould on his head, and a Rod of gould in his hand.

Highest of all in the most eminent seate of the Tryumphall sat, side to side, the cœlestiall Goddesse, *Honour*; and the earthy Deity, *Plutus*; or Riches. His attire; a short robe of gould, frindg'd; his wide sleeues turn'd vp, and out-showd his naked armes: his Head and Beard sprinckl'd with showrs of gould: his Buskins, clinckant, as his other attire. The Ornaments of Honor were these: a rich full robe of blew silke girt about her, a mantle of siluer worne ouerthwart, ful gathered, and descending in folds behind: a vaile of net lawne, enbrodered with Oos and Spangl'd; her tresses in tucks, braided with siluer: The hinder part shadowing in waues her shoulders.

These, thus perticularly, and with proprietie adorn'd, were 'strongly attended with a full Guard of two hundred Halbardiers: two Marshals (being choice Gentlemen, of either house) Commaunder-like attir'd, to and fro coursing, to keepe all in their orders.

A showe at all parts so nouell, conceitfull and glorious, as hath not in this land, (to the proper vse and obiect it had porpos'd) beene euer before beheld. Nor did those honorable Inns of Court, at any time in that kinde, such acceptable seruice to the sacred Maiesty of this kingdome, nor were return'd by many degrees, with so thrice gratious, and royall entertainment and honor. But, (as aboue sayd) all these so marching to the Court at White Hall, the King, Bride, & Bridegroom, with all the Lords of the most honord priuy Councel, and our chief Nobility, stood in the Gallery before the Tilt-yeard, to behold their arriuall; who, for the more ful satisfaction of his Maiesties view, made one turn about the yeard, and dismounted: being then honorably attended through the Gallery to a Chamber appointed, where they were to make ready for their performance in the Hall, &c.

The King beeing come forth, the Maskers ascended vnseene to their scœne. Then for the works.

First there appear'd at the lower end of the Hall, an Artificiall Rock, whose top was neere as high as the hall it selfe. This Rock, was in the vndermost part craggy, and full of hollow places, in whose concaues were contriu'd, two winding paire of staires, by whose greeces the Persons aboue might make their descents, and all the way be seene: all this Rocke grew by degrees vp into a gold-colour; and was run quite through, with veines of golde: On the one side whereof, eminently raised on a faire hill, was erected a siluer Temple of an octangle figure, whose Pillars were of a compos'd order, and bore vp an Architraue, Freese, and Cornish: Ouer which stood a continued Plinthe; whereon were aduanc't Statues of siluer: Aboue this, was placed a bastarde Order of Architecture, wherein were keru'd Compartements: In one of which was written in great golde Capitalls, *HONORIS FANVM*. Aboue all, was a *Coupolo*, or Type, which seem'd to be scal'd with siluer Plates.

For finishing, of all, vpon a Pedistall, was fixt a round stone of siluer, from which grew a paire of golden wings, both saign'd to bee Fortunes: the the round stone (when her feet trod it) euer affirm'd

to be rouling; figuring her inconftancy : the golden
wings, denoting thofe nimble Powres, that pompoufly
beare her about the world; On that Temple (erected
to her daughter, *Honor*; and figuring this kingdome)
put off by her, and fixt, for affured figne fhe would
neuer forfake it.

About this Temple, hung Feftones wreath'd with
filuer from one Pillars head to another. Befides, the
Freefe was enricht with keruings, all fhewing Greatnes
and Magnificence.

On the other fide of the Rocke, grewe a Groue,
in whofe vtmoft part appear'd a vaft, wither'd, and
hollow Tree, being the bare receptacle of the
Baboonerie.

Thefe following fhould in duty haue had their proper places, after euery fitted fpeech of the Actors; but
being preuented by the vnexpected hafte of the Printer, which he neuer let me know, and neuer fending
me a proofe, till he had paft thofe fpeeches; I had no
reafon to imagine hee could haue been fo forward.
His fault is therfore to be fupplied by the obferuation,
and reference of the Reader, who will eafily perceiue,
where they were to bee inferted.

After the fpeech of *Plutus* (who as you may fee
after, firft entred) the middle part of the Rocke began
to moue, and being come fome fiue paces vp towards
the King, it fplit in peeces with a great crack; and
out brake *Capriccio*, as before defcribed. The
peeces of the Rocke vanifht, and he fpake as in his
place.

At the finging of the firft Song, full, which was fung
by the Virginian Priefts; called the Phœbades, to fixe
Lutes (being vfed as an Orphean vertue, for the ftate
of the Mines opening) : the vpper part of the Rock
was fodainly turn'd to a Cloude, difcouering a rich
and refulgent Mine of golde; in which the twelue
Maskers were triumphantly feated: their Torch-bearers
attending before them. All the lights being fo ordred,
that though none were feen, yet had their luftre fuch

vertue, that by it, the leaſt ſpangle or ſpark of the Maſkers rich habites, might with eaſe and cleereneſſe be diſcerned as far off as the ſeate.

Ouer this golden Mine, in an Euening sky, the ruddy Sunne was ſeen ready to be ſet; and behind the tops of certaine white Cliffes, by degrees deſcended, caſting vp a banke of Cloudes; in which, a while hee was hidden: but then glorioufly ſhining, gaue that vſually-obſeru'd good Omen, of ſucceeding faire weather.

Before he was fully ſet, the Phœbades (ſhewing the cuſtome of the Indians to adore the Sunne ſetting) began their obſeruance with the Song, to whoſe place, wee muſt referre you for the manner and words; All the time they were ſinging; the Torch-bearers holding vp their Torches to the Sun; to whome the Prieſts themſelues, and the reſt, did as they ſung obeiſance: Which was anſwred by other Muſique and voices, at at the commandement of *Honor*, with al' obſeruances vſ'd to the King &c. As in the following places.

TO answer certaine insolent obiections made against the length of my speeches, and narrations; being (for the probability of all accidents, rising from the inuention of this Maske; and their aplication, to the persons, and places: for whome, and by whome it was presented) not conuenient, but necessary; I am enforct to affirme this; That: as there is no Poem nor Oration so generall; but hath his one perticular proposition; Nor no riuer so extrauagantly ample, but hath his neuer-so-narrow fountaine, worthy to be namd; so all these courtly, and honoriug inuentions (hauing Poesie, and Oration in them, and a fountaine, to be expresst, from whence their Riuers flow) should expressiuely-arise; out of the places, and persons for; and by whome they are presented; without which limits, they are luxurious, and paine. But what rules soeuer are set downe, to any Art, or Act (though, without their obseruation; No Art, nor Act, is true, and worthy) yet they are nothing the more followd; or those few that follow them credited. Euery vulgarly-esteemd vpstart; dares breake the dreadfull dignity of antient and autenticall Poesie: and presume Luciferously, to proclame in place thereof, repugnant precepts of their owne spaune. Truth, and Worth, haue no faces, to enamour the Lycentious, but vaine-glory, and humor. The same body: the same beauty, a thousand men seeing: Onely the man whose bloud is fitted, hath that which hee calls his soule, *enamourd. And this, out of infallible cauſe; for, men vnderſtand not theſe of* Mænander —— eſt morbus oportunitas

Animæ, quod ictus, vulnus accipit graue.

But the cauſe of all Mens being enamourd with Truth. And of her ſlight reſpect, in others; is the diuine Freedom; *one touching with his aprehenſiue finger, the other, paſſing. The Hill of the Muſes (which all men muſt clime in the regular way, to Truth) is ſaid of ould, to be forcked. And the two points of it, parting at the Top; are* Inſania, *and,* diuinus furor. Inſania, *is that which euery Ranck-brainde writer; and iudge of Poeticall writing, is rapt withal; when hee preſumes either to w ite or cenſure the height of Poeſie; and that transports him with humor, vaine-glory and pride, moſt prophane and ſacrilegious: when* diuinus furor; *makes gentle, and noble, the neuer ſo truly-inſpired writer* ——

Emollit mores nec finit eſſe feros.

And the mild beames of the moſt holy inflamer; eaſely, and ſweetly enter, with all vnderſtanding ſharpeneſſe, the ſoft, and ſincerely humane; but with no Time; No Study; No meanes vnder heauen: any arrogant, all-occupation deuourer (that will Chandler-like ſet vp with all wares; ſelling, Poeſies Nectar and Ambroſia; as wel as muſterd, and vineagar.) The chaſt and reſtraind beames of humble truth will euer enter; but onely graſe and glaunce at them: and the further fly them.

The aplicable argument of
the Maſke.

Honor, is ſo much reſpected, and ador'd; that ſhee hath a Temple erected to her, like a Goddeſſe; a Virgine Prieſt conſecrated to her (which is *Eunomia*, or Lawe; ſince none ſhould dare acceſſe to Honor, but by Vertue; of which Lawe being the rule, muſt needes be a chiefe) and a Herrald (call'd *Phemis*, or Fame) to proclame her inſtitutions, and commandements. To amplefie yet more the diuine graces of this Goddeſſe; *Plutus*, (or Riches) being by *Ariſtophanes*, *Lucian*, &c. preſented naturally blind, deformd, and dull witted; is here by his loue of Honor, made ſee, made ſightly, made ingenious; made liberall: And all this conuerted and conſecrate to the moſt worthy celebration of theſe ſacred Nuptialls; all iſſuing (to conclude the neceſſary application) from an honorable Temple. &c.

Non eſt certa fides, quam non Iniuria verſat.
———————— Fallit portus & ipſe fidem.

THE NAMES OF THE SPEAKERS.

Honour, a Goddeſſe.
Plutus, (or Riches) a God.
Eunomia (or law) Prieſt of honor.
Phemis, Honors Herrald.
Capriccio, a man of wit, &c.

THE PRESENTMENT.

Plutus *appear'd furuaying the worke with this ſpeech.*

PLVTVS.

Ockes? Nothing but Rockes in theſe masking deuices? Is Inuention ſo poore ſhee muſt needes euer dwell amongſt Rocks? But it may worthily haue chaunc'd (being ſo often preſented) that their vaine Cuſtome is now become the neceſſarie hand of heauen, transforming into Rocks, ſome ſtonie hearted Ladies, courted in former masks; for whoſe loues, ſome of their repulſt ſeruants haue periſht : or perhaps ſome of my flintie-hearted Vſurers haue beene heere metamorphoſed; betwixt whom and Ladies, there is reſemblance enough: Ladies vſing to take intereſt, beſides their principall, as much as Vſurers. See, it is ſo; and now is the time of reſtoring them to their naturall ſhapes : It moues, opens, excellent! This metamorphoſis I intend to ouer-heare.

A ROCK, MOOVING

and breaking with a cracke about Capriccio, *he enters with a payre of Bellows on his head, a spur in one hand, and a peece of golde Ore in the other, &c.*

He speakes, vt sequitur.

CAPRICCIO.

How hard this world is to a man of wit? hee must eate through maine Rockes for his food, or fast; a restles and tormenting stone, his wit is to him: the very stone of *Sisyphus* in hell; nay, the Philosophers stone, makes not a man more wretched: A man must be a second *Proteus*, and turne himselfe into all shapes (like *Vlisses*) to winde through the straites of this pinching vale of miserie; I haue turn'd my selfe into a Tailor, a Man, a Gentleman, a Nobleman, a Worthy man; but had neuer the witte to turne my selfe into an Alder-man. There are manie shapes to perish in, but one to liue in, and tha's an Aldermans: Tis not for a man of wit to take any rich Figure vpon him: your bould, proud, ignorant, that's braue and clinkant, that findes crownes put into his shooes euery morning by the Fayries and will neuer tell; whose Wit is humor, whose Iudgement is fashion, whose Pride is emptinesse, Birth his full man, that is in all things fomething, in Sum totall, nothing. He fhall liue in the land of *Spruce*, milke and hony flowing into his mouth fleeping.

PLVTVS.

This is no transformation, but an intrufion into my golden mines: I will heare him further.

CAPRIC.

This breach of Rockes I haue made, in needy purfuite of the blind Deity, Riches: who is myraculoufly ariued here. For (acording to our rare men of wit) heauen ftanding, and earth mouing, her motion (being circular) hath brought one of the moft remote parts of the world, to touch at this all-exceeding Iland: which a man of wit would imagine muft needs moue circularly with the reft of the world, and fo euer maintaine an equal diftance. But, Poets (our chiefe men of wit) anfwere that point directly; moft ingenioufly affirming: That this Ile is (for the excellency of it) diuided from the world (*diuifus ab orbe Britannus*) and that though the whole World befides moues; yet this Ile ftands fixt on her owne feete, and defies the Worlds mutability, which this rare accident of the arriuall of Riches, in one of his furtheft-off-fcituate dominions, moft demonftratiuely proues.

PLVTVS.

This is a man of wit indeede, and knows of all our arriuals.

CAPRIC.

With this dull Deity Riches, a rich Iland lying in the South-fea, called *Pæana*, (of the *Pæans* (or fongs) fung to the Sun, whom they there adore (being for ftrength and riches, called the Nauill of that South-fea) is by earths round motion mou'd neere this Brittan Shore. In which Ifland (beeing yet in command of the Virginian continent.) A troupe of the nobleſt Virginians inhabiting; attended hether the God of Riches, all triumphantly ſhyning in a Mine of gould. For hearing of the moſt royal ſolemnity, of theſe ſacred Nuptialls; they croſt the Ocean in their honor, and are here arriu'd. A poore ſnatch at ſome of the goulden Ore, that the feete of riches haue turnd vp as he trod here, my poore hand hath purchaſt; and hope the Remainder of a greater worke, wilbe ſhortly extant.

PLVT.

You Sir, that are miching about my goulden Mines here.

CAPR.

What, can you ſee Sir? you haue heretofore beene preſented blinde: like your Mother Fortune; and your Brother Loue.

PLVT.

But now Sir, you ſee I ſee.

CAPR.

By what good meanes, I beſeech you Sir.

PLVT.

That meanes, I may vouchſafe you hereafter; meane ſpace, what are you?

CAPR.

I am Sir a kinde of Man; A Man of wit: with whom your worſhip has nothing to do I thinke.

PLVT.

No Sir, nor will haue any thing to doe with him: A Man of wit? whats that? A Begger.

CAPR.

And yet no Diuell Sir.

PLV.

As I am, you meane.

CAPR.

Indeede fir your Kingdome is vnder the Earth.

PLVT.

That's true, for Riches is the *Atlas* that holdes it vp, it would finke elfe.

CAPR.

Tis rather a wonder, it finks not with you Sir, y'are fo finfully, and damnably heauy.

PLVT.

Sinfull? and damnable? what a Puritane? Thefe Bellowes you weare on your head, fhew with what matter your braine is pufft vp Sir: A Religion-forger I fee you are, and prefume of infpiration from thefe Bellowes; with which yee ftudy to blow vp the fetled gouernments of kingdomes.

CAPR.

Your worfhip knockes at a wrong dore Sir, I dwell farre from the perfon you fpeak of.

PLVT.

What may you be then, beeing a man of wit? a Buffon, a Iefter. Before I would take vpon mee the title of a man of wit, and bee baffl'd by euery man of wifedome for a Buffon; I would turne Banckrout, or fet vp a Tobacco fhop, change clokes with an Alchemift, or ferue an Vfurer, bee a watering poft for euery Groome; ftand the pufh of euery rafcall wit; enter lifts of iefts with trencher-fooles, and bee foold downe by them, or (which is worfe) put them downe in fooling : are thefe the qualities a man of wit fhould run proud of ?

CAPR.

Your worfhip I fee has obtaind wit, with fight, which I hope yet my poor wit wil well be able to anfwer; for touching my iefting, I haue heard of fome Courtiers, that haue run themfelues out of their ftates with Iufting; and why may not I then raife my felfe in the State with iefting ? An honeft Shoomaker, (in in a liberall Kings time) was knighted for making a cleáne boote, and is it impofsible, that I for breaking a cleane Ieft, fhould bee aduaunc't in Court, or Counfaile ? or at leaft, ferued out for an Ambaffador to a dull Climate ? Iefts, and Merriments are but wild weedes in a rank foile, which being well manured, yield the wholefom crop of wifdome and difcretion at time ath' yeare.

PLV.

Nay, nay, I commend thy iudgement for cutting thy cote fo iuft to the bredth of thy fhoulders; he that cannot be a courfer in the field, let him learne to play the Iack-an-Apes in the Chamber, hee that cannot perfonate the wife-man well amongft wifards, let him learne to play the foole well amongft dizzards.

CAPR.

Tis pafsing miraculous, that your dul and blind worfhip fhould fo fodainly turne both fightfull, and witfull.

PLVT.

The Riddle of that myracle, I may chance diffolue to you in fequell; meane time, what name fuftain'ft thou ? and what toies are thefe thou bear'ft fo phantaftically about thee ?

CAPR.

Thefe, toies Sir, are the Enfignes that difcouer my name and qualitie : my name being *Capriccio*, and I weare thefe Bellowes on my head, to fhew I can puffe vp with glory all thofe that affect mee : and befides, beare this fpurre, to fhew I can fpur-gall, euen the beft that contemne me.

PLVT.

A dangerous fellowe, But what makeft thou (poore man of wit) at thefe pompous Nuptials ;

CAPRIC.

Sir, I come hether with a charge ; To doe thefe Nuptial's, I hope, very acceptable feruice ; And my charge is ; A company of accomplifht Trauailers; that are excellent at Antemaskes ; and will tender a taft of thair quallity, if your worfhip pleafe.

PLVT.

Excellent well pleafd ; of what vertue are they befides.

CAPR.

Paffing graue Sir, yet exceeding acute : witty, yet not ridiculous ; neuer laugh at their owne iefts : laborious yet not bafe, hauing cut out the skirts of the whole world, in amorous queft of your gould and filuer.

PLVT.

They fhal haue enough ; cal them : I befeech thee call them : how farre hence abide they ?

CAPR.

Sir (being by another eminent qualitie the admired fouldiers of the world) in contempt of foftnes, and delicacie, they lie on the naturally hard boords of that naked tree; and will your worſhip aſſure them rewards fit for perſons of their freight.

PLVT.

Doſt thou doubt my reward beeing pleaſed?

CAPR.

I know Sir, a man may ſooner win your reward, for pleaſing you, thē deſeruing you. But you great wiſe perſons, haue a fetch of State; to employ with countenance, and encouragement, but reward with auſterity and diſgrace, ſaue your purſes, and loſe your honours.

PLVT.

To aſſure thee of reward, I will now ſatiſfie thee touching the miraculous cauſe, both of my ſight and wit, and which conſequently moues mee to humanity, and bounty; And all this, onely this; my late being in loue, with the louely Goddeſſe Honor.

CAPRIC.

If your Worſhipp loue Honor, indeed, Sir you muſt needes be bountifull. But where is the rare Goddeſſe you ſpeake of to be ſeene?

PLVTVS.

In that Rich Temple, where Fortune fixt thoſe her goulden wings, thou feeſt; And that rowling ſtone ſhe vſ'd to tread vpon, for ſigne ſhee would neuer for-ſake this Kingdome; There is ador'd, the worthy Goddeſſe Honor. The ſwetneſſe of whoſe voice, when I firſt heard her perſwaſions, both to my ſelf, and the *Virginian* Princes arriu'd here, to doe honor and homage, to theſe heauenly Nuptialls, ſo moſt powerfully enamour'd mee, that the fire of my loue flew vp to the fight of mine eyes: that haue lighted within mee a whole firmament of Bounty, which may fecurely affure the, thy reward is certaine: & therefore call thy accomplifht company to their Autemaske.

CAPRIC.

See Sir, The time, fet for their apperance, being expir'd; they appeere to their feruice of them-felues.

Enter the Baboones after whofe dance, being Anticke, and delightful, they returned to their Tree, when Plutus fpake to Capriccius.

PLVTVS.

Gramercy now *Capriccio*, take thy men of complement, and trauaile with them to other marriages. My Riches to thy Wit; they will get fomething fome-where.

CAPR.

Whats this?

PLVT.

A ftraine of Wit beyond a Man of Wit. I haue imployd you, and the grace of that, is reward enough; hence; packe, with your complemental Fardle: The fight of an attendant for reward, is abominable in the eyes of a turne-feru'd Politician, and I feare, will ftrike me blinde againe. I can not abide thefe bellowes of thy head, they and thy men of wit haue melted my

Mines with them, and confum'd me, yet take thy life and be gone. *Neptune* let thy predeceffor, *Vlyffes*, liue after all his flaine companions, but to make him die more miferably liuing: gaue him vp to fhip-wracks, enchantments; men of wit are but enchanted, there is no fuch thing as wit in this world. So, take a tree, inure thy fouldiers to hardnes, tis honorable, though not clinkant.

CAPR.

Can this be poffible?

PLVT.

Alas! poore man of wit, how want of reward daunts thy vertue? But becaufe I muft fend none away difcontented, from thefe all-pleafing Nuptials; take this wedge of golde, and wedge thy felfe into the world with it, renouncing that loofe wit of thine, t'will fpoile thy complexion.

CAPR.

Honor, and all *Argus* eyes, to Earths all-commaunding Riches. Pluto *etiam cedit* Iupiter.

Exit Capr.

After this lowe Induction, by thefe *fucceeding degrees, the chiefe Maskers* were aduanc't to their difcouerie

PLVTVS.

<small>Plutus, cals to Eunomia.</small> Thefe humble obiects can no high eyes drawe, *Eunomia*? (or the facred power of Lawe) Daughter of *Ioue*, and Goddeffe Honors Prieft; Appeare to *Plutus*, and his loue affift.

EVN.

<small>Eunomia in the Temple gates.</small> What would the god of Riches?

Temple, and Lincolns Inne.

PLVT.
Ioine with Honor:
In purpos'd grace of thefe great Nuptials;
And fince to Honor none fhould dare acceffe,
But helpt by vertues hand (thy felfe, chafte *Loue*
Being *Vertues* Rule, and her directfull light)
Help me to th' honor of her fpeech and fight.

EVN.
Thy will fhal ftraight be honour'd; all that feek
Acceffe to Honor, by cleer virtues beame,
Her grace preuents their pains, and comes to them.

Loud Mufick, and Honor appears, *defcending with her Herrald* Phemis, *and* Eunomia (her Prieft) before her. The Mufique ceafing *Plutus* fpake.

PLVT.
Crowne of all merit, Goddefs, and my Loue;
Tis now high time, that th' end for which we come
Should be endeuor'd in our vtmoft right,
Done to the fweetnes of this Nuptiall night.

HON.
Plutus? The Princes of the Virgine land,
Whom I made croffe Britan Ocean
To this moft famed Ile, of all the world,
To do due homage to the facred Nuptials
Of *Loue* and *Beauty*, celebrated here,
By this Howre of the holy Eeuen I know,
Are ready to performe the rites they owe
To fetting *Phœbus*; which (for greater State
To their apparance) their firft act aduances.
And with fongs Vfhers their fucceeding dances,
Herrald! giue fummons to the Virgine Knights
No longer to delay their purpos'd Rites.

HER.

Knights of the Virgine Land, whom bewties lights
Would glorifie with their inflaming fights ;
Keep now obscur'd no more your faire intent,
To adde your Beames to this nights ornament,
The golden-winged *Howre* strikes now a Plaine,
And calls out all the pompe ye entertaine ;
The Princely Bride-groome, and the Brides bright
    eyes,
Sparkle with grace to your discoueries.

At these words, the Phœbades (or Priests of the Sunne) appear'd first with sixe Lutes, and sixe voices, and sung to the opening of the Mine and Maskers discouery, this ful Song.

The first Song.

O*Pe Earth thy wombe of golde*
    Shew Heauen thy cope of starres.
All glad Aspects unfolde,
    Shine out, and cleere our Cares :
        Kisse Heauen and Earth, and so combine
        In all mixt ioy our Nuptiall Twine.

This Song ended, a Mount opened, and spred like a Skie, in which appear'd a Sunne setting ; beneath which, sate the twelue Maskers, in a Mine of golde ; twelue Torch-bearers holding their torches before them, after which Honor, *&c.*

HON.

Se now the setting Sun, casts vp his bank,
And showes his bright head at his Seas repaire,
For signe that all daies future shall be faire.

PLVT.

May he that rules al nightes & dayes confirme it.

HON.

Behold the Sunnes faire Preifts the *Phœbades*,
Their euening feruice in an Hymne addreffe
To *Phœbus* fetting; which we now fhall heare,
And fee the formes of their deuotions there.

The Phœbades fing the first Stance of the
fecond fong, *vt fequitur*.

One alone 1.

Defcend (faire Sun) and fweetly reft,
  In Tethis *Criftal armes, thy toyle,*
Fall burning on her Marble breft,
  And make with Loue her billowes boyle.

Another alone. 2.

Blow blow, fweet windes, O blow away,
  Al vapours from the fined ayre:
That to his golden head no Ray,
  May languifh with the leaft empaire.

CHO.

Dance Tethis, *and thy loues red beames,*
  Embrace with Ioy he now difcends:
Burnes burnes with loue to drinke thy ftreames,
  and on him endles youth attends.

After this Stance, Honor &c.

HON.

This fuperftitious Hymne, fung to the Sunne,
Let vs encounter with fit duties done
To our cleere Phœbus; whofe true piety,
Enioyes from heauen an earthly deity.

Other Mufique, and voyces; and this fecond Stance was fung, directing their obferuance to the King.

One alone   1.

Rife, rife O Phœbus, euer rife,
 defcend not to th' inconstant ftreame,
But grace with endles light, our fkyes,
 to thee that Sun is but a beame.

Another   2.

Dance Ladies in our Sunnes bright rayes,
 in which the Bride and Bridegroome fhine:
Cleere fable night with your eyes dayes,
 and fet firme lights on Hymens fhrine.

CHO.

O may our Sun not fet before,
 he fees his endles feed arife:
And deck his triple crowned fhore,
 with fprings of humane Deities.

This ended the Phœbades fung the third Stance.

1. Set Set (great Sun) our rifing loue
  fhall euer celebrate thy grace:
 Whom entring the high court of Ioue,
  each God greetes rifing from his place.

2. When thow thy filuer bow dost bend,
  all ftart afide and dread thy draughtes:
 How can we thee enough commend,
  commanding all worlds with thy fhafts?

CHO.

Blest was thy mother bearing thee,
　And Phœbe that delights in darts :
Thou artful Songes doſt ſet ; and ſhee
　winds horns, loues hounds, & high pallmd harts.

After this Honor.

HON.

Againe our Muſique and conclude this Song,
To him, to whom all Phœbus beames belong :

The other voyces ſung to other Muſike the
　　　　third ſtance.

1   *Riſe stil (cleere Sun) and neuer ſet,*
　　but be to Earth her only light :
　All other Kings in thy beames met,
　　are cloudes and darke effects of night.

2.

As when the Roſie Morn doth riſe,
　　Like Miſts, all giue thy wiſedome waie ;
　A learned King, is, as in skies,
　　To poore dimme ſtars, the flaming day,

CHO.

Bleſt was thy Mother, bearing Thee,
　　Thee only Relick of her Race,
　Made by thy vertues beames a Tree,
　　Whoſe armes ſhall all the Earth embrace.

This done *Eunomia* ſpake to the Maskers set
　　　　yet aboue.

EVN.

Virginian Princes, ye muſt now renounce
Your ſuperſtitious worſhip of theſe Sunnes,

The Masque of the middle

Subiect to cloudy darknings and defcents,
And of your fit deuotions, turne the euents
To this our Britan *Phœbus*, whofe bright skie
(Enlightned with a Chriftian Piety)
Is neuer fubiect to black Errors night,
And hath already offer'd heauens true light,
To your darke Region; which acknowledge now;
Defcend, and to him all your homage vow.

With this the Torch-bearers defcended, and performed another Antemaske, dancing with Torches lighted at both ends; which done, the Maskers defcended, and fell into their dances, two of which being paft, and others with the Ladies.

Honor fpake.

<small>The Bride and Bridegroome were figured in</small> Mufique! your voyces, now tune fweet and hie,
<small>Loue and Beauty.</small> And finge the Nuptiall *Hymn* of Love, and Beauty.
Twinns, as of one age, fo to one defire
<small>Twinns of which Hippocrates fpeakes.</small> May both their bloods giue, an vnparted fire. And as thofe twinns that Fame giues all her prife,
Combind their lifes power in fuch *Symphathies*;
That one being merry; mirth the other grac't:
If one felt forrow, th' other griefe embrac't.
If one were healthfull; Health the other pleafd:
If one were ficke: the other was difeafd;
And all waies ioynd in fuch a conftant troth
That one like caufe had like effect in both,
<small>Called Twynns being both of an Age.</small> So may thefe Nuptiall Twynnes, their whole liues ftore,
Spend in fuch euen parts, neuer grieuing more,
Then may the more fet off their ioyes diuine;
As after the clouds, the Sunne, doth clereft fhine.

This fayd, this Song of *Loue*, and *Bewty* was fung; fingle.

Bright Panthæa *borne to* Pan,
Of the Noblest Race of Man,
    Her white hand to Eros *giuing,*

With a kiſse, ioin'd Heauen to Earth
And begot ſo faire a birth,
   As yet neuer grac't the liuing.

CHO.

A Twinne that all worlds did adorne,
For ſo were Loue *and* Bewty *borne.*

2.

Both ſo lou'd, they did contend
Which the other ſhould tranſcend,
   Doing either, grace, and kindnes;
Loue *from* Bewty *did remoue,*
Lightnes call'd her ſtaine in loue,
   Bewtie *took from* Loue *his blindneſs;*

CHO.

Loue *ſparks made flames in* Bewties *ſkie,*
And Bewtie *blew vp* Loue *as hie.*

3

Virtue then commixt her fire;
To which Bountie *did aſpire,*
   Innocence a Crowne conferring;
Mine, and Thine, were then vnuſde,
All things common: Nought abuſde,
   Freely earth her frutage bearing.

CHO.

Nought then was car'd for, that could fade,
And thus the golden world was made.

The Masque of the middle

This sung, the Maskers danc't againe with the Ladies, after which *Honor*.

HON.

Now may the bleſſings of the golden age,
Swimme in theſe Nuptials, euen to holy rage,
A Hymn to Sleep prefer, and all the ioyes
That in his Empire are of deareſt choice,
Betwixt his golden ſlumbers euer flow,
In theſe; And Theirs, in Springs ás endleſs growe.

This ſayd, the laſt Song was ſung full.

The laſt Song.

Now ſleepe, binde faſt, the flood of Ayre,
 ſtrike all things dumb and deafe,
And, to diſturbbe our Nuptiall paire,
 Let ſtir no Aſpen leafe.
Send flocks of golden Dreames
 That all true ioyes preſage,
Bring, in thy oyly ſtreames,
 The milke and hony Age.
  Now cloſe the world-round ſphere of bliſſe,
  And fill it with a heauenly kiſſe.

After this *Plutus* to the Maskers.

PLVT.

Come Virgine Knights, the homage ye haue done,
To *Loue* and *Bewty*, and our Britan Sun,
Kinde *Honor*, will requite with holy feaſts
In her faire Temple; and her loued Gueſts,
Giues mee the grace t'inuite, when ſhe and I
(*Honor* and *Riches*) will eternally
A league in fauour of this night combine,
In which *Loues* ſecond hallowed Tapers ſhine;

Whofe Ioies, may Heauen & Earth as highly pleafe
As thofe two nights that got great *Hercules*.

The fpeech ended; they concluded with a dance, that brought them off; *Plutus*, with *Honor* and the reft conducting them vp to the Temple of *Honor*.

FINIS.

A Hymne to Hymen for the moſt time-
fitted Nuptialls of our
thrice gracious Princeſſe
Elizabeth, &c.

SInge, Singe a Rapture to all Nuptial eares,
  Bright *Hymens* torches, drunke vp *Parcæs* tears:
  Sweete *Hymen*; *Hymen*, Mightieſt of Gods,
Attoning of all-taming blood the odds;
Two into One, contracting; One to Two
Dilating, which no other God can doe.
Mak'ſt ſure, with change, and lett'ſt the married try,
Of Man and woman, the Variety.
And as a flower, halfe ſcorcht with daies long
  Simil.   heate.
Thirſts for refreſhing, with Nights cooling ſweate,
The wings of *Zephire*, fanning ſtill her face,
No chere can ad to her heart-thirſty grace;

A Hymn to Hymen.

Yet weares fhe gainft thofe fires that make her fade,
Her thicke hayrs proofe, al hyd, in Midnights fhade;
Her Helth, is all in dews; Hope, all in fhowres,
Whofe want bewailde, fhe pines in all her powres:
So Loue-fcorch't Virgines, nourifh quenchles fires;
The Fathers cares;. the Mothers kind defires.
Their Gould, and Garments, of the neweft guife,
Can nothing comfort their fcorcht Phantafies,
But, taken rauifh't vp, in *Hymens* armes,
His Circkle holds, for all their anguifh, charms:

Simil. ad eandem explicat. Then, as a glad Graft, in the fpring Sunne fhines,
That all the helps, of Earth, & Heauen combines
In Her fweet grouth: Puts in the Morning on
Her cherefull ayres; the Sunnes rich fires, at Noone;
At Euen the fweete deaws, and at Night with ftarrs,
In all their vertuous influences fhares;
So, in the Bridegroomes fweet embrace; the Bride,
All varied Ioies tafts, in their naked pride:
To which the richeft weedes: are weedes, to flowres;
Come *Hymen* then: com clofe thefe Nuptial howres
With all yeares comforts. Come; each virgin keepes
Her odorous kiffes for thee; Goulden fleepes
Will, in their humors, neuer fteepe an eie,
Till thou inuit'ft them with thy Harmony.
Why ftaieft thou? fee each Virgin doth prepare
Embraces for thee; Her white brefts laies bare
To tempt thy foft hand; let's fuch glances flie
As make ftarres fhoote,-to imitate her eye.
Puts Arts attires on, that put Natures doune:
Singes, Dances, fets on euery foote a Crowne,
Sighes, in her fongs, and dances; kiffeth Ayre
Till Rites, and words paft, thou in deedes repair;
The whole court Io fings: Io, the Ayre:
Io, the flouds, and fields: Io, moft faire,
Moft fweet, moft happy *Hymen*; Come: away;
With all thy Comforts come; old Matrons pray,
With young Maides Languors; Birds bill, build, and breed

To teach thee thy kinde, euery flowre and weed
Looks vp to gratulate thy long'd for fruites ;
Thrice giuen, are free, and timely-granted suites :
There is a seed by thee now to be sowne,
In whose fruit Earth, shall see her glories show'n,
At all parts perfect; and must therfore loose
No minutes time ; from times vse all fruite flowes ;
And as the tender Hyacinth, that growes   Simil.
Where *Phœbus* most his golden beames bestowes,
Is propt with care ; is water'd euery howre ;
The sweet windes adding their encreasing powre,
The scattered drops of Nights refreshing dew,
Hasting the full grace, of his glorious hew,
Which once disclosing, must be gatherd straight,
Or hew, and Odor both, will lose their height ;
So, of a Virgine, high, and richly kept,
The grace and sweetnes full growne must be reap't,
Or, forth her spirits fly, in empty Ayre ;
The sooner fading ; the more sweete and faire.
Gentle, O Gentle *Hymen*, be not then
Cruell, That kindest art to Maids, and Men ;
These two, One Twynn are ; and their mutuall blisse,
Not in thy beames, but in thy Bosome is.
Nor can their hands fast, their harts ioyes make sweet ;
Their harts, in brests are ; and their Brests must
   meete.
Let there be Peace, yet Murmur ; and that noise,
Beget of peace, the Nuptiall battailes ioyes.
Let Peace grow cruell, and take wrake of all,
The warrs delay brought thy full Festiuall.
Harke, harke, O now the sweete Twyn murmur
   sounds ;
Hymen is come, and all his heate abounds ;
Shut all Dores ; None, but *Hymens* lights aduance.
No sound styr ; let, dumb Ioy, enioy a trance.
Sing, sing a Rapture to all Nuptiall eares,
Bright *Hymens* Torches drunke up *Parcæs* teares.

AND

POMPEY:

A Roman Tragedy, declaring their Warres.

Out of whose euents is euicted this Propoſition.

Only a iuſt man is a freeman.

By George Chapman.

LONDON:

Printed by Thomas Harper, and are to be ſold by *Godfrey Emondſon,* and *Thomas Alchorne.*
M.DC.XXXI.

TO
THE RIGHT HONO-
rable, his exceeding good Lord, the
Earle of *Middlesex, &c.*

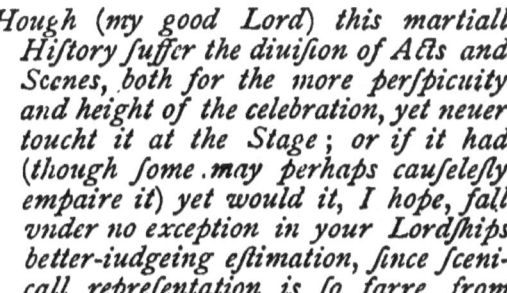

Hough (my good Lord) this martiall Hiſtory ſuffer the diuiſion of Acts and Scenes, both for the more perſpicuity and height of the celebration, yet neuer toucht it at the Stage; or if it had (though ſome may perhaps cauſeleſly empaire it) yet would it, I hope, fall vnder no exception in your Lordſhips better-iudgeing eſtimation, ſince ſceni-call repreſentation is ſo farre from giuing iuſt cauſe of any leaſt dimimution; that the perſonall and exact life it giues to any Hiſtory, or other ſuch delineation of humane actions, ads to them luſter, ſpirit and apprehenſion, which the only ſection of Acts and Scenes makes mee ſtand vpon thus much, ſince that only in ſome preciſianiſmes will require a little preuention: And the haſty proſe the ſtile auoides, obtaine to the more temperate and ſtai'd numerous elocu-tion, ſome aſsiſtance to the acceptation and grace of it. Though ingeniouſly my gratitude confeſſeth (my Lord) it is not ſuch as hereafter J vow to your honor; being written ſo long ſince; and had not the timely ripeneſſe of that age that (J thank God) J yet finde no fault with all for any old defects.

Good my Lord vouchſafe your idle minutes may admit ſome ſlight glances at this, till ſome worke of more nouelty and faſhion may conferre this the more liking of your honors more worthy deſeruings ; To which his bounden affection vowes all ſeruices.

Euer your Lordſhips

GEO. CHAPMAN.

The Argument.

POmpey and *Cæsar* bring their Armies fo neare *Rome*, that the Senate except againſt them. *Cæsar* vnduly and ambitiouſly commanding his forces. *Pompey* more for feare of *Cæſars* violence to the State, then mou'd with any affectation of his own greatneſſe. Their oppoſite pleadings, out of which admirable narrations are made, which yet not conducing to their ends, warre ends them. In which at firſt *Cæsar* is forc't to fly, whom *Pompey* not purſuing with ſuch wings as fitted a ſpeeding Conqueror; his victory was preuented, and he vnhappily diſhonor'd. Whoſe ill fortune his moſt louing and learned wife *Cornelia* trauailde after, with paines ſolemne and carefull enough; whom the two *Lentuli* and others attended, till ſhe miſerably found him, and ſaw him monſtrouſly murthered.

Both the Conſuls and *Cato* are ſlaughterd with their owne invincible hands; and *Cæsar* (in ſpight of all his fortune) without his victory, victor.

ONELY A IVST MAN IS A FREE MAN.
Act 1.   Scene 1.

Cato, Athenodorus, Porcius, Statilius.

Cat. Now will the two Suns of our Romane
Heauen
(*Pompey & Cæsar*) in their Tropicke
burning,
With their contention, all the clouds assemble
That threaten tempests to our peace & Empire,
Which we shall shortly see poure down in bloud,
Civill and naturall, wilde and barbarous turning.
  Ath. From whence presage you this?
  Cat. From both their Armies,
Now gathered neere our Italie, contending
To enter seuerally : *Pompeys* brought so neere
By Romes consent; for feare of tyranous *Cæsar*,
Which *Cæsar* fearing to be done in fauour
Of *Pompey*, and his passage to the Empire;
Hath brought on his for interuention.

And fuch a flocke of Puttocks follow *Cæsar*,
For fall of his ill-difpofed Purfe
(That neuer yet fpar'd Croffe to Aquiline vertue)
As well may make all ciuill fpirits fufpicious.
Looke how againft great raines, a ftanding Poole
Of Paddockes, Todes, and water-Snakes put vp
Their fpeckl'd throates aboue the venemous Lake,
Croking and gafping for fome frefh falne drops
To quench their poifond thirft ; being neere to ftifle
With clotterd purgings of their owne foule bane ;
So ftill, where *Cæsar* goes, there thruft vp head,
Impoftors, Flatterers, Fauorites, and Bawdes,
Buffons, Intelligencers, felect wits ;
Clofe Murtherers, Montibanckes, and decaied Theeues,
To gaine their banefull liues reliefes from him.
From Britaine, Belgia, France, and Germanie,
The fcum of either Countrie, (chus'd by him,
To be his blacke Guard, and red Agents here)
Swarming about him.

 Porc. And all thefe are faid
To be fuborn'd, in chiefe, againft your felfe ;
Since *Cæsar* chiefly feares, that you will fit
This day his oppofite ; in the caufe for which
Both you were fent for home ; and he hath ftolne
Acceffe fo foone here ; *Pompeys* whole reft raifde
To his encounter ; and on both fides, Rome
In generall vproare.

 Stat. Which Sir, if you faw,
And knew, how for the danger, all fufpect
To this your worthieft friend (for that knowne free-
 dome
His fpirit will vfe this day, 'gainft both the Riuals,
His wife and familie mourne, no food, no comfort
Allowd them for his danger) you would vfe
Your vtmoft powrs to ftay him from the Senate,
All this daies Seffion.

 Cat. Hee's too wife, *Statilius*,
For all is nothing.

 Stnt. Nothing Sir ? I faw

Castor and *Pollux* Temple, thrust vp full,
With all the damn'd crew you haue lately nam'd :
The market place and suburbs swarming with them :
And where the Senate sit, are Ruffians pointed
To keepe from entring the degrees that goe
Vp to the Bench ; all other but the Consuls,
Cæsar and *Pompey*, and the Senators,
And all for no cause, but to keepe out *Cato*,
With any violence, any villanie ;
And is this nothing Sir ? Is his One life,
On whom all good liues, and their goods depend,
In Romes whole Empire ! All the Iustice there
That's free, and simple ; all such virtues too,
And all such knowledge ; Nothing, nothing, all !

   Cat. Away *Statilius* ; how long shall thy loue
Exceede thy knowledge of me, and the Gods ?
Whose rights thou wrongst for my right ? haue not I
Their powers to guard me, in a cause of theirs ?
Their iustice, and integrity included,
In what I stand for ? he that feares the Gods,
For guard of any goodnesse ; all things feares ;
Earth, Seas, and Aire ; Heauen, darknesse, broade
    day-light,
Rumor, and Silence, and his very shade :
And what an Aspen soule hath such a creature ?
How dangerous to his soule is such a feare ?
In whose cold fits, is all heauens iustice shaken
To his faint thoughts ; and all the goodnesse there
Due to all good men, by the gods owne vowes,
Nay, by the firmenesse of their endlesse Being,
All which shall faile as soone as any one
Good to a good man in them : for his goodnesse
Proceeds from them, and is a beame of theirs.
O neuer more, *Statilius*, may this feare
Taint thy bould bosome, for thy selfe, or friend,
More then the gods are fearefull to defend.

   Athen. Come ; let him goe, *Statilius* ; and your
    fright ;

This man hath inward guard, paſt your yong ſight.
Exeunt.

Enter Minutius, manet Cato.

Cat. Welcome; come ſtand by me in what is fit
For our poore Cities ſafety; nor reſpect
Her proudeſt foes corruption, or our danger
Of what ſeene face ſoeuer.
  Min. I am yours.
But what alas, Sir, can the weakneſſe doe
Againſt our whole State of vs only two?
You know our Statiſts ſpirits are ſo corrupt
And ſeruile to the greateſt; that what croſſeth
Them, or their owne particular wealth, or honor,
They will not enterpriſe to ſaue the Empire.
  Cat. I know it; yet let vs doe like our ſelues.
Exeunt.

Enter ſome bearing Axes, bundles of rods, bare; before two Conſuls, Cæſar and Metellus; Anthonius, and Marcellus in couples; Senators, People, Souldiers, &c. following. The Conſuls enter the Degrees, with Anthonius, and Marcellus: Cæſar ſtaying a while without with Metellus who hath a paper in his hand.

  Cæſ. Moue you for entring only *Pompeys* army;
Which if you gaine for him; for me, all iuſtice
Will ioyne with my requeſt of entring mine.
  Met. Tis like ſo, and I purpoſe to enforce it.
  Cæſ. But might we not win *Cato* to our friendſhip
By honoring ſpeeches, nor perſwaſiue gifts?
  Met. Not poſſible.
  Cæſ. Nor by enforciue vſage?
  Met. Not all the violence that can be vſde,
Of power, or ſet authority can ſtirre him,
Much leſſe faire words win, or rewards corrupt him;
And therefore all meanes we muſt vſe to keepe him
From off the Bench.

Cæſar *and* Pompey.

Cæſ. Giue you the courſe for that,
And if he offer entry, I haue fellowes
Will ſerue your will on him, at my giuen ſignall.

They aſcend:
Enter Pompey, Gabinius, Vibius, Demetrius, with
papers. Enter the Liſts, aſcend and ſit.
After whom enter Cato, Minutius,
Athenodorus, Statilius, Porcius.

Cat. He is the man that ſits ſo cloſe to *Cæſar*,
And holds the law there, whiſpering; ſee the Cowherd
Hath guards of arm'd men got, againſt one naked.
Ile part their whiſpering virtue.
1   Hold, keepe out.
2. What? honor'd *Cato*? enter, chuſe thy place.
Cat. Come in;
He drawes him in and ſits betwixt Cæſar and Metellus.
—Away vnworthy groomes.
3. No more.
Cæſ. What ſhould one ſay to him?
Met. He will be Stoicall.
Cat. Where fit place is not giuen, it muſt be taken.
4. Doe, take it *Cato*; feare no greateſt of them;
Thou ſeek'ſt the peoples good; and theſe their owne.
5. Braue *Cato*! what a countenance he puts on?
Let's giue his noble will, our vtmoſt power.
6. Be bould in all thy will; for being iuſt,
Thou maiſt defie the gods.
Cat. Said like a God.
Met. We muſt endure theſe people.
Caeſ. Doe; begin.
Met. Conſuls, and reuerend Fathers; And ye
   people,
Whoſe voyces are the voyces of the Gods;
I here haue drawne a law, by good conſent,
For entring into *Italy*, the army
Of *Romes* great *Pompey*: that his forces here,

As well as he, great *Rome*, may reſt ſecure
From danger of the yet ſtill ſmoaking fire,
Of *Catilines* abhorr'd conſpiracy :
Of which the very chiefe are left aliue,
Only chaſtiſde, but with a gentle priſon.
    Cat. Put them to death then, and ſtrike dead our
    feare,
That well you vrge, by their vnfit furuiuall.
Rather then keepe it quick ; and two liues giue it,
By entertaining *Pompeys* army too.
That giues as great cauſe of our feare, as they.
For their conſpiracy, onely was to make
One Tyrant ouer all the State of *Rome.*
And *Pompeys* army, ſufferd to be entred,
Is, to make him, or giue him meanes to be ſo.
    Met. It followes not.
    Cat. In purpoſe ; clearely Sir,
Which Ile illuſtrate, with a cleare example.
If it be day, the Sunne's aboue the Earth ;
Which followes not (youle anſwere) for 'tis day
When firſt the morning breakes ; and yet is then
The body of the Sunne beneath the Earth ;
But he is virtually aboue it too,
Becauſe his beames are there ; and who then knowes
    not
His golden body will ſoone after mount.
So *Pompeys* army entred *Italy*,
Yet *Pompey's* not in *Rome* ; but *Pompey's* beames
Who ſees not there ? and conſequently, he
Is in all meanes enthron'd in th' Emperie.
    Met. Examples proue not, we will haue the army
Of *Pompey* entred.
    Cato. We ? which we intend you ?
Haue you already bought the peoples voices ?
Or beare our Conſuls or our Senate here
So ſmall loue to their Country ; that their wills
Beyond their Countrys right are ſo peruerſe,
To giue a Tyrant here entire command ?
Which I haue prou'd as cleare as day, they doe,

If either the Conspirators suruiuing
Be let to liue; or *Pompeys* army entred;
Both which, beat one sole path; and threat one danger.
   Cæs. Consuls, and honor'd Fathers; The sole entry
Of *Pompeys* army, Ile not yet examine:
But for the great Conspirators yet liuing,
(Which *Cato* will conclude as one selfe danger,
To our deare Country; and deterre all therefore
That loue their Country, from their liues defence
I see no reason why such danger hangs
On their sau'd liues; being still safe kept in prison;
And since close prison, to a Roman freedome,
Ten fold torments more, then directest death,
Who can be thought to loue the lesse his Country,
That seekes to saue their liues? And lest my selfe
(Thus speaking for them) be vniustly toucht
With any lesse doubt of my Countryes loue,
Why (reuerend Fathers) may it be esteem'd
Selfe praise in me, to proue my selfe a chiefe
Both in my loue of her; and in desert
Of her like loue in me: For he that does
Most honour to his Mistrisse; well may boast
(Without least question) that he loues her most.
And though things long since done, were long since known,
And so may seeme superfluous to repeat;
Yet being forgotten, as things neuer done,
Their repetition needful is, in iustice,
T'enflame the shame of that obliuion:
For hoping it will seeme no lesse empaire
To others acts, to truely tell mine owne;
Put all together; I haue past them all
That by their acts can boast themselues to be
Their Countries louers: first in those wilde kingdomes
Subdu'd to *Rome*, by my vnwearied toyles.
Which I dissuag'd and made nobly ciuill.

The Tragedy of

Next, in the multitude of thofe rude Realmes
That fo I fafhiond ; and to *Romes* yong Empire
Of old haue added : Then the battailes numbred
This hand hath fought, and wonne for her, with all
Thofe infinites of dreadfull enemies
(I flue in them : Twice fifteene hundred thoufand
All able Souldiers) I haue driuen at once
Before my forces : and in fundry onfets,
A thoufand thoufand of them, put to fword :
Befides, I tooke in leffe then ten yeares time,
By ftrong affault, aboue eight hundred Cities,
Three hundred feuerall Nations, in that fpace,
Subduing to my Countrey ; all which feruice,
I truft, may intereft me in her loue,
Publique, and generall enough, to aquit me
Of any felfe-loue ; paft her common good :
For any motion of particular iuftice
(By which her generall Empire is maintaind)
That I can make for thofe accufed prifoners,
Which is but by the way ; that fo the reafon
Metellus makes for entring *Pompeys* armie,
May not more weighty feeme, then to agree
With thofe imprifon'd nobles, vitall fafeties.
Which granted, or but yeelded fit to be,
May well extenuate the neceffity
Of entring *Pompeys* armie.
    Cat. All that need
I tooke away before ; and reafons gaue
For a neceffity to keepe it out
Whofe entry (I thinke) he himfelfe affects not.
Since I as well thinke he affects not th' Empire,
And both thofe thoughts hold ; fince he loues his
    Country,
In my great hopes of him too well to feeke
His fole rule of her, when fo many foules,
So hard a taske approue it ; nor my hopes
Of his fincere loue to his Country, build
On fandier grounds then *Cæfars* ; fince he can
As good Cards fhew for it as *Cæfar* did,

And quit therein the clofe afperfion
Of his ambition, feeking to imploy
His army in the breaft of *Italy*.
 Pomp. Let me not thus (imperiall Bench and Senate)
Feele my felfe beat about the eares, and toft
With others breathes to any coaft they pleafe :
And not put fome ftay to my errors in them.
The gods can witneffe that not my ambition
Hath brought to queftion th' entry of my army,
And therefore not fufpected the effect,
Of which that entry is fuppofde the caufe :
Which is a will in me, to giue my power
The rule of *Romes* fole Empire ; that moft ftrangely
Would put my will in others powers ; and powers
(Vnforfeit by my fault) in others wills.
My felfe-loue, out of which all this muft rife :
I will not wrong the knowne proofes of my loue
To this my natiue Cities publique good,
To quit, or thinke of ; nor repeat thofe proofes
Confirm'd in thofe three triumphs I haue made ;
For conqueft of the whole inhabited world ;
Firft *Affrick*, *Europe*, and then *Afia*,
Which neuer Confull but my felfe could boaft.
Nor can blinde Fortune vaunt her partiall hand,
In any part of all my feruices,
Though fome haue faid, fhe was the page of *Cæfar*,
Both fayling, marching, fighting, and preparing
His fights in very order of his battailes :
The parts fhe plaid for him inuerting nature,
As giuing calmneffe to th' enraged fea ;
Impofing Summers weather on fterne winter ;
Winging the floweft foot he did command,
And his moft Cowherd making fierce of hand.
And all this euer when the force of man
Was quite exceeded in it all ; and fhe
In th' inftant adding her cleare deity.
Yet, her for me, I both difclaime and fcorne ;
And where all fortune is renounc't, no reafon

Will thinke one man transferd with affectation
Of all *Romes* Empire ; for he muſt haue fortune
That goes beyond a man ; and where ſo many
Their hand-fulls finde with it ; the one is mad
That vndergoes it : and where that is clear'd ;
Th' imputed meanes to it, which is my ſute
For entry of mine army, I confute.
 Cat. What reſts then, this of all parts being dif-
  claimd ?
 Met. My part, Sir, reſts, that let great *Pompey*
  beare
What ſpirit he liſts ; 'tis needfull yet for *Rome,*
That this Law be eſtabliſht for his army.
 Cæſ. Tis then as needfull to admit in mine ;
Or elſe let both lay downe our armes ; for elſe
To take my charge off, and leaue *Pompey* his ;
You wrongfully accuſe me to intend
A tyranny amongſt ye : and ſhall giue
Pompey full meanes to be himſelfe a tyrant.
 Anth. Can this be anſwer'd ?
 1. *Conſ.* Is it then your wils
That *Pompey* ſhall ceaſe armes ?
 Anth. What elſe ?
 Omnes. No, no.
 2. *Conſ.* Shall *Cæſar* ceaſe his armes ?
 Omn. I, I.
 Anth. For ſhame
Then yeeld to this cleare equity, that both
May leaue their armes.
 Omn. We indifferent ſtand.
 Met. Read but this law, and you ſhall ſee a differ-
  ence
Twixt equity and your indifferency ;
All mens obiections anſwered ; Read it Notary.
 Cat. He ſhall not read it.
 Met. I will read it then.
 Min. Nor thou ſhalt read it, being a thing ſo vaine,
Pretending cauſe for *Pompeys* armies entry,
That only by thy Complices and thee ;

Tis forg'd to fet the Senate in an vproare.
   Met. I haue it Sir, in memory, and will fpeake it.
   Cat. Thou fhalt be dumbe as foone.
   Cæf. Pull downe this *Cato*,
Author of factions, and to prifon with him.
   Gen. Come downe Sir.   *He drawes,*
   Pom. Hence ye mercenary Ruffians. *and all draw.*
   1. *Conf.* What outrage fhew you? fheath your
     infolent fwords,
Or be proclaim'd your Countreys foes and traytors.
   Pom. How infolent a part was this in you,
To offer the imprifonment of *Cato*?
When there is right in him (were forme fo anfwer'd
With termes and place) to fend vs both to prifon?
If, of our owne ambitions, we fhould offer
Th' entry of our armies; for who knowes
That, of vs both, the beft friend to his Country,
And freeft from his owne particular ends;
(Being in his power) would not affume the Empire,
And hauing it, could rule the State fo well
As now 'tis gouer'nd, for the common good?
   Cæf. Accufe your felfe, Sir, (if your confcience
     vrge it)
Or of ambition, or corruption,
Or infufficiency to rule the Empire,
And found not me with your Lead.
   Pom. Lead? tis Gold,
And fpirit of Gold too; to the politique droffe
With which falfe *Cæfar* founds men; and for which
His praife and honour crownes them; who founds not
The inmoft fand of *Cæfar*? for but fand
Is all the rope of your great parts affected.
You fpeake well, and are learn'd; and golden fpeech
Did Nature neuer giue man; but to guild
A copper foule in him; and all that learning
That heartily is fpent in painting fpeech,
Is merely painted, and no folid knowledge.
But y'aue another praife for temperance,

Which nought commends your free choice to be temperate.
For so you must be; at least in your meales,
Since y'aue a malady that tyes you to it;
For feare of daily fals in your aspirings.
And your disease the gods nere gaue to man;
But such a one, as had a spirit too great
For all his bodies passages to serue it,
Which notes th' excesse of your ambition.
The malady chancing where the pores and passages
Through which the spirit of a man is borne,
So narrow are, and straight, that oftentimes
They intercept it quite, and choake it vp.
And yet because the greatnesse of it notes
A heat mere fleshly, and of bloods ranck fire,
Goates are of all beasts subiect'st to it most.
   Cæs. Your selfe might haue it then, if those faults cause it;
But deales this man ingeniously, to tax
Men with a frailty that the gods inflict?
   Pomp. The gods inflict on men, diseases neuer,
Or other outward maimes; but to decipher,
Correct, and order some rude vice within them:
And why decipher they it, but to make
Men note, and shun, and tax it to th' extreame?
Nor will I see my Countryes hopes abusde,
In any man commanding in her Empire;
If my more tryall of him, makes me see more
Into his intricasies; and my freedome
Hath spirit to speake more, then obseruers seruile.
   Cæs. Be free, Sir, of your insight and your speech;
And speak, and see more, then the world besides;
I must remember I haue heard of one,
That fame gaue out, could see thorow Oke and stone:
And of another set in *Sicily*,
That could discerne the Carthaginian Nauy,
And number them distinctly, leauing harbor,
Though full a day and nights saile distant thence:
But these things (Reuerend Fathers) I conceiue,

Hardly appeare to you worth graue beliefe:
And therefore fince fuch ftrange things haue beene feene
In my fo deepe and foule detractions,
By only Lyncean *Pompey*; who was moft
Lou'd and beleeu'd of *Romes* moft famous whore,
Infamous *Flora*; by fo fine a man
As *Galba*, or *Sarmentus*; any iefter
Or flatterer may draw through a Ladyes Ring;
By one that all his Souldiers call in fcorne
Great *Agamemnon*, or the King of men;
I reft vnmou'd with him; and yeeld to you
To right my wrongs, or his abufe allow.

 Cat. My Lords, ye make all *Rome* amaz'd to heare.

 Pom. Away, Ile heare no more; I heare it thunder
My Lords; All you that loue the good of *Rome*,
I charge ye, follow me; all fuch as ftay,
Are friends to *Cæsar*, and their Countreys foes.

 Cæs. Th' euent will fall out contrary, my Lords.

 1. *Conf.* Goe, thou art a thiefe to *Rome*, difcharge thine army,
Or be proclaim'd, forthwith, her open foe.

 2. *Conf.* *Pompey*, I charge thee, helpe thy iniur'd Country
With what powers thou haft arm'd, and leuy more.

 The Ruffians. Warre, warre, O *Cæsar*.

 Sen. and Peop. Peace, peace, worthy *Pompey*.

Act II.   Scene I.

Enter Fronto all ragg'd, in an ouergrowne red Beard, black head, with a Halter in his hand, looking about.

WArres, warres, and preſſes, fly in fire about;
 No more can I lurke in my laſie corners,
Nor ſhifting courſes: and with honeſt meanes
To rack my miſerable life out, more,
The rack is not ſo fearefull; when diſhoneſt
And villanous faſhions faile me; can I hope
To liue with virtuous? or to raiſe my fortunes
By creeping vp in Souldierly degrees?
Since villany varied thorow all his figures,
Will put no better caſe on me then this;
Deſpaire! come ſeaſe me: I had able meanes;
And ſpent all in the ſwinge of lewd affections;
Plung'd in all riot, and the rage of blood;
In full aſſurance that being knaue enough,
Barbarous enough, baſe, ignorant enough,
I needs muſt haue enough, while this world laſted;
Yet, ſince I am a poore, and ragged knaue,
My rags diſgrace my knauery ſo, that none
Will thinke I am knaue; as if good clothes
Were knacks to know a knaue; when all men know
He has no liuing? which knacks ſince my knauery
Can ſhew no more; and only ſhew is all
That this world cares for; Ile ſtep out of all
The cares 'tis ſteept in.   *He offers to hang himſelfe.*

Thunder, and the Gulfe opens, flames iſſuing; and Ophioneus aſcending, with the face, wings, and taile of a Dragon; a skin coate all ſpeckled on the throat.

Oph.   Hold Raſcall, hang thy ſelfe in theſe dayes?

Cæsar *and* Pompey.   141

The only time that euer was for a Rafcall to liue in ?
Fron. How chance I cannot liue then ?
Oph. Either th'art not rafcall nor villaine enough;
Or elfe thou doft not pretend honefty
And piety enough to difguife it.
Fro. That's certaine, for euery affe does that.
What art thou ?
Oph. O villaine worfe then thou.
Fro. And doft breathe?
Oph. I fpeake, thou hear'ft, I moue, my pulfe beates
Faft as thine.
Fro. And wherefore liu'ft thou ?
Oph. The world's out of frame, a thoufand Rulers
Wrefting it this way, and that, with as many
Religions; when, as heauens vpper Sphere is mou'd
Onely by one; fo fhould the Sphere of earth be, and
Ile haue it fo.
Fro. How canft thou ? what art thou ?
Oph. My fhape may tell thee.
Fro. No man ?
Oph. Man ? no, fpawne of a clot, none of that curfed
Crew, damn'd in the maffe it felfe; plagu'd in his birth,
Confinde to creepe below, and wreftle with the Elements;
Teach himfelfe tortures; kill himfelfe, hang himfelfe;
No fuch gally flaue, but at warre with heauen;
Spurning the power of the gods, command the Elements.
Fro. What maift thou be theu ?
Oph. An endleffe friend of thine; an immortall deuill.
Fro. Heauen bleffe vs.
Oph. Nay then, forth, goe, hang thy felfe, and thou talk'ft
Of heauen once.
Fro. I haue done; what deuill art thou ?

Oph. Read the old ſtoick *Pherecides*, that tels thee
Me truly, and ſayes that I *Ophioneus* (for ſo is
My name.
   Fro. *Ophioneus*? what's that?
   Oph. Deuiliſh Serpent, by interpretation; was generall
Captaine of that rebellious hoſt of ſpirits that
Wag'd warre with heauen.
   Fro. And ſo were hurl'd downe to hell.
   Oph. We were ſo; and yet haue the rule of earth; and cares
Any man for the worſt of hell then?
   Fro. Why ſhould he?
   Oph. Well ſaid; what's thy name now?
   Fro. My name is *Fronto*.
   Oph. *Fronto*? A good one; and has *Fronto* liu'd thus long
In *Rome*? loſt his ſtate at dice? murther'd his
Brother for his meanes? ſpent all? run thorow worſe
Offices ſince? beene a Promoter? a Purueyor? a Pander?
A Sumner? a Sergeant? an Intelligencer? and at laſt
Hang thy ſelfe?
   Fro. How the deuill knowes he all this?
   Oph. Why thou art a moſt greene Plouer in policy, I
Perceiue; and maiſt drinke Colts-foote, for all thy
Horſemane beard: S'light, what need haſt
Thou to hang thy ſelfe? as if there were a dearth
Of hangmen in the land? Thou liu'ſt in a good cheape
State, a man may be hang'd here for a little, or
Nothing. What's the reaſon of thy deſperation?
   Gro. My idle diſſolute life, is thruſt out of all his corners
By this ſearching tumult now on foot in *Rome*.
—————————————— *Cæſar* now and *Pompey*
Are both for battaile: *Pompey* (in his feare
Of *Cæſars* greater force) is ſending hence

Cæsar *and* Pompey.

His wife and children, and he bent to fly.

Enter Pompey running over the Stage with his wife and children, Gabinius, Demetrius, Vibius, Pages; other Senators, the Confuls aud all following.

See, all are on their wings; and all the City
In fuch an vproare, as if fire and fword
Were ranfacking, and ruining their houfes,
No idle perfon now can lurke neare *Rome*,
All muft to armes; or fhake their heeles beneath
Her martiall halters; whofe officious pride
Ile fhun, and vfe mine owne fwinge: I be forc't
To helpe my Countrey, when it forceth me
To this paft-helping pickle?

   Oph. Goe to, thou fhalt ferue me; chufe thy profeffion;
And what cloth thou wouldft wifh to haue thy Coat
Cut out on.

   Fro. I can name none.
   Oph. Shall I be thy learn'd Counfaile?
   Fro. None better.
   Oph. Be an Archflamen then, to one of the Gods.
   Fro. Archflamen? what's that?
   Oph. A Prieft.
   Fro. A Prieft? that nere was Clerke?
   Oph. No Clerke? what then?
The greateft Clerks are not the wifeft men.
Nor skils it for degrees in a knaue, or a fooles preferment,
Thou fhalt rife by fortune: let defert rife leifurely
Enough, and by degrees; fortune preferres headlong,
And comes like riches to a man; huge riches being
Got with little paines; and little with huge paines.
   And
For difcharge of the Priefthood, what thou wantft
In learning, thou fhalt take out in goodfellowfhip:
Thou fhalt equiuocate with the Sophifter, prate with

The Lawyer, fcrape with the Vfurer, drinke with the
Dutchman, fweare with the French man, cheat
With the Englifh man, brag with the Scot, and
Turne all this to Religion, *Hoc eft regnum
Deorum Gentibus.*
 Fro. All this I can doe to a haire.
 Oph. Very good, wilt thou fhew thy felfe deepely
learn'd too,
And to liue licentioufly here, care for nothing here-
 after ?
 Fro. Not for hell ?
 Oph. For hell ? foft Sir ; hop'ft thou to purchafe
hell
With only dicing or whoring away thy liuing ?
Murthering thy brother, and fo forth ? No there
Remaine works of a higher hand and deeper braine,
To obtaine hell. Thinkft thou earths great
Potentates haue gotten their places there with
Any fingle act of murther, poyfoning, adultery,
And the reft ? No ; tis a purchafe for all manner
Of villany ; efpecially, that may be priuiledg'd
By Authority ; colourd with holineffe, and enioyd
With pleafure.
 Fro. O this were moft honourable and admirable.
 Oph. Why fuch an admirable honorable villane
 fhalt
Thou be.
 Fro. Is't poffible ?
 Oph. Make no doubt on't ; Ile infpire thee.
 Fro. Sacred and puiffant.   *He kneeles.*
 Oph. Away ; Companion and friend, giue me thy
Hand ; fay, doft not loue me ? art not enamourd
Of my acquaintance ?
 Fro. Proteft I am.
 Oph. Well faid, proteft and tis enough. And know
 for
Infallible ; I haue promotion for thee ; both here, and
Hereafter ; which not one great one amongft
Millions fhall euer afpire to. *Alexander,* nor great

Cyrus, retaine thofe titles in hell, that they did
On earth.
 Fron. No? *Oph.* No: he that fold Seacoale
  here, fhall be
A Baron there; he that was a cheating
Rogue here, fhall be a Iuftice of peace there;
A knaue here, a knight there. In the meane
Space, learne what it is to liue; and thou fhalt
Haue Chopines at commandment to any height
Of life thou canft wifh.
 Fro. I feare my fall is too low.
 Oph. Too low foole? haft thou not heard of
  Vulcans falling
Out of heauen? Light a thy legges, and no matter
Thou thou halt'ft with thy beft friend euer after; tis
The more comely and fafhionable. Better goe lame
In the fafhion with *Pompey*, then neuer fo vpright,
Quite out of the fafhion with *Cato*.
 Fro. Yet you cannot change the old fafhion (they
  fay)
And hide your clouen feet.
 Oph. No? I can weare Rofes that fhall fpread
  quite
Ouer them.
 Fro. For loue of the fafhion doe then.
 Oph. Goe to; I will hereafter.
 Fro. But for the Priefthood you offer me, I affect
  it not.
 Oph. No? what faift thou to a rich office then?
 Fro. The only fecond meanes to raife a rafcall
In the earth.
 Oph. Goe to; Ile helpe thee to the beft ith earth
  then:
And that's in *Sicilia*; the very ftorehoufe of the
Romanes, where the Lord chiefe Cenfor there
Lyes now a dying; whofe foule I will haue; and
Thou fhalt haue his office.
 Fro. Excellent; was euer great office better
  fupplied?   *Exeunt.*

          K

The Tragedy of

Nuntius.
Now is the mighty Empreſſe of the earth
(Great *Rome*) faſt lockt vp in her fancied ſtrength,
All broke in vproares ; fearing the iuſt gods
In plagues will drowne her ſo abuſed bleſſings.
In which feare, all without her wals, fly in ;
By both their iarring Champions ruſhing out ;
And thoſe that were within, as faſt fly forth ;
The Conſuls both are fled without one rite
Of ſacrifice ſubmitted to the gods,
As euer heretofore their cuſtome was
When they began the bloody frights of warre.
In which our two great Souldiers now encountring,
Since both left *Rome*, oppos'd in bitter skirmiſh,
Pompey (not willing yet to hazard battaile,
By *Catos* counſaile, vrging good cauſe) fled :
Which firing *Cæſars* ſpirit ; he purſu'd
So home, and fiercely, that great *Pompey* skorning
The heart he tooke, by his aduiſed flight,
Deſpiſde aduice as much as his purſuite.
And as in *Lybia*, an aged Lion,
Vrg'd from his peacefull couert, feares the light,
With his vnready and diſeaſ'd appearance,
Giues way to chace a while, and coldly hunts,
Till with the youthfull hunters wanton heat,
He all his coole wrath frets into a flame :
And then his ſides he ſwinges with his Sterne,
To laſh his ſtrenth vp, let's downe all his browes
About his burning eyes ; erects his mane,
Breakes all his throat in thunders, and to wreake
His hunters inſolence, his heart euen barking ;
He frees his fury, turnes, and ruſhes back
With ſuch a gaſtly horror, that in heapes,
His proud foes fly, and he that ſtation keepes :
So *Pompeys* coole ſpirits, put to all their heat
By *Cæſars* hard purſuit he turnd freſh head,
And flew vpon his foe with ſuch a rapture
As tooke vp into furies, all friends feares ;
Who fir'd with his firſt turning, all turnd head,

And gaue fo fierce a charge, their followers fled,
Whofe inftant iffue on their both fides, fee,
And after fet out fuch a tragedy,
As all the Princes of the earth may come
To take their patternes by the fpirits of *Rome*.

*Alarme, after which enter Cæfar following Craffi-
nius calling to the Souldiers.*

Craff. Stay cowherd, fly ye *Cæfars* fortunes?
Cæf. Forbeare, foolifh *Craffinius*, we contend in vaine
To ftay thefe vapours, and muft raife our Campe.
Craff. How fhall we rife (my Lord) but all in vp-
roares,
Being ftill purfude?

Enter Acilius.

The purfuit ftayes, my Lord,
Pompey hath founded a retreat, refigning
His time to you to vfe, in inftant rayfing
Your ill-lodg'd army, pitching now where fortune
May good amends make for her fault to day.
Cæf. It was not fortunes fault, but mine *Acilius*,
To giue my foe charge, being fo neare the fea,
Where well I knew the eminence of his ftrength,
And fhould haue driuen th' encounter further off;
Bearing before me fuch a goodly Country,
So plentifull, and rich, in all things fit
To haue fuppli'd my armies want with victuals,
And th' able Cities too, to ftrengthen it,
Of *Macedon* and *Theffaly*, where now
I rather was befieg'd for want of food,
Then did affault with fighting force of armes.

Enter Anthony, Vibius, with others.

Ant. See, Sir, here's one friend of your foes recouer'd.
Cæf. Vibius? In happy houre.

Vib. For me vnhappy.
Cæf. What? brought againſt your will?
Vib. Elſe had not come.
Ant. Sir, hee's your priſoner, but had made you his,
Had all the reſt purſu'd the chace like him;
He draue on like a fury; paſt all friends,
But we that tooke him quick in his engagement.
Cæf. O *Vibius*, you deſerue to pay a ranſome
Of infinite rate, for had your Generall ioyn'd
In your addreſſion, or knowne how to conquer;
This day had prou'd him the ſupreame of *Cæſar.*¹
Vib. Knowne how to conquer? His fiue hundred Conqueſts
Atchieu'd ere this day, make that doubt vnfit
For him that flyes him; for, of iſſues doubtfull
Who can at all times put on for the beſt?
If I were mad, muſt hee his army venture
In my engagement? Nor are Generalls euer
Their powers diſpoſers, by their proper Angels,
But truſt againſt them, oftentimes, their Counſailes,
Wherein, I doubt not, *Cæſars* ſelfe hath err'd
Sometimes as well as *Pompey.*
Cæf. Or done worſe,
In diſobeying my Counſaile (*Vibius*)
Of which, this dayes abuſed light is witneſſe;
By which I might haue ſeene a courſe ſecure
Of this diſcomfiture.
Ant. Amends fits euer
Aboue repentance, what's done, wiſh not vndone;
But that prepared patience that you know
Beſt fits a ſouldier charg'd with hardeſt fortunes;
Asks ſtill your vſe, ſince powers ſtill temperate kept
Ope ſtill the clearer eyes by one faults ſight
To place the next act, in the ſurer right.
Cæf. You prompt me nobly Sir, repayring in me
Mine owne ſtayes practice, out of whoſe repoſe,
The ſtrong convulſions of my ſpirits forc't me
Thus farre beyond my temper; but good *Vibius*,

Cæfar *and* Pompey.

Be ranſom'd with my loue, and haſte to *Pompey*,
Entreating him from me, that we may meet,
And for that reaſon which I know this day
(Was giuen by *Cato*, for his purſutes ſtay
Which was preuention of our Romane blood)
Propoſe my offer of our hearty peace.
That being reconcil'd, and mutuall faith
Giuen on our either part, not three dayes light
May further ſhew vs foes, but (both our armies
Diſperſt in Gariſons) we may returne
Within that time to *Italy*, ſuch friends
As in our Countryes loue, containe our ſplenes.

  Vit. Tis offerd, Sir, 'boue the rate of *Cæfar*,
In other men, but in what I approue
Beneath his merits: which I will not faile
T' enforce at full to *Pompey*, nor forget
In any time the gratitude of my ſeruice. *Vi. ſalutes Ant. and the other, & exit.*

  Cæſ. Your loue, Sir, and your friendſhip.

  Ant. This prepares a good induction to the change of fortune,
In this dayes iſſue, if the pride it kindles
In *Pompeys* vaines, makes him deny a peace
So gently offerd: for her alterd hand
Works neuer ſurer from her ill to good
On his ſide ſhe hath hurt, and on the other
With other changes, then when meanes are vſde
To keepe her conſtant, yet retire refuſde.

  Caſ. I try no ſuch concluſion, but deſire
Directly peace. In meane ſpace Ile prepare
For other iſſue in my vtmoſt meanes;
Whoſe hopes now reſting at *Brunduſium*,
In that part of my army, with *Sabinus*,
I wonder he ſo long delaies to bring me,
And muſt in perſon haſte him, if this Euen
I heare not from him.

  Craſſ. That (I hope) flyes farre
Your full intent, my Lord, ſince *Pompeys* navie
You know, lies houering all alongſt thoſe ſeas,
In too much danger, for what ayde ſoeuer

The Tragedy of

You can procure to paſſe your perſon ſafe.
  Acil. Which doubt may proue the cauſe that ſtayes
    Sabinus;
And, if with ſhipping fit to paſſe your army,
He yet ſtraines time to venture, I preſume
You will not paſſe your perſon with ſuch Conuoy
Of thoſe poore veſſels, as may ſerue you here.
  Cæſ. How ſhall I helpe it ? ſhall I ſuffer this
Torment of his delay ? and rack ſuſpitions
Worſe then aſſur'd deſtructions through my thoughts.
  Anth. Paſt doubt he will be here ; I left all orderd,
And full agreement made with him to make
All vtmoſt haſte, no leaſt let once ſuſpected.
  Cæſ. Suſpected ? what ſuſpection ſhould feare a
    friend
In ſuch aſſur'd ſtreights from his friends enlargement.
If twere his ſouldiers ſafeties he ſo tenders,
Were it not better they ſhould ſinke by ſea,
Then wrack their number, King and cauſe aſhore ?
Their ſtay is worth their ruine, ſhould we liue,
If they in fault were ? if their leader ! he
Should dye the deaths of all ; in meane ſpace, I
That ſhould not, beare all, fly the fight in ſhame,
Thou eye of nature, and abortiue night
Fall dead amongſt vs : with defects, defects
Muſt ſerue proportion ; iuſtice neuer can
Be elſe reſtor'd, nor right the wrongs of man. *Exeunt.*

Pompey, Cato, Gabinius, Demetrius, Athenodorus,
Porcius, Statilius.

  Pomp. This charge of our fierce foe, the friendly
    gods
Haue in our ſtrengthen'd ſpirits beaten back
With happy iſſue, and his forces leſſen'd,
Of two and thirty Enſignes forc't from him,
Two thouſand ſouldiers ſlaine.
  Cat. O boaſt not that,
Their loſſe is yours, my Lord.

Pomp. I boaſt it not,
But only name the number.
   Gab. Which right well
You might haue raiſde ſo high, that on their tops
Your Throne was offer'd, euer t'ouerlooke
Subuerted *Cæſar*, had you beene ſo bleſt
To giue ſuch honor to your Captaines Counſailes
As their alacrities did long to merit
With proofefull action.
   Dem. O twas ill neglected.
   Stat. It was deferr'd with reaſon, which not yet
Th' euent ſo cleare is to confute.
   Pom. If twere,
Our likelieſt then was, not to hazard battaile,
Th' aduenture being ſo caſuall ; if compar'd
With our more certaine meanes to his ſubuerſion ?
For finding now our army amply ſtorde
With all things fit to tarry ſurer time,
Reaſon thought better to extend to length
The warre betwixt vs ; that his little ſtrength
May by degrees proue none ; which vrged now,
(Conſiſting of his beſt and ableſt ſouldiers)
We ſhould haue found at one direct ſet battaile
Of matchleſſe valours ; their defects of victuall
Not tyring yet enough on their tough nerues,
Where, on the other part, to put them ſtill
In motion, and remotion, here and there ;
Enforcing them to fortifying ſtill
Where euer they ſet downe ; to ſiege a wall,
Keepe watch all night in armour : their moſt part
Can neuer beare it, by their yeares oppreſſion ;
Spent heretofore too much in thoſe ſteele toyles.
   Cat. I ſo aduiſde, and yet repent it not,
But much reioyce in ſo much ſaued blood
As had beene pour'd out in the ſtroke of battaile,
Whoſe fury thus preuented, comprehends
Your Countreys good, and Empires ; in whoſe care
Let me beſeech you that in all this warre,
You ſack no City, ſubiect to our Rule,

Nor put to fword one Citizen of *Rome* ;
But when the needfull fury of the fword
Can make no fit diftinction in maine battaile,
That you will pleafe ftill to prolong the ftroke
Of abfolute decifion to thefe iarres,
Confidering you fhall ftrike it with a man
Of much skill and experience, and one
That will his Conqueft fell at infinite rate,
If that muft end your difference ; but I doubt
There will come humble offer on his part,
Of honor'd peace to you, for whofe fweet name
So cryed out to you in our late-met Senate,
Loft no fit offer of that wifhed treaty.
Take pity on your Countreys blood as much
As poffible may ftand without the danger
Of hindering her iuftice on her foes,
Which all the gods to your full wifh difpofe.
   Pom. Why will you leaue vs? whither will you
     goe
To keepe your worthyeft perfon in more fafety
Then in my army, fo deuoted to you ?
   Cat. My perfon is the leaft, my Lord, I value ;
I am commanded by our powerfull Senate,
To view the Cities, and the kingdomes fcituate
About your either army, that which fide
Soeuer conquer, no difordered ftraglers
Puft with the Conqueft, or by need impeld,
May take their fwinge more then the care of one
May curb and order in thefe neighbor confines
My chiefe paffe yet refolues for Vtica.
   Pom. Your paffe (my trueft friend, and worthy
     Father)
May all good powers make fafe, and always anfwer
Your infinite merits, with their like protection.
In which, I make no doubt but we fhall meet
With mutuall greetings, or for abfolute conqueft
Or peace preuenting that our bloody ftroke,
Nor let our parting be difhonor'd fo,
As not to take into our nobleft notice

Cæfar *and* Pompey.

Your felfe (moft learned and admired Father)
Whofe merits, if I liue, fhall lack no honor.
Porcius, Statilius, though your fpirits with mine
Would highly chere me, yet ye fhall beftow them
In much more worthy conduct ; but loue me,
And wifh me conqueft, for your Countreys fake.

   Sta. Our liues fhall feale our loues, Sir, with worft deaths
Aduentur'd in your feruice.

   Pom. Y'are my friends.
                       Exeunt Cat. Athen. Por. Sat.
Thefe friends thus gone, tis more then time we minded
Our loft friend *Vibius.*

   Gab. You can want no friends,
See, our two Confuls, Sir, betwixt them bringing
The worthy *Brutus*

      Enter two Confuls leading Brutus betwixt them.

   1. *Conf.* We attend (my Lord)
With no meane friend, to fpirit your next encounter,
Six thoufand of our choice Patrician youths
Brought in his conduct.

   2. *Conf.* And though neuer yet
He hath faluted you with any word
Or looke of flendreft loue in his whole life,
Since that long time fince, of his fathers death
By your hand authord ; yet fee, at your need
He comes to ferue you freely for his Country.

   Pom. His friendly prefence, making vp a third
With both your perfons, I as gladly welcome,
As if *Ioues* triple flame had guilt this field,
And lightn'd on my right hand, from his fhield.

   Bru. I well affure my felfe, Sir, that no thought
In your ingenious conftruction, touches
At the afperfion that my tendred feruice
Proceeds from my defpaire of elfewhere fafety.
But that my Countreys fafety owning iuftly
My whole habilities of life and fortunes,

And you the ableſt fautor of her ſafty,
Her loue, and (for your loue of her) your owne
Only makes ſacred to your vſe my offering.
 Pom. Farre fly all other thought from my conſtruction,
And due acceptance of the liberall honor,
Your loue hath done me, which the gods are witneſſe,
I take as ſtirr'd vp in you by their fauours,
Nor leſſe eſteeme it then an offering holy;
Since, as of all things, man is ſaid the meaſure,
So your full merits meaſure forth a man.
 1. *Conf.* See yet, my Lord, more friends.
 2 *Conf.* Fiue Kings, your ſeruants.

Enter fiue Kings.

 Hib. Conqueſt and all grace crowne the gracious *Pompey*,
To ſerue whom in the ſacred Romane ſafety,
My ſelfe, *Iberias* King, preſent my forces.
 Theſſ. And I that hold the tributary Throne
Of Grecian *Theſſaly*, ſubmit my homage,
To *Rome*, and *Pompey*.
 Cil. So *Cilicia* too.
 Epir. And ſo *Epirus*.
 Thra. Laſtly I from Thrace
Preſent the duties of my power and ſeruice.
 Pom. Your royall aides deſerue of *Rome* and *Pompey*
Our vtmoſt honors. O may now our fortune
Not ballance her broad breaſt twixt two light wings,
Nor on a ſlippery globe ſuſtaine her ſteps,
But as the Spartans ſay, the Paphian Queene
(The flood *Eurotas* paſſing) laid aſide
Her Glaſſe, her Ceſton, and her amorous graces,
And in *Lycurgus* fauor; arm'd her beauties
With Shield and Iaueline, ſo may fortune now,
The flood of all our enemies forces paſſing
With her faire Enſignes, and arriu'd at ours,

Cæsar *and* Pompey.

Difplume her fhoulders, caft off her wing'd fhooes,
Her faithleffe, and ftill-rowling ftone fpurne from her,
And enter our powers as fhe may remaine
Our firme affiftent : that the generall aydes,
Fauours, and honors you performe to *Rome*,
May make her build with you her endleffe home.
 Omn. The gods vouchfafe it ; and our caufes right.
 Dem. What fuddaine Shade is this ? obferue my
  Lords,
The night, methinks, comes on before her houre.
       Thunder and lightning.
 Gab. Nor truft me if my thoughts conceiue not fo.
 Bru. What thin clouds fly the winds, like fwifteft
  fhafts
Along aires middle region.
 1 *Conf.* They prefage
Vnufuall tempefts.
 2. *Conf.* And tis their repaire,
That timeleffe darken thus the gloomy ayre.
 Pom. Let's force no *omen* from it, but avoid
The vapors furies now by *Ioue* employd.

Thunder continued, and Cæfar enters difguifde.

The wrathfull tempeft of the angry night,
Where hell flyes mufl'd vp in clouds of pitch,
Mingl'd with Sulphure, and thofe dreadfull bolts,
The Cyclops Ram in *Ioues* Artillery,
Hath roufde the furies, arm'd in all their horrors,
Vp to the enuious feas, in fpight of *Cæfar*.
O night, O ielous night, of all the nobleft
Beauties, and glories, where the gods haue ftroke
Their foure digeftions, from thy gaftly Chaos,
Blufh thus to drowne them all in this houre fign'd
By the neceffity of fate for *Cæfar*.
I that haue ranfackt all the world for worth,
To forme in man the image of the gods,

Muſt like them haue the power to check the worſt
Of all things vnder their celeſtiall Empire,
Stoope it, and burſt it, or breake through it all,
With vſe and ſafety, till the Crowne be ſet
On all my actions; that the hand of nature
In all her worſt works ayming at an end,
May in a maſter-peece of hers be ſeru'd
With tops, and ſtate fit for his virtuous Crowne:
Not lift arts thus farre vp in glorious frame,
To let them vaniſh thus in ſmoke and ſhame.
This riuer *Anius* (in whoſe mouth now lyes
A Pynnace I would paſſe in, to fetch on
My armies dull reſt from *Brunduſium*)
That is at all times elſe exceeding calme,
(By reaſon of a purling winde that flyes
Off from the ſhore each morning, driuing vp
The billows farre to ſea) in this night yet,
Beares ſuch a terrible gale; put off from ſea,
As beats the land wind back, and thruſts the flood,
Vp in ſuch vproare, that no boat dare ſtirre.
And on it is diſperſt all *Pompeys* nauy
To make my perill yet more enuious.
Shall I yet ſhrinke for all? were all, yet more?
There is a certaine need that I muſt giue
Way to my paſſe; none, knowne, that I muſt liue.

Enter Maſter of a ſhip with Sailors

Maſt. What battaile is there fought now in the
ayre.
That threats the wrack of nature?
  Cæſ. Maſter? come.
Shall we thruſt through it all?
  Maſt. What loſt man,
Art thou in hopes and fortunes, that dar'ſt make
So deſperate a motion.
  Cæſ. Launch man, and all thy feares fraight dif-
auow,
Thou carrieſt *Cæſar* and his fortunes now.

Act III.   Scene I.

Pompey, two *Confuls*, *fiue Kings*, *Brutus*, *Gabinius*,
Demetrius.

Now to *Pharfalia*, where the fmarting ftrokes
Of our refolu'd contention muft refound,
(My Lords and friends of *Rome*) I giue you all
Such welcome as the fpirit of all my fortunes,
Conquefts, and triumphs (now come for their crowne)
Can crowne your fauours with, and ferue the hopes
Of my deare Country, to her vtmoft wifh;
I can but fet vp all my being to giue
So good an end to my forerunning Acts;
The powers in me that formd them hauing loft
No leaft time fince, in gathering skill to better;
But like fo many Bees haue brought me home,
The fweet of what foeuer flowers haue growne
In all the meades, and gardens of the world.
All which hath growne ftill, as the time encreafe
In which twas gather'd, and with which it ftemm'd.
That what decay foeuer blood inferr'd,
Might with my mindes ftore, be fuppli'd, and cher'd,
All which, in one fire of this inftant fight
Ile burne, and facrifice to euery cinder
In facred offering to my Countreys loue,
And therefore what euent foeuer fort,
As I no praife will looke for, but the good
Freely beftow on all; (if good fucceed)
So if aduerfe fate fall, I wifh no blame,
But th' ill befalne me, made my fortunes fhame,
Not mine, nor my fault.
    1 *Conf.*   We too well loue *Pompey*,
To doe him that iniuftice.

Bru. Who more thirsts
The Conquest, then resolues to beare the foile?
  Pom. Said *Brutus*-like, giue feuerall witneſſe all,
That you acquit me whatſoeuer fall.
  2 Conſ. Particular men particular fates muſt beare,
Who feeles his owne wounds leſſe, to wound another?
  Theſſ. Leaue him the worſt whoſe beſt is left
    vndone,
He only conquers whoſe minde ſtill is one.
  Epir. Free mindes, like dice, fall ſquare, what ere
    the caſt.
  Ibir. Who on him felfe fole ſtands, ſtands folely
    faſt.
  Thra. He's neuer downe, whoſe minde fights ſtill
    aloft.
  Cil. Who cares for vp or downe, when all's but
    thought.
  Gab. To things euents doth no mans power extend.
  Dem. Since gods rule all, who any thing would
    mend.
  Pom. Ye ſweetly eaſe my charge, your ſelues vn-
    burthening.
Return'd not yet our trumpet, ſent to know
Of *Vibius* certaine ſtate?
  Gab. Not yet, my Lord.
  Pomp. Too long protract we all meanes to recouer
His perſon quick or dead, for I ſtill thinke
His loſſe ſeru'd fate, before we blew retreat;
Though ſome affirme him ſeene, ſoone after fighting.
  Dem. Not after, Sir, (I heard) but ere it ended.
  Gab. He bore a great minde to extend our purſuit
Much further then it was; and ſeru'd that day
(When you had, like the true head of a battaile,
Led all the body in that glorious turne)
Vpon a farre-off Squadron that ſtood faſt
In conduct of the great *Marc Anthony*,
When all the reſt were fled, ſo paſt a man
That in their tough receipt of him, I ſaw him
Thrice breake thorow all with eaſe, and paſſe as faire

Cæsar *and* Pompey.

As he had all beene fire, and they but ayre.
Pom. He ſtuck at laſt yet, in their midſt, it ſeem'd.
Gab. So haue I ſeen a fire drake glide at midnight
Before a dying man to point his graue,
And in it ſtick and hide.
Dem. He comes yet ſafe.

*A Trumpet ſounds, and enters before Vibius,
with others.*

Pom. O *Vibius*, welcome, what a priſoner?
With mighty *Cæſar*, and ſo quickly ranſom'd?
Vib. I Sir, my ranſome, needed little time,
Either to gaine agreement for the value,
Or the disburſment, ſince in *Cæſars* grace
We both concluded.
Pom. Was his grace ſo free.
Vib. For your reſpect, Sir.
Pom. Nay, Sir, for his glory.
That the maine Conqueſt he ſo ſurely builds on,
(Which euer is forerun with petty fortunes)
Take not effect, by taking any friend
From all the moſt, my poore defence can make,
But muſt be compleat, by his perfect owne.
Vib. I know, Sir, you more nobly rate the freedome
He freely gaue your friend; then to peruert it
So paſt his wiſdome: that knowes much too well
Th' vncertaine ſtate of Conqueſt; to raiſe frames
Of ſuch preſumption on her fickle wings,
And chiefely in a loſſe ſo late, and grieuous,
Beſides, your forces farre exceeding his,
His whole powers being but two and twenty thouſand:
And yours full foure and fourty thouſand ſtrong:
For all which yet, he ſtood as farre from feare
In my enlargement, as the confident glory
You pleaſe to put on him; and had this end
In my ſo kinde diſmiſſion, that as kindely
I might ſolicite a ſure peace betwixt you.
Pom. A peace? Is't poſſible?

Vib. Come, doe not ſhew this wanton incredulity too.

Tom. Beleeue me I was farre from ſuch a thought
In his high ſtomack : *Cato* prophecied then.
What thinke my Lords our Conſuls, and friend *Brutus*?

Omn. An offer happy.

Bru. Were it plaine and hearty.

Pom. I, there's the true inſpecton to his proſpect.

Bru. This ſtreight of his perhaps may need a ſleight
Of ſome hid ſtratagem, to bring him off.

Pom. Deuices of a new fordge to entrap me?
I reſt in *Cæſars* ſhades? walke his ſtrow'd paths?
Sleepe in his quiet waues? Ile ſooner truſt
Hibernian Boggs, and quickſands; and hell mouth
Take for my ſanctuary: in bad parts
That no extreames will better, natures finger
Hath markt him to me, to take heed of him.
What thinks my *Brutus*?

Bru. Tis your beſt and ſafeſt.

Pom. This offer'd peace of his is ſure a ſnare
To make our warre the bloodier, whoſe fit feare
Makes me I dare not now (in thoughts maturer
Then late enclin'de me) put in vſe the Counſaile
Your noble father *Cato* (parting) gaue me,
Whoſe much too tendèr ſhunning innocent blood,
This battaile hazards now, that muſt coſt more.

1 *Conſ.* It does, and therefore now no more deferre it.

Pom. Say all men ſo?

Omn. We doe.

Pom. I grieue ye doe,
Becauſe I rather wiſh to erre with *Cato*
Then with the truth goe of the world beſides;
But ſince it ſhall abide this other ſtroke,
Ye gods that our great Romane *Genius*
Haue made, not giue vs one dayes conqueſt only,
Nor grow in conqueſts for ſome little time,
As did the *Genius* of the *Macedons*;

Cæfar *and* Pompey.

Nor be by land great only, like *Laconians*;
Nor yet by fea alone, as was th' *Athenians*;
Nor flowly ftirr'd vp, like the Perfian Angell;
Nor rockt afleepe foone, like the Ionian fpirit.
But made our Romane *Genius*, fiery, watchfull,
And euen from *Romes* prime, ioynd his youth with hers,
Grow as fhe grew, and firme as earth abide,
By her encreafing pomp, at fea, and fhore,
In peace, in battaile; againft *Greece* as well
As our Barbarian foes; command yet further
Ye firme and iuft gods, our affiftfull Angell
For *Rome*, and *Pompey*, who now fights for *Rome*;
That all thefe royall Lawes, to vs, and iuftice
Of common fafety, may the felfe-loue drowne
Of tyrannous *Cæfar*; and my care for all
Your Altars crown'd with endleffe feftiuall.   *Exeunt.*

*Cæfar, Anthony, a Soothfayer, Craffinius,
Acilius, with others.*

Cæf. Say (facred Southfayer) and informe the truth,
What liking haft thou of our facrifice?
  Sooth. Imperiall *Cæfar*, at your facred charge,
I drew a milke white Oxe into the Temple,
And turning there his face into the eaft,
(Fearefully fhaking at the fhining light)
Downe fell his horned forehead to his hoofe,
When I began to greet him with the ftroke,
That fhould prepare him for the holy rites,
With hydeous roares he laid out fuch a throat
As made the fecret lurkings of the god
To anfwer ecco-like, in threatning founds:
I ftroke againe at him, and then he flept,
His life-blood boyling out at euery wound
In ftreames as cleare as any liquid Ruby,
And there began to alter my prefage,
The other ill fignes, fhewing th'other fortune,
Of your laft skirmifh, which farre oppofite now

L

Proues, ill beginnings good euents forefhew.
For now the beaft cut vp, and laid on th' Altar,
His lims were all lickt up with inftant flames,
Not like the Elementall fire that burnes
In houfhold vfes, lamely ftruggling vp,
This way and that way winding as it rifes,
But (right and vpright) reacht his proper fphere
Where burnes the fire eternall and fincere.

 Cæf. And what may that prefage?
 Sooth. That euen the fpirit
Of heauens pure flame flew downe and rauifht vp
Your offerings blaze in that religious inftant,
Which fhewes th' alacritie and cheerefull virtue
Of heauens free bounty, doing good in time,
And with what fwiftneffe true deuotions clime.

 Omn. The gods be honor'd.
 Sooth. O behold with wonder,
The facred blaze is like a torch enlightned,
Directly burning iuft aboue your campe!

 Omn. Miraculous.
 Sooth. Beleeue it, with all thanks:
The Romane *Genius* is alterd now,
And armes for *Cæfar.*

 Cæf. Soothfayer be for euer
Reuerenc't of *Cæfar.* O *Marc Anthony,*
I thought to raife my camp, and all my tents,
Tooke downe for fwift remotion to *Scotuffa.*
Shall now our purpofe hold?

 Anth. Againft the gods?
They grace in th' inftant, and in th' inftant we
Muft adde our parts, and be in th' vfe as free.

 Craff. See Sir, the fcouts returne.

Enter two fcouts.

 Cæf. What newes, my friends?
 1 *Scou.* Arme, arme, my Lord, the voward of the foe
Is rang'd already.
 2 *Scou.* Anfwer them, and arme:
You cannot fet your reft of battell vp

Cæsar *and* Pompey. 163

In happyer houre; for I this night beheld
A ſtrange confuſion in your enemies campe,
The ſouldiers taking armes in all diſmay,
And hurling them againe as faſt to earth.
Euery way routing; as th' alarme were then
Giuen to their army. A moſt cauſeleſſe feare
Diſperſt quite through them.
  Cæſ. Then twas *Ioue* himſelfe
That with his ſecret finger ſtirr'd in them.
  Craſſ. Other preſages of ſucceſſe (my Lord)
Haue ſtrangely hapn'd in the adiacent Cities,
To this your army: for in *Tralleis*,
Within a Temple, built to Victory,
There ſtands a ſtatue of your forme and name,
Neare whoſe firme baſe, euen from the marble paue-
  ment,
There ſprang a Palme tree vp, in this laſt night,
That ſeemes to crowne your ſtatue with his boughs,
Spred in wrapt ſhadowes round about your browes.
  Cæſ. The ſigne, *Craſſinius*, is moſt ſtrange and
  gracefull,
Nor could get iſſue, but by power diuine;
Yet will not that, nor all abodes beſides
(Of neuer ſuch kinde promiſe of ſucceſſe)
Perforne it without tough acts of our owne.
No care, no nerue the leſſe to be emploid;
No offering to the gods, no vowes, no prayers:
Secure and idle ſpirits neuer thriue
When moſt the gods for their aduancements ſtriue.
And therefore tell me what abodes thou buildſt on
In any ſpirit to act, enflam'd in thee,
Or in our Souldiers ſeene reſolu'd addreſſes?
  Craſſ. Great and firy virtue. And this day
Be ſure (great *Cæſar*) of effects as great
In abſolute conqueſt; to which are prepar'd
Enforcements reſolute, from this arm'd hand,
Which thou ſhalt praiſe me for aliue or dead.
  Cæſ. Aliue (ye gods vouchſafe) and my true vowes
For life in him (great heauen) for all my foes

The Tragedy of

(Being naturall Romans) fo farre ioyntly heare
As may not hurt our Conqueft ; as with feare
Which thou already ftrangely haft diffufde
Through all their army; which extend to flight
Without one bloody ftroke of force and fight.
    Cnth. Tis time, my Lord, you put in forme your
    battell.
    Cæf. Since we muft fight then, and no offerd peace
Will take with *Pompey :* I rejoyce to fee
This long-time lookt for, and moft happy day,
In which we now fhall fight, with men, not hunger,
With toyles, not fweats of blood through yeares extended,
This one day feruing to decide all iarres
Twixt me and *Pompey.* Hang out of my tent
My Crimfine coat of armes, to giue my fouldiers
That euer-fure figne of refolu'd-for fight.
    Craff. Thefe hands fhall giue that figne to all their
    longings.   *Exit Craff.*
    Cæf. My Lord, my army, I thinke beft to order
In three full Squadrons: of which let me pray
Your felfe would take on you the left wings charge ;
My felfe will lead the right wing, and my place
Of fight elect in my tenth legion :
My battell by *Domitius Calvinus*
Shall take direction.

*The Cote of Armes is hung out, and the
Souldiers fhoute within.*

    An. Heark, your fouldiers fhoute
For ioy to fee your bloody Cote of Armes
Affure their fight this morning.
    Cæf. O bleft Euen
Bring on them worthy comforts. And ye gods
Performe your good prefages in euents
Of fit crowne for our difcipline, and deeds
Wrought vp by conqueft ; that my vfe of it
May wipe the hatefull and vnworthy ftaine

Of Tyrant from my Temples, and exchange it
For fautor of my Country, ye haue giuen
That title to thofe poore and fearefull fowles
That euery found puts vp, in frights and cryes;
Euen then, when all *Romes* powers were weake and
  heartlefs,
When traiterous fires, and fierce Barbarian fwords,
Rapines, and foule-expiring flaughters fild
Her houfes, Temples, all her ayre, and earth.
To me then (whom your bounties haue enform'd
With fuch a fpirit as defpifeth feare;
Commands in either fortune, knowes, and armes
Againft the worft of fate; and therefore can
Difpofe bleft meanes, encourag'd to the beft)
Much more vouchfafe that honor; chiefely now,
When *Rome* wants only this dayes conqueft giuen me
To make her happy, to confirme the brightneffe
That yet fhe fhines in ouer all the world;
In Empire, riches, ftrife of all the Arts,
In gifts of Cities, and of kingdomes fent her;
In Crownes laid at her feet, in euery grace
That fhores, and feas, floods, Iflands, Continents,
Groues, fields, hills, mines, and metals can produce;
All which I (victor) will encreafe, I vow
By all my good, acknowledg'd giuen by you.

Act IIII   Scene I.

Pompey in hafte, Brutus, Gabinius, Vibius following.

THe poyfon fteep't in euery vaine of Empire,
  In all the world, meet now in onely me,
Thunder and lighten me to death; and make
My fenfes feed the flame, my foule the crack.

Was euer foueraigne Captaine of fo many
Armies and Nations, fo oppreſt as I,
With one hoſts headſtrong outrage ? vrging fight,
Yet fly about my campe in panick terrors ;
No reaſon vnder heauen fuggeſting caufe.
And what is this but euen the gods deterring
My iudgement from enforcing fight this morne ?
The new-fled night made day with Meteors,
Fir'd ouer *Cæfars* campe, and falne in mine,
As pointing out the terrible euents
Yet in fufpence ; but where they threat their fall
Speake not thefe prodigies with fiery tongues,
And eloquence that fhould not moue but rauifh
All found mindes, from thus tempting the iuſt gods,
And fpitting out their faire premoniſhing flames
With brackifh rheumes of ruder and brainfick number,
What's infinitely more, thus wild, thus mad
For one poore fortune of a beaten few ;
To halfe fo many ſtaid, and dreadfull fouldiers ?
Long train'd, long foughten ? able, nimble, perfect
To turne and winde aduantage euery way ?
Encreafe with little, and enforce with none ?
Made bold as Lyons, gaunt as famifht wolues,
With ſtill-feru'd flaughters, and continuall toyles.

Bru. You fhould not, Sir, forfake your owne wife
    Counfell,
Your owne experienc't difcipline, owne practife,
Owne god-infpired infight to all changes,
Of Protean fortune, and her zany, warre,
For hoſts, and hels of fuch ; What man will thinke
The beſt of them, not mad ; to fee them range
So vp and downe your campe, already fuing
For offices falne, by *Cæfars* built-on fall,
Before one ſtroke be ſtruck ? *Domitius, Spinther,*
Your father *Scipio* now preparing friends
For *Cæfars* place of vniverfall Bifhop ?
Are you th'obferued rule, and vouch example ;
Who euer would commend Phyfitians,
That would not follow the difeaſ'd defires

Of their sick patients? yet incurre your selfe
The faults that you so much abhorre in others.
    Pom. I cannot, Sir, abide mens open mouthes,
Nor be ill spoken of; nor haue my counsels
And circumspections, turnd on me for feares,
With mocks and scandals that would make a man
Of lead, a lightning; in the desperat'st onset
That euer trampled vnder death, his life.
I beare the touch of feare for all their safeties,
Or for mine owne? enlarge with twice as many
Selfe-liues, selfe-fortunes? they shall sinke beneath
Their owne credulities, before I crosse them.
Come, haste, dispose our battaile.
    Vib. Good my Lord,
Against your *Genius* warre not for the world.
    Pom. By all worlds he that moues me next to beare
Their scofs and imputations of my feare
For any cause, shall beare this sword to hell.
Away, to battaile; good my Lord lead you
The whole six thousand of our yong Patricians,
Plac't in the left wing to enuiron *Cæsar*.
My father *Scipio* shall lead the battaile;
Domitius the left wing; I the right
Against *Marc Anthony*. Take now your fils
Ye beastly doters on your barbarous wills.
                                               Exeunt.

Alarme, excursions, of al: *The fiue Kings driuen ouer
   the Stage, Crassinius chiefely pursuing*: *At the
   dore enter againe the fiue Kings. The
   battell continued within.*

    Epir. Fly, fly, the day was lost before twas fought.
    Thess. The Romans feard their shadowes.
    Cil. Were there euer
Such monstrous confidences, as last night
Their Cups and musique shew'd? Before the morning
Made such amazes ere one stroke was struck?
    Iber. It made great *Pompey* mad, which who could
    mend?

The gods had hand in it.
  Tra. It made the Confuls
Run on their fwords to fee't. The braue Patricians
Fled with their fpoyled faces, arrowes fticking
As fhot from heauen at them.
  Theff. Twas the charge
That *Cæfar* gaue againft them.
  Epir. Come, away,
Leaue all, and wonder at this fatall day.
Exeunt.

*The fight neerer; and enter, Craffineus, a fword, as
  thruft through his face; he fals. To him Pompey
  and Cæfar fighting: Pompey giues way,
    Cæfar follows, and enters at
        another dore.*

  Cæf. Purfue, purfue; the gods forefhew'd their powers,
Which we gaue iffue, and the day is ours.
Craffineus? O looke vp: he does, and fhewes
Death in his broken eyes; which *Cæfars* hands
Shall doe the honor of eternall clofure.
Too well thou keptft thy word, that thou this day
Wouldft doe me feruice to our victory,
Which in thy life or death I fhould behold,
And praife thee for; I doe, and muft admire
Thy matchles valour; euer euer reft
Thy manly lineaments, which in a tombe
Erected to thy noble name and virtues,
Ile curiofly preferue with balmes, and fpices,
In eminent place of thefe Pharfalian fields,
Infcrib'd with this true foule of funerall.

Epitaph:

Craffineus *fought for fame, and died for* Rome,
Whofe publique weale fprings from this priuate tombe.

  Enter fome taking him off, whom Cæfar helps.

Cæsar *and* Pompey.

Enter Pompey, Demetrius, with black robes in their hands, broad hats, &c.

Pom. Thus haue the Gods their iuſtice, men their wils,
And I, by mens wils rulde ; my ſelfe renouncing,
Am by my Angell and the gods abhorr'd ;
Who drew me, like a vapour, vp to heauen
To daſh me like a tempeſt 'gainſt the earth :
O the deſerued terrors that attend
On humane confidence ! had euer men
Such outrage of preſumption to be victors
Before they arm'd ? To ſend to *Rome* before
For houſes neare the market place, their tents
Strowd all with flowers, and noſegayes ; tables couer'd
With cups and banquets ; bayes and mirtle garlands,
As ready to doe ſacrifice for conqueſt
Rather then arme them for fit fight t'enforc it ;
Which when I ſaw, I knew as well th' euent
As now I feele it, and becauſe I rag'd
In that preſage, my *Genius* ſhewing me clearely
(As in a mirror) all this curſed iſſue ;
And therefore vrg'd all meanes to put it off
For this day, or from theſe fields to ſome other,
Or from this ominous confidence, till I ſaw
Their ſpirits fettl'd in ſome grauer knowledge
Of what belong'd to ſuch a deare deciſion ;
They ſpotted me with feare, with loue of glory,
To keepe in my command ſo many Kings,
So great an army ; all the helliſh blaſtings
That could be breath'd on me, to ſtrike me blinde
Of honor, ſpirit and ſoule : And ſhould I then
Saue them that would in ſpight of heauen be ruinde ?
And, in their ſafeties ruine me and mine
In euerlaſting rage of their detraction.
   Dem. Vour ſafety and owne honor did deſerue
Reſpect paſt all their values ; O my Lord
Would you ?
   Pom. Vpbraid me not ; goe to, goe on.

Dem. No ;. Ile not rub the wound. The mifery is,
The gods for any error in a man
(Which they might rectify, and fhould ; becaufe
That man maintain'd the right) fhould fuffer wrong
To be thus infolent, thus grac't, thus bleft ?
 Pom. O the ftrange carriage of their acts, by which
Men order theirs ; and their deuotions in them ;
Much rather ftriving to entangle men
In pathleffe error, then with regular right
Confirme their reafons, and their pieties light.
For now Sir, whatfoeuer was forefhowne
By heauen, or prodigy ; ten parts more for vs,
Forewarning vs, deterring vs, and all
Our blinde and brainleffe frenzies, then for *Cæfar* ;
All yet will be afcribde to his regard
Giuen by the gods for his good parts, preferring
Their gloffe (being ftarck impoftures) to the iuftice,
Loue, honor, piety, of our lawes and Countrey.
Though I thinke thefe are arguments enow
For my acquitall, that for all thefe fought.
 Dem. Y'are cleare, my Lord.
 Pom. Gods helpe me, as I am ;
What euer my vntoucht command of millions
Through all my eight and fifty yeares, hath woonne,
This one day (in the worlds efteeme) hath loft.
So vile is praife and difpraife by euent.
For I am ftill my felfe in euery worth
The world could grace me with, had this dayes Euen
In one blaze ioyn'd, with all my other Conquefts.
And fhall my comforts in my well-knowne felfe
Faile me for their falfe fires, *Demetrius* ?
 Dem. O no, my Lord.
 Pom. Take griefe for them, as if
The rotten-hearted world could fteepe my foule
In filthy putrifraction of their owne ?
Since their applaufes faile me ? that are hiffes
To euery found acceptance ? I confeffe,
That till th' affaire was paft, my paffions flam'd,
But now tis helpleffe, and no caufe in me,

Rest in these embers my vnmoued soule,
With any outward change, this dystick minding;
No man should more allow his owne losse, woes,
(Being past his fault) then any stranger does.
And for the worlds false loues, and ayry honors,
What soule that euer lou'd them most in life,
(Once feuer'd from this breathing sepulchre)
Againe came and appearde in any kind
Their kinde admirer still, or did the state
Of any best man here, associate?
And euery true soule should be here so feuer'd
From loue of such men, as here drowne their soules
As all the world does?   *Cato* sole accepted,
To whom Ile fly now, and my wife in way
(Poore Lady, and poore children, worse then father-
  lesse)
Visit, and comfort.   Come *Demetrius*,   *They disguise*
We now must sute our habites to our fortunes   *themselues.*
And since these changes euer chance to greatest.
Nor desire to be
(Doe fortune, to exceed it, what she can)
A *Pompey*, or a *Cæsar*, but a man.   *Exeunt.*

Enter Cæsar, Anthony, Acilius, with souldiers.

Cæs. O We haue slaine, not conquerd, Roman
  blood
Peruerts th' euent, and desperate blood let out
With their owne swords.   Did euer men before
Enuy their owne liues, since another liu'd
Whom they would willfully conceiue their foe,
And forge a Tyrant merely in their feares
To iustifie their slaughters?   Consuls? furies.
  Ant.   Be, Sir, their faults their griefes! The greater
  number
Were only slaues, that left their bloods to ruth,
And altogether, but six thousand slaine.
  Cæs. How euer many; gods and men can witnesse·
Themselues enforc't it, much against the most

I could enforce on *Pompey* for our peace.
Of all flaine, yet, if *Brutus* only liu'd,
I fhould be comforted, for his life fau'd
Would weigh the whole fix thoufand that are loft.
But much I feare his death, becaufe the battell
Full ftricken now, he yet abides vnfound.

    Acil. I faw him fighting neare the battels end,
But fuddainly giue off, as bent to fly.

Enter Brutus.

    Anth. He comes here, fee Sir.
    Bru. I fubmit to *Cæfar*
My life and fortunes.
    Cæf. A more welcome fortune
Is *Brutus*, then my conqueft.
    Bru. Sir, I fought
Againft your conqueft, and your felfe ; and merit
(I muft acknowledge) a much fterner welcome.
    Cæf. You fought with me, Sir, for I know your armes
Were taken for your Country, not for *Pompey* :
And for my Country I fought, nothing leffe
Then he, or both the mighty-ftomak't Confuls ;
Both whom (I heare) haue flaine themfelues before
They would enioy life in the good of *Cæfar*.
But I am nothing worfe, how ill foeuer
They, and the great authority of *Rome*
Would faine enforce me by their mere fufpitions.
Lou'd they their Country better then her *Brutus* ?
Or knew what fitted nobleffe, and a Romane
With freer fouls then *Brutus*. Thofe that liue
Shall fee in *Cæfars* iuftice, and what euer
Might make me worthy both their liues and loues,
That I haue loft the one without my merit,
And they the other with no Roman fpirit.
Are you empair'd to liue, and ioy my loue ?
Only requite me, *Brutus*, loue but *Cæfar*,
And be in all the powers of *Cæfar*, *Cæfar*.
In wnich free wifh, I ioyne your father *Cato* ;

Cæsar *and* Pompey..

For whom Ile haſte to *Vtica*, and pray
His loue may ſtrengthen my ſucceſſe to day. *Exeunt.*

*Porcius in haſte, Marcillius bare, following. Porcius
diſcouers a bed, and a ſword hanging by it which he
takes downe.*

   Mar. To what vſe take you that (my Lord?)
   Por. Take you
No note that I take it, nor let any ſeruant,
Beſides your ſelfe, of all my fathers neareſt,
Serue any mood he ſerues, with any knowledge
Of this or any other. *Cæſar* comes
And giues his army wings to reach this towne.
Not for the townes ſake, but to ſaue my father.
Whom iuſtly he ſuſpects to be reſolu'd
Of any violence to his life, before
He will preſerue it by a Tyrants fauour.
For *Pompey* hath miſcarried, and is fled.
Be true to me, and to my fathers life;
And doe not tell him; nor his fury ſerue
With any other.
   Mar. I will dye, my Lord,
Ere I obſerue it.
   Por. O my Lord and father.

*Cato, Athenodorus, Statilius.
Cato with a booke in his hand.*

   Cat. What feares fly here on all ſides? what wilde
     lookes
Are ſquinted at me from mens mere ſuſpicions
That I am wilde my ſelfe, and would enforce
What will be taken from me by the Tyrant.
   Ath. No: Would you only aske life, he would
     thinke
His owne life giuen more ſtrength in giuing yours
   Cat. I aske my life of him?
   Stat. Aske what's his owne?

Of him he scornes should haue the least drop in it
At his disposure.
 Cat. No, *Statilius*.
Men that haue forfeit liues by breaking lawes,
Or haue beene ouercome, may beg their liues,
But I haue euer beene in euery iustice
Better then *Cæsar*, and was neuer conquer'd,
Or made to fly for life, as *Cæsar* was.
But haue beene victor euer, to my wish,
Gainst whomsoeuer euer hath opposde;
Where *Cæsar* now is conquer'd in his Conquest,
In the ambition, he til now denide;
Taking vpon him to giue life, when death
Is tenfold due to his most tyrannous selfe.
No right, no power giuen him to raise an army,
Which in despight of *Rome* he leades about
Slaughtering her loyall subiects, like an outlaw,
Nor is he better. Tongue, shew, falshood are,
To bloodiest deaths his parts so much admir'd,
Vaineglory, villany; and at best you can,
Fed with the parings of a worthy man.
My fame affirme my life receiu'd from him?
Ile rather make a beast my second father.
 Stat. The gods auert from euery Roman minde
The name of slaue to any Tyrants power.
Why was man euer iust, but to be free,
'Gainst all iniustice? and to beare about him
As well all meanes to freedome euery houre,
As euery houre he should be arm'd for death,
Which only is his freedome?
 Ath. But *Statilius*
Death is not free for any mans election,
Till nature, or the law, impose it on him.
 Cat. Must a man goe to law then, when he may
Enioy his owne in peace? If I can vse
Mine owne my selfe, must I of force, reserue it
To serue a Tyrant with it? All iust men
Not only may enlarge their liues, but must,
From all rule tyrannous, or liue vniust.

Ath. By death muſt they enlarge their liues ?
Cat. By death.
Ath. A man's not bound to that.
Cat. Ile proue he is.
Are not the liues of all men bound to iuſtice ?
Ath. They are.
Cat. And therefore not to ſerue iniuſtice :
Iuſtice it ſelfe ought euer to be free,
And therefore euery iuſt man being a part
Of that free iuſtice, ſhould be free as it.
Ath. Then wherefore is there law for death ?
Cat. That all
That know not what law is, nor freely can
Performe the fitting iuſtice of a man
In kingdomes common good, may be enforc't.
But is not euery iuſt man to him ſelfe
The perfect'ſt law ?
Ath. Suppoſe.
Cat. Then to himſelfe
Is euery iuſt mans life ſubordinate.
Againe, Sir ; Is not our free ſoule infuſ'd
To euery body in her abſolute end
To rule that body ? in which abſolute rule
Is ſhe not abſolutely Empreſſe of it ?
And being Empreſſe, may ſhe not diſpoſe
It, and the life in it, at her iuſt pleaſure ?
Ath. Not to deſtroy it.
Cat. No ; ſhe not deſtroyes it
When ſhe diſliues it ; that their freedomes may
Goe firme together, like their powers and organs,
Rather then let it liue a rebell to her,
Prophaning that diuine coniunction
Twixt her and it ; nay, a diſiunction making
Betwixt them worſe then death ; in killing quick
That which in iuſt death liues : being dead to her
If to her rule dead, and to her aliue,
If dying in her iuſt rule.
Ath. The body liues not
When death hath reft it.

Cat.   Yet tis free, and kept
Fit for reiunction in mans second life ;
Which dying rebell to the soule, is farre
Vnfit to ioyne with her in perfect life.
   Ath.   It shall not ioyne with her againe.
   Cat.   It shall.
   Ath.   In reason shall it ?
   Cat.   In apparant reason ;
Which Ile proue clearely.
   Stat.   Heare, and iudge it Sir.
   Cat.   As nature works in all things to an end,
So in th' appropriate honor of that end,
All things precedent haue their naturall frame ;
And therefore is there a proportion
Betwixt the ends of those things and their primes :
For else there could not be in their creation,
Alwayes, or for the most part, that firme forme
In their still like existence ; that we see
In each full creature.   What proportion then
Hath an immortall with a mortall substance ?
And therefore the mortality to which
A man is subiect ; rather is a sleepe,
Then bestiall death ; since sleepe and death are call'd
The twins of nature.   For if absolute death
And bestiall sease the body of a man,
Then is there no proportion in his parts,
His soule being free from death, which otherwise
Retaines diuine proportion.   For as sleepe
No disproportion holds with humane soules,
But aptly quickens the proportion
Twixt them and bodies, making bodies fitter
To giue vp formes to soules, which is their end :
So death (twin-borne of sleepe) resoluing all
Mans bodies heauy parts ; in lighter nature
Makes a reunion with the spritely soule ;
When in a second life their beings giuen,
Holds this proportion firme, in highest heauen.
   Ath.   Hold you our bodies shall reuiue, resuming
Our soules againe to heauen ?

Cat. Paſt doubt, though others
Thinke heauen a world too high for our low reaches.
Not knowing the ſacred fence of him that ſings,
Ioue can let downe a golden chaine from heauen,
Which tyed to earth, ſhall fetch vp earth and ſeas;
And what's that golden chaine, but our pure ſoules,
A golden beame of him, let downe by him,
That gouern'd with his grace, and drawne by him,
Can hoiſt this earthy body vp to him,
The ſea, and ayre, and all the elements
Compreſt in it: not while tis thus concret,
But fin'd by death, and then giuen heauenly heat.
    Ath. Your happy expoſition of that place
(Whoſe ſacred depth I neuer heard ſo ſounded)
Euicts glad grant from me you hold a truth.
    Stat. Is't not a manly truth, and mere diuine?
    Cat. Tis a good chearefull doctrine for good men.
But (ſonne and ſeruants) this is only argu'd
To ſpend our deare time well, and no life vrgeth
To any violence further then his owner
And grauer men hold fit. Lets talke of *Cæſar*,
He's the great ſubiect of all talke, and he
Is hotly haſting on. Is ſupper ready?
    Mar. It is, my Lord.
    Cat. Why then let's in and eat;
Our coole ſubmiſſion will quench *Cæſars* heat.
    Sta. Submiſſion? here's for him.
    Cat. *Statilius*,
My reaſons muſt not ſtrengthen you in error,
Nor learn'd *Athenodorus* gentle yeelding.
Talke with ſome other deepe Philoſophers.
Or ſome diuine Prieſt of the knowing gods,
And heare their reaſons, in meane time come ſup.
                            Exeunt.
                 Cato going out arme in arme
                betwixt Athen. and Statilius.

Act V. Scene I.

*Enter Vshers, with the two Lentuli, and Septimius
before Cornelia; Cyris, Telesilla, Lælia, Drusus,
with others, following, Cornelia, Septimius
and the two Lentuli reading letters.*

 Cor. So may my comforts for this good newes thriue
As I am thankfull for them to the Gods.
Ioyes vnexpected, and in desperate plight,
Are still most sweet, and proue from whence they
 come;
When earths still Moonelike confidence, in ioy,
Is at her full. True ioy descending farre
From past her sphere, and from that highest heauen
That moues and is not mou'd : how farre was I
From hope of these euents, when fearefull dreames
Of Harpies tearing out my heart? of armies
Terribly ioyning? Cities, kingdomes falling,
And all on me? prou'd sleepe, not twin to death,
But to me, death it selfe? yet waking then,
These letters; full of as much chearefull life,
I found closde in my hand. O gods how iustly
Ye laugh at all things earthly? at all feares
That rise not from your iudgements? at all ioyes,
Not drawne directly from your selues, and in ye,
Distrust in man is faith, trust in him ruine.
Why write great learned men? men merely rapt
With sacred rage, of confidence, beleefe?
Vndanted spirits? inexorable fate
And all feare treading on? tis all but ayre,
If any comfort be, tis in despaire.
 1 Len. You learned Ladies may hold any thing.

Cæsar *and* Pompey.

2 Lent. Now madam is your walk from coach come neare
The promontory, where you late commanded
A Sentinell fhould ftand to fee from thence
If either with a nauy, brought by fea,
Or traine by land ; great *Pompey* comes to greet you
As in your letters, he neare this time promifde.

Cor. O may this Ifle of *Lesbos*, compaft in
With the *Ægæan* fea, that doth diuide
Europe from *Afia.* (The fweet literate world
From the Barbarian) from my barbarous dreames
Diuide my deareft husband and his fortunes.

2 Len. He's bufied now with ordering offices.
By this time, madam, fits your honor'd father *He looks in his letter.*
In *Cæfars* chaire of vniuerfall Bifhop.
Domitius Ænobarbas, is made Confull,
Spynther his Confort ; and *Phaonius*
Tribune, or Pretor.

Septimius with a letter.

Sep. Thefe were only fought
Before the battaile, not obtaind ; nor mouing
My father but in fhadowes.

Corn. Why fhould men
Tempt fate with fuch firme confidence ? feeking places
Before the power that fhould difpofe could grant them ?
For then the ftroke of battaile was not ftruck.

1 Len. Nay, that was fure enough. *Phyfitians* know
When fick mens eyes are broken, they muft dye.
Your letters telling you his victory
Loft in the skirmifh, which I know hath broken
Both the eyes and heart of *Cæfar* : for as men
Healthfull through all their liues to grey-hayr'd age,
When fickneffe takes them once, they feldom fcape :
So *Cæfar* victor in his general fights

Till this late skirmifh, could no aduerfe blow
Suftaine without his vtter ouerthrow.
 2 Lent. See, madam, now ; your Sentinell : en-
    quire.
 Cor. Seeft thou no fleet yet (Sentinell) nor tráine
That may be thought great *Pompeys* ?
 Sen. Not yet, madame.
 1 Len. Seeft thou no trauellers addreft this way ?
In any number on this Lesbian fhore ?
 Sent. I fee fome not worth note ; a couple comming
This way, on foot, that are not now farre hence.
 2 Lent. Come they apace ? like meffengers with
    newes ?
 Sent. No, nothing like (my Lord) nor are their
    habites
Of any fuch mens fafhions ; being long mantles,
And fable hew'd ; their heads all hid in hats
Of parching *Theffaly*, broad brimm'd, high crown'd.
 Cor. Thefe ferue not our hopes.
 Sent. Now I fee a fhip,
A kenning hence ; that ftrikes into the hauen.
 Cor. One onely fhip ?
 Sen. One only, madam, yet.
 Cor. That fhould not be my Lord.
 1 Lent. Your Lord ? no madam.
 Sen. She now lets out arm'd men vpon the land.
 2 Lent. Arm'd men ? with drum and colours ?
 Sen. No, my Lord,
But bright in armes, yet beare halfe pikes, or bead-
    hookes.
 1 Lent. Thefe can be no plumes in the traine of
    Pompey.
 Cor. Ile fee him in his letter, once againe.
 Sen. Now, madam, come the two I faw on foot.

Enter Pompey and Demetrius.

 Dem. See your Princeffe, Sir, come thus farre
from the City in her coach, to encounter your promift
comming

Cæfar *and* Pompey. 181

About this time in your laſt letters.
Pom. The world is alter'd ſince *Demetrius* ;
(offer to goe by.
1 *Lent.* See, madam, two Theſſalian Augurs it
ſeemes
By their habits. Call, and enquire if either by their
Skils or trauels, they know no newes of your husband.
Cor. My friends? a word.
Dem. With vs, madam?
Cor. Yes. Are you of *Theſſaly*?
Dem. I, madam, and all the world beſides.
Cor. Your Country is great.
Dem. And our portions little.
Cor. Are you Augures?
Dem. *Augures madam? yes a kinde of Augures, alias*
Wizerds, that goe vp and downe the world, teaching
How to turne ill to good.
Cor. Can you doe that?
Dem. I, madam, you haue no worke for vs, haue
you?
No ill to turne good, I meane?
Cor. Yes; the abſence of my husband.
Dem. What's he?
Cor. *Pompey* the great.
Dem. Wherein is he great?
Cor. In his command of the world.
Dem. Then he's great in others. Take him without his
Addition (great) what is he then?
Cor. *Pompey*.
Dem. Not your husband then?
Cor. Nothing the leſſe for his greatneſſe.
Dem. Not in his right; but in your comforts he is.
Cor. His right is my comfort.
Dem. What's his wrong?
Cor. My ſorrow.
Dem. And that's ill.
Cor. Yes.

Dem. Y'are come to the vſe of our Profeſſion,
madam,
Would you haue that ill turnd good? that
Sorrow turnd comfort?
Cor. Why is my Lord wrong'd?
Cor. We profeſſe not that knowledge, madam:
Supoſe he were.
Cor. Not I.
Dem. Youle ſuppoſe him good.
Cor. He is ſo.
Dem. Then muſt you needs ſuppoſe him wrong'd;
for
All goodneſſe is wrong'd in this world.
Cor. What call you wrong?
Dem. Ill fortune, afflićtion.
Cor. Thinke you my Lord afflićted?
Dem. If I thinke him good (madam) I muſt. Vn-
leſſe he
Be worldly good, and then, either he is ill, or has ill:
Since, as no ſugar is without poyſon: ſo is no worldly
Good without ill. Euen naturally nouriſht in it, like a
Houſhold thiefe, which is the worſt of all theeues.
Cor. Then he is not worldly, but truly good.
Dem. He's too great to be truly good; for worldly
greatnes
Is the chiefe worldly goodneſſe; and all worldly good-
neſſe
(I prou'd before) has ill in it: which true good has not.
Cor. If he rule well with his greatneſſe; wherein
is he ill?
Dem. But great Rulers are like Carpenters that
weare their
Rules at their backs ſtill: and therefore to make good
your
True good in him, y'ad better ſuppoſe him little, or
meane.
For in the meane only is the true good.
Pom. But euery great Lady muſt haue her husband
Great ſtill, or her loue will be little.

Cor. I am none of thofe great Ladyes.

1 *Len.* She's a Philofophreffe Augure, and can turne
Ill to good as well as you.

Pom. I would then, not honor, but adore her: could you
Submit your felfe chearefully to your husband,
Suppofing him falne?

Cor. If he fubmit himfelfe chearfully to his fortune.

Pom. Tis the greateft greatnes in the world you vndertake.

Cor. I would be fo great, if he were.

Pom. In fuppofition.

Cor, In fact.

Pom. Be no woman, but a Goddeffe then; & make good thy greatneffe;
I am chearfully falne; be chearfull.

Cor. I am: and welcome, as the world were clofde
In thefe embraces.

Pom. Is it poffible?
A woman, lofing greatneffe, ftill as good,
As at her greateft? O gods, was I euer
Great till this minute?

Amb. Len. Pompey?

Pom. View me better.

Amb. Len. Conquerd by *Cæfar?*

Pom. Not I, but mine army.
No fault in me, in it: no conqueft of me:
I tread this low earth as I trod on *Cæfar.*
Muft I not hold my felfe, though lofe the world?
Nor lofe I leffe; a world loft at one clap,
Tis more then *Ioue* euer thundred with.
What glory is it to haue my hand hurle
So vaft a volley through the groning ayre?
And is't not great, to turne griefes thus to ioyes,
That breake the hearts of others?

Amb. Len. O tis *Ioue*-like.

Pom. It is to imitate *Ioue,* that from the wounds
Of fofteft clouds, beats vp the terribleft founds.

I now am good, for good men ſtill haue leaſt,
That twixt themſelues and God might riſe their reſt.
   Cor. O *Pompey, Pompey* : neuer Great till now.
   Pom. O my *Cornelia* : let vs ſtill be good,
And we ſhall ſtill be great : and greater farre
In euery ſolid grace, then when the tumor
And bile of rotten obſeruation ſweld vs.
Griefes for wants outward, are without our cure,
Greatneſſe, not of it ſelfe, is neuer ſure.
Before, we went vpon heauen, rather treading
The virtues of it vnderfoot, in making
The vicious world our heauen ; then walking there
Euen here, as knowing that our home ; contemning
All forg'd heauens here raiſde ; ſetting hills on hills.
Vulcan from heauen fell, yet on's feet did light,
And ſtood no leſſe a god then at his height ;
At loweſt, things lye faſt ; we now are like
The two Poles propping heauen, on which heauen
    moues ;
And they are fixt, and quiet, being aboue
All motion farre ; we reſt aboue the heauens.
   Cor. O, I more ioy, t'embrace my Lord thus fixt,
Then he had brought me ten inconſtant conqueſts.
   1 *Len.* Miraculous ſtanding in a fall ſo great,
Would *Cæſar* knew Sir, how you conquerd him
In your conuiction.
   Pom. Tis enough for me
That *Pompey* knows it. I will ſtand no more
On others legs : nor build one ioy without me.
If euer I be worth a houſe againe,
Ile build all inward : not a light ſhall ope
The common outway : no expence, no art,
No ornament, no dore will I vſe there,
But raiſe all plaine, and rudely, like a rampier,
Againſt the falſe ſociety of men
That ſtill batters
All reaſon peecemeale. And for earthy greatneſſe
All heauenly comforts rarifies to ayre,
Ile therefore liue in darke, and all my light,

Cæſar *and* Pompey.

Like Ancient Temples, let in at my top.
This were to turne ones back to all the world,
And only looke at heauen. *Empedocles*
Recur'd a mortall plague through all his Country,
With ſtopping vp the yawning of a hill,
From whence the hollow and vnwholſome South
Exhald his venomd vapor. And what elſe
Is any King, given ouer to his luſts,
But euen the poyſon'd cleft of that crackt mountaine,
That all his kingdome plagues with his example ?
Which I haue ſtopt now, and ſo cur'd my Country
Of ſuch a ſenſuall peſtilence :
When therefore our diſeaſ'de affections
Harmefull to humane freedome ; and ſtormelike
Inferring darkneſſe to th' infected minde
Oppreſſe our comforts : tis but letting in
The light of reaſon, and a purer ſpirit,
Take in another way ; like roomes that fight
With windowes gainſt the winde, yet let in light.
    Amb. Len. My Lord, we ſeru'd before, but now
    adore you.
    Sen. My Lord, the arm'd men I diſcou'rd lately
Vnſhipt, and landed ; now are trooping neare.
    Pom. What arm'd men are they ?
    1 *Len.* Some, my Lord, that lately
The Sentinell diſcouer'd, but not knew.
    Sen. Now all the ſea (my Lords) is hid with ſhips,
Another Promontory flanking this,
Some furlong hence, is climb'd, and full of people,
That eaſily may ſee hither ; it ſeemes looking
What theſe ſo neare intend : Take heed, they come.

Enter Achillas, Septius, Saluius, with ſouldiers.

    Arch. Haile to *Romes* great Commander; to whom
    Ægypt
(Not long ſince ſeated in his kingdome by thee,
And ſent to by thee in thy paſſage by)
Sends vs with anſwer : which withdraw and heare.

Pom. Ile kiffe my children firft.
Sep. Bleffe me, my Lord.
Pom. I will, and *Cyris*, my poore daughter too.
Euen that high hand that hurld me downe thus low,
Keepe you from rifing high : I heare : now tell me.
I thinke (my friend) you once feru'd vnder me :

Septius only nods with his head.

Pom. Nod onely ? not a word daigne ? what are
thefe ?
Cornelia ? I am now not worth mens words.
Ach. Pleafe you receiue your ayde, Sir ?
Pom. I, I come.
Exit Pom. They draw and follow.
Cor. Why draw they ? See, my Lords; attend them
vfhers.
Sen. O they haue flaine great *Pompey.*
Cor. O my husband.
Sept. Cyr. Mother, take comfort.
Enter Pompey bleeding.
O my Lord and father.
Pom. See heauens your fufferings, is my Countries
loue,
The iuftice of an Empire ; pietie ;
Worth this end in their leader : laft yet life .
And bring the gods off fairer : after this
Who will adore, or ferue the deities ?
He hides his face with his robe.

Enter the Murtherers.

Ach. Helpe hale him off: and take his head for
Cæfar.
Sep. Mother ? O faue us ; *Pompey* ? O my father.

*Enter the two Lentuli and Demetrius bleeding,
and kneele about Cornelia.*

1 *Len.* Yet fals not heauen ? Madam, O make
good

Your late great fpirits; all the world will fay,
You know not how to beare aduerfe euents,
If now you languifh.
 Omn. Take her to her coach.
They beare her out.

Cato with a booke in his hand.

O Beaftly apprehenders of things manly,
And merely heauenly : they with all the reafons
I vfde for iuft mens liberties, to beare
Their liues and deaths vp in their owne free hands ;
Feare ftill my refolution though I feeme
To giue it off like them : and now am woonne
To thinke my life in lawes rule, not mine owne,
When once it comes to death ; as if the law
Made for a fort of outlawes, muft bound me
In their fubiection ; as if I could
Be rackt out of my vaines, to liue in others ;
As fo I muft, if others rule my life ;
And publique power keepe all the right of death,
As if men needes muft ferue the place of iuftice ;
The forme, and idoll, and renounce it felfe ?
Our felues, and all our rights in God and goodneffe ?
Our whole contents and freedomes to difpofe,
All in the ioyes and wayes of arrant rogues ?
No ftay but their wilde errors, to fuftaine vs ?
No forges but their throats to vent our breaths ?
To forme our liues in, and repofe our deaths ?
See, they haue got my fword. Who's there ?

Enter Marcillius bare.

 Mar. My Lord.
 at. Who tooke my fword hence ? Dumb ? I doe
  not aske
For any vfe or care of it : but hope
I may be anfwered. Goe Sir, let me haue it.
Exit Mar.

Poore flaues, how terrible this death is to them?
If men would fleepe, they would be wroth with all
That interrupt them: Phyfick take to take
The golden reft it brings: both pay and pray
For good, and foundeft naps: all friends confenting
In thofe kinde inuocations; praying all
Good reft, the gods vouchfafe you; but when death
(Sleepes naturall brother) comes; (that's nothing worfe,
But better; being more rich; and keepes the ftore;
Sleepe euer fickle, wayward ftill, and poore)
O how men grudge, and fhake, and feare, and fly
His fterne approaches? all their comforts taken
In faith, and knowledge of the bliffe and beauties
That watch their wakings in an endleffe life:
Dround in the paines and horrors of their fenfe
Suftainde but for an houre; be all the earth
Rapt with this error, Ile purfue my reafon,
And hold that as my light and fiery pillar,
Th' eternall law of heauen and earth no firmer.
But while I feeke to conquer conquering *Cæfar*,
My foft-fplen'd feruants ouerrule and curb me.
          He knocks, and Brutus enters.
Where's he I fent to fetch and place my fword
Where late I left it? Dumb to? Come another!
                    Enter Cleanthes.
Where's my fword hung here?
  Cle. My Lord, I know not.   *Ent. Marcilius.*
  Cat. The reft, come in there. Where's the fword
    I charg'd you
To giue his place againe? Ile breake your lips ope,
Spight of my freedome; all my feruants, friends;
My fonne and all, will needs betray me naked
To th' armed malice of a foe fo fierce
And Beare-like, mankinde of the blood of virtue.
O gods, who euer faw me thus contemn'd?
Goe call my fonne in; tell him, that the leffe
He fhewes himfelfe my fonne, the leffe Ile care
To liue his father.

Cæsar *and* Pompey.   189

Enter Athenodorus, Porçius : *Porcius kneeling*; *Brutus, Cleanthes and Marcilius by him.*

  Por. I befeech you, Sir,
Reft patient of my duty, and my loue ;
Your other children think on, our poore mother,
Your family, your Country.
  Cat. If the gods
Giue ouer all, Ile fly the world with them.
Athenodorus, I admire the changes,
I note in heauenly prouidence. When *Pompey*
Did all things out of courfe, paft right, paft reafon,
He ftood inuincible againft the world :
Yet, now his cares grew pious, and his powers
Set all vp for his Countrey, he is conquered.
  Ath. The gods wills fecret are, nor muft we mea-
    fure
Their chaft-referued deepes by our dry fhallowes.
Sufficeth vs, we are entirely fuch
As twixt them and our confciences we know
Their graces, in our virtues, fhall prefent
Vnfpotted with the earth ; to'th high throne
That ouerlookes vs : for this gyant world
Let's not contend with it, when heauen it felfe
Failes to reforme it : why fhould we affect
The leaft hand ouer it, in that ambition ?
A heape tis of digefted villany ;
Virtue in labor with eternall Chaos
Preft to a liuing death, and rackt beneath it.
Her throwes vnpitied ; euery worthy man
Limb by limb fawne out of her virgine wombe,
To liue here peecemeall tortur'd, fly life then ;
Your life and death made prefidents for men.   *Exit.*
  Cat. Ye heare (my mafters) what a life this is,
And vfe much reafon to refpect it fo.
But mine fhall ferue ye. Yet reftore my fword,
Left too much ye prefume, and I conceiue
Ye front me like my fortunes. Where's *Statilius* ?

The Tragedy of

Por. I think Sir, gone with the three hundred
    Romans
In *Lucius Cæsars* charge, to ferue the victor.
    Cat. And would not take his leaue of his poore
    friend?
Then the Philofophers haue ftoop't his fpirit,
Which I admire, in one fo free, and knowing,
And fuch a fiery hater of bafe life,
Befides, being fuch a vow'd and noted foe
To our great Conqueror. But I aduifde him
To fpare his youth, and liue.
    Por. My brother *Brutus*
Is gone to *Cæfar.*
    Cat. *Brutus?* Of mine honor
(Although he be my fonne in law) I muft fay
There went as worthy, and as learned a Prefident
As liues in *Romes* whole rule, for all lifes actions;
And yet your fifter *Porcia* (his wife)
Would fcarce haue done this. But (for you my fonne)
Howeuer *Cæfar* deales with me; be counfailde
By your experienc't father, not to touch
At any action of the publique weale,
Nor any rule beare neare her politique fterne:
For, to be vpright, and fincere therein
Like *Catos* fonne, the times corruption
Will neuer beare it: and, to footh the time,
You fhall doe bafely, and vnworthy your life;
Which, to the gods I wifh, may outweigh mine
In euery virtue; howfoeuer ill
You thriue in honor.
    Por. I, my Lord, fhall gladly
Obey that counfell.
    Cat. And what needed you
Vrge my kinde care of any charge that nature
Impofes on me? haue I euer fhowne
Loues leaft defect to you? or any dues
The moft indulgent father (being difcreet)
Could doe his deareft blood? doe you me right
In iudgement, and in honor; and difpence

With paffionate nature: goe, negleƈt me not,
But fend my fword in. Goe, tis I that charge you.
  Cor. O my Lord, and father, come, aduife me.
                                          Exeunt.
  Cat. What haue I now to thinke on in this world?
No one thought of the world, I goe each minute
Difcharg'd of all cares that may fit my freedome.
The next world, and my foule, then let me ferue
With her laſt vtterance ; that my body may
With fweetneffe of the paffage drowne the fowre
That death will mix with it : the Confuls foules
That flew themfelues fo nobly, fcorning life
Led vnder Tyrants Scepters, mine would fee.
For we fhall know each other ; and paſt death
Retaine thofe formes of knowledge learn'd in life ;
Since, if what here we learne, we there fhall lofe,
Our immortality were not life, but time.
And that our foules in reafon are immortall,
Their naturall and proper obieƈts proue ;
Which immortallity and knowledge are.
For to that obieƈt euer is referr'd
The nature of the foule, in which the aƈts
Of her high faculties are ſtill employde.
And that true obieƈt muſt her powers obtaine
To which they are in natures aime direƈted.
Since twere abfurd to haue her fet an obieƈt
Which poffibly fhe neuer can afpire.

      Enter a Page with his fword taken out before.

  Pag. Your fword, my Lord.
  Cat. O is it found? lay downe
Vpon the bed (my boy) *Exit Pa.* Poore men ; a
    boy
Muſt be prefenter; manhood at no hand
Muſt ferue fo foule a faƈt ; for fo are calde
(In common mouths) mens faireſt aƈts of all.
Vnfheath ; is't fharpe? tis fweet. Now I am fafe,
Come *Cæfar*, quickly now, or lofe your vaffall.

Now wing thee, deare foule, and receiue her heauen.
The earth, the ayre, and feas I know, and all
The ioyes, and horrors of their peace and warres,
And now will fee the gods ftate, and the ftarres.

*He fals upon his fword, and enter Statilius at
another fide of the Stage with his fword
drawne, Porcius, Brutus, Cleanthes
and Marcilius holding his hands.*

    Stat.   Cato? my Lord?
    Por. I fweare (*Statilius*)
He's forth, and gone to feeke you, charging me
To feeke elfewhere, left you had flaine your felfe;
And by his loue entreated you would liue.
    Sta. I fweare by all the gods, Ile run his fortunes.
    Por. You may, you may; but fhun the victor now,
Who neare is, and will make vs all his flaues.
    Sta. He fhall himfelfe be mine firft, and my flaues.
                                                    Exit.
    Por. Looke, looke in to my father, O (I feare)
He is no fight for me to beare and liue.   *Exit.*
    Omn. 3. O ruthfull fpectacle?
    Cle. He hath ript his entrals.
    Bru. Search, fearch; they may be found.
    Cle. They may, and are.
Giue leaue, my Lord, that I may few them vp
Being yet vnperifht.
    Ca. Stand off; now they are *He thrufts him back
not.*   *& plucks out his entrals.*
Have he my curfe that my lifes leaft part faues.
Iuft men are only free, the reft are flaues.
    Bru. Myrror of men.
    Mar. The gods enuied his goodneffe.

*Enter Cæfar, Anthony, Brutus, Acilius, with Lords
and Citizens of Vtica.*

    Cæf. Too late, too late; with all our hafte. O
Cato,

Cæsar *and* Pompey.

All my late Conqueſt, and my lifes whole acts,
Moſt crownde, moſt beautified, are blaſted all
With thy graue lifes expiring in their ſcorne.
Thy life was rule to all liues; and thy death
(Thus forcibly deſpiſing life) the quench
Of all liues glories.
   Ant. Vnreclaimed man?
How cenſures *Brutus* his ſterne fathers fact?
   Bru. Twas not well done.
   Cæſ. O cenſure not his acts;
Who knew as well what fitted man, as all men.

Enter Achilius, Septimius, Salvius, with Pompeys head.

   All kneeling. Your enemies head great *Cæſar.*
   Cæſ. Curſed monſters,
Wound not mine eyes with it, nor in my camp
Let any dare to view it; farre as nobleſſe
The den of barbariſme flies, and bliſſe
The bittereſt curſe of vext and tyranniſde nature,
Transferre it from me. Borne the plagues of virtue
How durſt ye poyſon thus my thoughts? to torture
Them with inſtant rapture.
   Omn. 3. Sacred *Cæſar.*
   Cæſ. Away with them; I vow by all my comforts,
Who ſlack ſeemes, or not fiery in my charge,
Shall ſuffer with them.
   All the ſouldiers. Out baſe murtherers;
Tortures, tortures for them: *hale them out.*
   Omn. Cruell *Cæſar.*
   Cæſ. Too milde with any torture.
   Bru. Let me craue
The eaſe of my hate on their one curſt life.
   Cæſ. Good *Brutus* take it; O you coole the poyſon
Theſe villaines flaming pou'rd vpon my ſpleen
To ſuffer with my lothings. If the blood
Of euery common Roman toucht ſo neare;
Shall I confirme the falſe brand of my tyranny

With being found a fautor of his murther
Whom my deare Country chufde to fight for her?
   Ant. Your patience Sir, their tortures well will quit
      you :
   Bru. Let my flaues vfe, Sir, be your prefident.
   Cæf. It fhall, I fweare: you doe me infinite honor.
O *Cato*, I enuy thy death, fince thou
Enuiedft my glory to preferue thy life.
Why fled his fonne and friend *Statilius*?
So farre I fly their hurt, that all my good
Shall fly to their defires. And (for himfelfe)
My Lords and Citizens of *Vtica*,
His much renowne of you, quit with your moft.
And by the fea, vpon fome eminent rock,
Erect his fumptuous tombe; on which aduance
With all fit ftate his ftatue; whofe right hand
Let hold his fword, where, may to all times reft
His bones as honor'd as his foule is bleft.

FINIS.

THE
TRAGEDY
OF
ALPHONSUS
EMPEROUR
OF
GERMANY

As it hath been very often Acted (with great applaufe) at the Privat houfe in BLACK-FRIERS by his late MAIESTIES Servants.

By *George Chapman* Gent.

LONDON,
Printed for HUMPHREY MOSELEY, and are to be fold at his Shopp at the Princes-Arms in St. *Pauls* Church-yard 1654.

To the Reader

I Shall not need to befpeak thee Courteous, if thou haft feen this Piece prefented with all the Elegance of Life and Action on the *Black-Friers* Stage; But if it be a Stranger to thee, give me leave to prepare thy acceptation, by telling thee, it was receiv'd with general applaufe, and thy judgement (I doubt not) will be fatisfied in the reading.

I will not raife thy Expectation further, nor delay thy Entertainment by a tedious Preface. The Defign is high, the Contrivement fubtle, and will deferve thy grave Attention in the perufall.

Farewell.

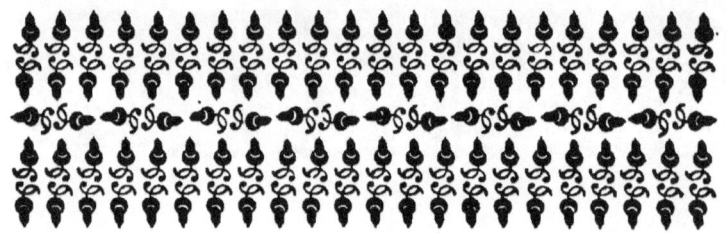

Dramatis Personæ.

Alphonsus Emperour of *Germany.*
King of *Bohemia.*
Bishop of *Mentz.*
Bishop of *Collen.*
Bishop of *Tryer.*
Pallatine of the *Rhein.*
Duke of *Saxon.*
Marquess of *Brandenburgh.*
} The seven Electors of the *German* Empire.

Prince *Edward* of *England.*
Richard Duke of *Cornwall.*
Lorenzo de Cipres, Secretary to the Emperour.
Alexander his Son, the Emperours Page.
Isabella the Empress.
Hedewick Daughter to the Duke of *Saxon.*
Captain of the Guard.
Souldiers.
Jaylor.
Two Boores.

ALPHONSUS

Emperour of *Germany*.

Enter Alphonsus *the Emperour in his night-gown, and his shirt, and a torch in his hand,* Alexander de Tripes *his Page following him.*

Al. Oy, give me the Master Key of all the doors.
To Bed again, and leave me to my self.
        Exit Alexder...
Is *Richard* come? have four Electors sworn
To make him Keisar in despite of me?
Why then *Alphonsus* it is time to wake.
No Englishman, thou art too hot at hand,
Too shallow braind to undermine my throne;
The Spanish Sun hath purifi'd my wit,
And dry'd up all grofs humours in my head,
That I am sighted as the King of Birds,
And can discern thy deepest Stratagems.
I am the lawful German Emperour,

Chosen, enstall'd, by general consent;
And they may tearm me Tyrant as they please,
I will be King, and Tyrant if I please;
For what is Empire but a Tyrannie?
And none but children use it otherwise.
Of seven Electors, four are falln away,
The other three I dare not greatly trust;
My Wife is Sister to mine enemy,
And therefore wisely to be dealt withall;
But why do I except in special,
When this position must be general,
That no man living must be credited,
Further than tends unto thy proper good.
But to the purpose of my silent walk;
Within this Chamber lyes my Secretary,
Lorenzo de Cipres, in whose learned brain
Is all the compass of the world containd;
And as the ignorant and simple age
Of our forefathers, blinded in their zeal,
Receiv'd dark answers from *Appollo's* shrine,
And honour'd him as Patron of their bliss;
So I, not muffled in simplicitie,
Zealous indeed of nothing but my good,
Hast to the *Augur* of my happiness,
To lay the ground of my ensuing Wars.
He learns his wisdom, not by flight of Birds,
By prying into sacrificed beasts,
By Hares that cross the way, by howling Wolves,
By gazing on the Starry Element,
Or vain imaginary calculations;
But from a setled wisdom in it self
Which teacheth to be void of passion.
To be Religious as the ravenous Wolf,
Who loves the Lamb for hunger, and for prey;
To threaten our inferiors with our looks;
To flatter our Superiors at our need;
To be an outward Saint, an inward Devill;
These are the lectures that my Master reads.
This Key commands all Chambers in the Court;

Emperour of Germany. 201

Now on a fudain will I try his wit,
I know my comming is unlook'd for.
He opens the door and finds Lorenzo *fleep a loft.*
Nay fleep, *Lorenzo*, I will walk a while.
As nature in the framing of the world,
Ordain'd there fhould be *nihil vacuum*;
Even fo me thinks his wifdom fhould contrive,
That all his Study fhould be full of wit,
And every corner ftuft with fentences?
What's this? *Plato? Ariftotle?* tufh thefe are ordinary,
It feems this is a note but newly written. [*He reads a note which he finds among his Books.*

Una arbufta non alit duos Erithicos; *which being granted, the Roman Empire will not fuffice* Alphonfus *King of* Caftile, *and* Richard *Earl of* Cornwall *his competitor*; *thy wifdom teacheth thee to cleave to the ftrongeft*; Alphonfus *is in poffeffion, and therefore the ftrongeft, but he is in hatred with the Electors, and men rather honour the Sun rifing than the Sun going down.* I marry this is argued like himfelf, and now me thinks he wakes.

[*Lorenzo* Rifeth, and fnatches at his fword which hung by his Bed-fide.]

Loren. What are there thieves within the Emperour's Court?
Villain thou dy'ft; what mak'ft thou in my Chamber?
Alphon. How now *Lorenzo*, wilt thou flay thy Lord?
Loren. I do befeech your facred Majefty to pardon me,
I did not know your grace.
Alphon. Ly down *Lorenzo*, I will fit by thee,
The ayr is fharp and piercing; tremble not,
Had it been any other but our felf,
He muft have been a villain and a thief.
Loren. Alas my Lord! what means your excellence,
To walk by night in thefe fo dangerous times?

Alphon. Have I not reason now to walk and watch,
When I am compast with so many foes ?
They ward, they watch, they cast, and they conspire,
To win confederate Princes to their aid,
And batter down the Eagle from my creast.
O, my *Lorenzo*, if thou help me not,
Th' Imperial Crown is shaken from my head,
And giv'n from me unto an English Earl.
Thou knowest how all things stand as well as we,
Who are our enemies, and who our friends,
Who must be threatned, and who dallyed with,
Who won by words, and who by force of arms ;
For all the honour I have done to thee.
Now speak, and speak to purpose in the cause ;
Nay rest thy body, labour with thy brain,
And of thy words my self will be the scribe.

Loren. Why then my Lord, take Paper, Pen and Ink,
Write first this maxim, it shall do you good.
1. A Prince must be of the nature of the Lion and the Fox ; but not the one without the other.

Alphon. The Fox is subtil, but he wanteth force ;
The Lion strong, but scorneth policie ;
I'l imitate *Lysander* in this point,
And where the Lion's hide is thin and scant,
I'l firmly patch it with the Foxes fell.
Let it suffice I can be both in one.

Loren. 2. A Prince above all things must seem devout ; but there is nothing so dangerous to his state, as to regard his promise or his oath.

Alphon. Tush, fear not me, my promises are sound,
But he that trusts them shall be sure to fail.

Loren. Nay my good Lord, but that I know your Majesty,
To be a ready quickwitted Scholar,
I would bestow a comment on the text.
3. Trust not a reconciled friend ; for good turns cannot blot out old grudges.

Emperour of Germany. 203

Alphon. Then muſt I watch the Palatine of the *Rhein*,
I caus'd his Father to be put to death.
 Loren. Your Highneſs hath as little cauſe to truſt
The dangerous mighty Duke of *Saxony* ;
You know, you ſought to baniſh him the Land ;
And as for *Cullen*, was not he the firſt
That ſent for *Richard* into *Germany* ?
 Alphon. What's thy opinion of the other four ?
 Alphon. That *Bohemie* neither cares for one nor other,
But hopes this deadly ſtrife between you twain,
Will caſt th' Imperial Crown upon his head.
For *Trier* and *Brandenberg*, I think of them
As ſimple men that wiſh the common good ;
And as for *Mentz* I need not cenſure him,
Richard hath chain'd him in a golden bond,
And ſav'd his life from ignominious death.
 Alphon. Let it ſuffice, *Lorenzo*, that I know,
When *Churfurſt Mentz* was taken Priſoner,
By young victorious *Otho* Duke of *Brunſchweige*
That *Richard* Earl of *Cornwall* did disburſe
The ranſome of a King, a million,
To ſave his life, and rid him out of bands,
That ſum of gold did fill the *Brunſchweige* bags ;
But ſince my ſelf have rain'd a golden ſhower.
Of bright Hungarian Ducates and Cruſadoes,
Into the private Coffers of the Biſhop,
The Engliſh Angels took their wings and fled ;
My croſſes bleſs his Coffers, and plead for me,
His Voice is mine, bought with ten tun of Gold,
And at the meeting of the ſeven Electors,
His Princely double-dealing holineſs
Will ſpoyl the Engliſh Emperour of hope.
But I refer theſe matters to the ſequel.
Proceed *Lorenzo* forward to the next.
 Loren. I'm glad your grace hath dealt ſo cunningly,
With that victorious fickle minded Prelate ; for in
election his voice is firſt but to the next.

4. 'Tis more fafety for a Prince to be feared than loved.

Alphon. Love is an humour pleafeth him that loves;
Let me be hated, fo I pleafe my felf.
Love is an humour mild and changeable;
But fear engraves a reverence in the heart.

Loren. 5. To keep an ufurped Crown, a Prince muft fwear, forfwear, poyfon, murder, and commit all kind of villanies, provided it be cunningly kept from the eye of the world.

Alphon. But my *Lorenzo* that's the hardeft point,
It is not for a Prince to execute,
Phyficians and Apothecaries muft know,
And fervile fear or Counfel-breaking bribes,
Will from a Peafant in an hour extort
Enough to overthrow a Monarchy.

Loren. Therefore my Lord fet down this fixt and laft Article.

6. Be alwaies jealous of him that knows your fecrets,
And therefore it behooves you credit few;
And when you grow into the leaft fufpect,
With filent cunning muft you cut them off.
As for example, *Julio Lentulus*,
A moft renowned *Neapolitan*,
Gave me this Box of poyfon, t'was not long
But therewithall I fent him to his grave.

Alphon. And what's the fpecial vertue of the fame?
Loren. That it is twenty days before it works.
Alphon. But what is this?
Loren. This an infection that kils fuddainly;
This but a toy to caft a man afleep.
Alphon. How? being drunk?
Loren. No, being fmelt unto.
Alphon. Then fmell *Lorenzo*, I did break thy fleep;
And, for this time, this lecture fhall fuffice.
Loren. What have you done my Lord? y'ave made me fafe,
For ftirring hence thefe four and twenty hours.
Alphon. I fee this charms his fenfes fudainly.

Emperour of Germany.

How now *Lorenzo*, half afleep already?
Æneas Pilot by the God of dreams,
Was never lull'd into a founder trance;
And now *Alphonfus* over-read thy notes. [*He reads.*
Thefe are already at my fingers ends,
And left the world fhould find this little Schedule,
Thus will I rend the text, and after this,
On my behaviour fet fo fair a glofs,
That men fhall take me for a Convertite;
But fome may think, I fhould forget my part,
And have been over rafh in renting it,.
To put them out of doubt I ftudy fure,
I'le make a backward repetition,
In being jealous of my Counfel keepers,
This is the poyfon that kils fudainly,
So didft thou unto *Julius Lentulus*,
And blood with blood muft be requited thus.
Now am I fafe, and no man knows my Counfels.
Churfurft of *Mentz*, if now thou play thy part,
Erning thy gold with cunning workmanfhip,
Upon the Bemifh Kings ambition,
Richard fhall fhamefully fail of his hope,
And I with triumph keep my Emperie. *Exit.*

Enter the King of Bohemia, *the Bifhops of* Mentz,
Collen, Trier, *the Pallatine of the* Rhein,
The Duke of Saxon, *The Marquefs
of* Brandenburg.

Bohe. Churfurfts and Princes of the Election,
Since by the adverfe fortune of our age,
The facred and Imperial Majefty
Hath been ufurp'd by open Tyranny,
We the feven Pillars of the German Empire,
To whom fucceffively it doth belong
To make election of our Emperours,
Are here affembled to unité a new
Unto her former ftrength and glorious type,
Our half declining Roman Monarchy,

And in that hope, I *Henry* King of *Bohem*,
Churfurſt and Sewer to the Emperour,
Do take my ſeat next to the ſacred throne.
 Mentz. Next ſeat belongs to *Julius Florius*
Archbiſhop of *Mentz*, Chancelor of *Germany*,
By birth the Duke of fruitful *Pomerland.*
 Pal. The next place in election longs to me,
George Caſſimirus Palſgrave of the *Rhein*,
His Highneſs Taſter, and upon my knee
I vow a pure ſincere innated zeal
Unto my Country, and no wreſted hate,
Or private love ſhall blind mine intellect.
 Collen. Brave Duke of *Saxon*, Dutchlands greateſt hope,
Stir now or never, let the Spaniſh tyrant,
That hath diſhonoured us, murder'd our Friends,
And ſtain'd this ſeat with blood of innocents,
At laſt be chaſtis'd with the *Saxon* ſword,
And may *Albertus* Archbiſhop of *Collen*,
Chancelor of *Gallia* and the fourth Elector;
Be thought unworthy of his place and birth,
But he aſſiſt thee to his utmoſt power.
 Sax. Wiſdom, not words, muſt be the ſoveraign ſalve,
To ſearch and heal theſe grievous feſtred wounds,
And in that hope *Auguſtus* Duke of *Saxon*,
Arch-Marſhall to the Emperour, take my place.
 Trier. The like doth *Frederick* Arch-Biſhop of *Trier*,
Duke of *Lorrain*, Chancelour of *Italie.*
 Bran. The ſeventh and laſt is *Joachim Carolus*,
Marqueſs of *Brandenburg*, overworn with age,
Whoſe Office is to be the Treaſurer:
But Wars have made the Coffers like the Chair.
Peace bringeth plenty, Wars bring poverty;
Grant Heavens, this meeting may be to effect,
Eſtabliſh Peace, and cut off Tyrannie.

Enter the Emprefs Ifabella *King* John's *Daughter.*

Emprefs. Pardon my bold intrufion mighty *Chur-furfts*,
And let my words pierce deeply in your hearts.
O! I befeech you on my bended Knees,
I the poor miferable Emprefs,
A ftranger in this Land, unus'd to broyls,
Wife to the one, and Sifter to the other
That are Competitors for Soveraignty;
All that I pray, is, make a quiet end;
Make Peace between my Husband and my Brother.
O think how grief doth ftand on either fide,
If either party chance to be amifs;
My Husband is my Husband; but my Brother,
My heart doth melt to think he fhould mifcarry.
My Brother is my Brother; but my Husband,
O how my joynts do fhake fearing his wrong!
If both fhould dye in thefe uncertain broyls.
O me, why do I live to think upon't!
Bear with my interrupted fpeeches Lords,
Tears ftop my voice, your wifdoms know my meaning.
Alas I know my Brother *Richard*'s heart
Affects not Empire, he would rather choofe
To make return again to *Paleftine*,
And be a fcourge unto the Infidels;
As for my Lord, he is impatient,
The more my grief, the leffer is my hope.
Yet Princes thus he fends you word by me,
He will fubmit himfelf to your award,
And labour to amend what is amifs.
All I have faid, or can device to fay,
Is few words of great worth, Make unity.

Bohe. Madam, that we have fuffer'd you to kneel fo long,
Agrees not with your dignity nor ours;
Thus we excufe it, when we once are fet,
In folemn Councel of Election,
We may not rife till fomewhat be concluded.

So much for that : touching your earneſt ſute,
Your Majeſtie doth know how it concerns us,
Comfort your ſelf, as we do hope the beſt ;
But tell us, Madam, wher's your Husband now ?
 Empreſs.   I left him at his prayers, good my Lord.
 Saxon.   At prayers ? Madam that's a miracle.
 Pall.   Vndoubtedly your Highneſs did miſtake ;
'Twas ſure ſome Book of Conjuration ;
I think he never ſaid pray'r in his life.
 Empreſs.   Ah me, my fear, I fear, will take effect ;
Your hate to him, and love unto my Brother,
Will break my heart, and ſpoil th' Imperial peace.
 Mentz.   My Lord of *Saxon*, and Prince *Pallatine*,
This hard opinion yet is more than needs ;
But, gracious Madam, leave us to our ſelves.
 Empreſs.   I go, and Heav'n that holds the Hearts of Kings,
Direct your Counſels unto unity.   *Exit.*
 Bohe.   Now to the depth of that we have in hand ;
This is the queſtion, whether the King of *Spain*
Shall ſtill continue in the Royal throne,
Or yield it up unto *Plantagenet*,
Or we proceed unto a third Eelection.
 Saxon.   E're ſuch a viperous blood-thirſty Spaniard
Shall ſuck the hearts of our Nobility,
Th' Imperial Sword which *Saxony* doth bear,
Shall be unſheath'd to War againſt the world.
 Pall.   My hate is more than words can teſtifie,
Slave as he is he murdered my Father.
 Coll.   Prince *Richard* is the Champion of the world,
Learned, and mild, fit for the Government.
 Bohe.   And what have we to do with Engliſhmen ?
They are divided from our Continent.
But now that we may orderly proceed
To our high Office of Election,
To you my Lord of *Mentz* it doth belong,
Having firſt voice in this Imperial Synod,
To name a worthy man for Emperour.

Emperour of Germany.

Mentz. It may be thought, moſt grave and reverend Princes,
That in reſpect of divers ſums of gold,
Which *Richard* of meer charitable love,
Not as a bribe, but as a deed of Alms,
Disburs'd for me unto the Duke of *Brunſchweige*,
That I dare name no other man but he,
Or ſhould I nominate an other Prince,
Upon the contrary I may be thought
A moſt ingrateful wretch unto my Friend;
But private cauſe muſt yield to publick good;
Therefore me thinks it were the fitteſt courſe,
To chooſe the worthieſt upon this Bench.
 Bohem. We are all Germans, why ſhould we be yoak'd
Either by Engliſhmen or Spaniards?
 Saxo. The Earl of *Cornwall* by a full conſent
Was ſent for out of *England*.
 Mentz. Though he were,
Our later thoughts are purer than our firſt,
And to conclude, I think this end were beſt,
Since we have once choſen him Emperour,
That ſome great Prince of wiſdom and of power,
Whoſe countenance may overbear his pride,
Be joynd in equal Government with *Alphonſus*.
 Bohem. Your Holineſs hath ſoundly in few words
Set down a mean to quiet all theſe broyls.
 Trier. So may we hope for peace if he amend;
But ſhall Prince *Richard* then be joynd with him?
 Pal. Why ſhould your Highneſs ask that queſtion?
As if a Prince of ſo high Kingly Birth,
Would live in couples with ſo baſe a Cur?
 Bohe. Prince *Pallatine*, ſuch words do ill become thee.
 Saxon. He ſaid but right, and call'd a Dog a Dog.
 Bohe. His Birth is Princely.
 Saxo. His manners villanous,
And vertuous *Richard* ſcorns ſo baſe a yoak.

O

Bohe. My Lord of *Saxon*, give me leave to tell you,
Ambition blinds your judgement in this cafe;
You hope, if by your means *Richard* be Emperour,
He, in requital of fo great advancement,
Will make the long-defired Marriage up
Between the Prince of *England* and your Sifter,
And to that end *Edward* the Prince of *Wales*,
Hath born his Uncle Company to *Germany*.

Saxo. Why King of *Bohem* i'ft unknown to thee,
How oft the *Saxons* Sons have marryed Queens,
And Daughters Kings, yea mightieft Emperours?
If *Edward* like her beauty and behaviour,
He'l make no queftion of her Princely Birth;
But let that pafs, I fay, as erft I faid,
That vertuous *Richard* fcorns fo bafe a yoak.

Mentz. If *Richard* fcorn, fome one upon this Bench,
Whofe power may overbear *Alphonfus* pride,
Is to be named. What think you my Lords?

Saxon. I think it was a mighty mafs of Gold,
That made your grace of this opinion.

Mentz. My Lord of *Saxony*, you wrong me much,
And know I highly fcorn to take a bribe.

Pal. I think you fcorn indeed to have it known:
But to the purpofe, if it muft be fo,
Who is the fitteft man to joyn with him?

Collen. Firft with an Oxe to plough will I be yok'd.

Mentz. The fitteft is your grace in mine opinion.

Bohem. I am content, to ftay thefe mutinies,
To take upon me what you do impofe.

Saxon. Why here's a tempeft quickly overblown.
God give you joy my Lord of half the Empire;
For me I will not meddle in the matter,
But warn your Majeftie to have a care,
And vigilant refpect unto your perfon,
I'l hie me home to fortifie my Towns,
Not to offend, but to defend my felf.

Palf. Ha' with you Cofin, and adieu my Lords,

I am afraid this fuddain knitted Peace,
Will turn unto a tedious lafting War;
Only thus much we do requeft you all,
Deal honourably with the Earl of *Cornwall*,
And fo adieu.   *Exeunt.* Saxon. *and* Palf.
  Brand. I like not this ftrange Farewel of the Dukes.
  Bohem. In all elections fome are malcontent.
It doth concern us now with fpeed to know,
How the Competitors will like of this,
And therefore you my Lord Archbifhop of *Trier*,
Impart this order of arbitrament
Unto the Emperour bid him be content,
To ftand content with half or lofe the whole,
My Lord of *Mentz* go you unto Prince *Richard*,
And tell him flatly here's no Crown, nor Empire
For Englifh Iflanders; tell him, 'twere his beft,
To hie him home to help the King his Brother,
Againft the Earl of *Leicefter* and the Barons.
  Collen. My Lord of *Mentz*, fweet words will qualifie,
When bitter tearms will adde unto his rage.
'Tis no fmall hope that hath deceiv'd the Duke;
Therefore be mild; I know an Englifhman,
Being flattered, is a Lamb, threatned, a Lion;
Tell him his charges what fo e're they are
Shalbe repaid with treble vantages;
Do this; we will expect their refolutions.
  Mentz. Brother of *Collen*, I entreat your grace
To take this charge upon you in my ftead;
For why I fhame to look him in the face.
  Collen. Your Holinefs fhall pardon me in this,
Had I the profit I would take the pains;
With fhame enough your Grace may bring the meffage.
  Mentz. Thus am I wrong'd, God knows, unguiltily.
  Brand. Then arm your countenance with innocency,
And boldly do the meffage to the Prince;
For no man elfe will be the meffenger.
  Mentz. Why then I muft, fince ther's no remedy.
                                              Exit Mentz.

Brand. If Heav'n that guides the hearts of mighty men,
Do calm the Winds of thefe great Potentates,
And make them like of this Arbitrament,
Sweet Peace will tryumph thorough Chriftendom,
And *Germany* fhall blefs this happy day.

Enter Alexander de Toledo *the Page.*

Alexand. O me moft miferable! O my dear Father!
Bohem. What means this paffionate accent? what art thou
That founds thefe acclamations in our ears?
Alex. Pardon me Princes, I have loft a Father,
O me, the name of Father kils my heart.
O! I fhall never fee my Father more,
H'as tane his leaue of me for age and age,
Collen. What was thy Father?
Alex. Ah me? whot was a not?
Noble, Rich, valiant, well-belov'd of all,
The glory and the wifdom of his age,
Chief Secretary to the Emperour.
Collen. *Lorenzo de Toledo*, is he dead?
Alex. Dead, ay me dead, ay me my life is dead,
Strangely this night bereft of breath and fenfe,
And I, poor I, am comforted in nothing,
But that the Emperour laments with me,
As I exclame, fo he, he rings his hands,
And makes me mad to fee his Majefty
Excruciate himfelf with endlefs forrow.
Collen. The happieft news that euer I did hear;
Thy Father was a villain murderer,
Witty, not wife, lov'd like a Scorpion,
Grown rich by the impoverifhing of others,
The chiefeft caufe of all thefe mutinies,
And *Cæfar*'s tutor to all villanie.
Alex. None but an open lyar terms him fo.
Col. What Boy, fo malepert?
Bohem. Good *Collen* bear with him, it was his Father,

Dutch-land is bleffed in *Lorenzo's* Death.
Brand. Did never live a viler minded man.
Exeunt. Manet Alex.
Alex. Nor King, nor *Churfurſt* ſhould be privileg'd
To call me Boy, and rayl upon my Father,
Were I wehrſafflig ; but in *Germany*,
A man muſt be a Boy at 40. years,
And dares not draw his weapon at a Dog,
Till being foundly box'd about the ears,
His Lord and Maſter gird him with a ſword ;
The time will come I ſhall be made a man,
Till then I'l pine with thought of dire revenge,
And live in Hell untill I take revenge.

ACT. II.

Enter Alphonſus, Richard *Earl of* Cornwall, Mentz, Trier, *Prince* Edward, Bohemia, Collen, Brandenburge, *Attendants, and Pages with a ſword.*

Bohem. Behold here comes the Princes hand in hand,
Pleas'd highly with the ſentence as it ſeems.
Alphon. Princes and Pillars of the Monarchy,
We do admire your wiſdoms in this cauſe,
And do accept the King of *Bohemia*,
As worthy partner in the Government.
Alas my Lords, I flatly now confeſs,
I was alone too weak to underprop
So great a burden as the Roman Empire,

And hope to make you all admire the courfe
That we intend in this conjunction.
 Richard. That I was call'd from *England* with confent
Of all the feven Electors to this place,
Your felves beft know, who wrote for me to come.
'Twas no ambition mov'd me to the journey,
But pitty of your half declining State ;
Which being likely now to be repayr'd,
By the united force of thefe two Kings,
I reft content to fee you fatisfied.
 Mentz. Brave Earl, wonder of Princely patience,
I hope your grace will not mif-think of me,
Who for your good, and for the Empires beft,
Bethought this means to fet the world at Peace.
 Edward. No doubt this means might have been thought upon,
Although your Holinefs had dy'd in Prifon.
 Mentz. Peace, peace young Prince, you want experience ;
Your Unckle knows what cares accompany,
And wait upon the Crowns of mightieft Kings,
And glad he is that he hath fhak'd it off.
 Edward. Heark in your ear my Lord, hear me one word,
Although it were more than a million,
Which thefe two Kings beftow'd upon your grace,
Mine Unckle *Richards* million fav'd your life.
 Mentz. Youwere beft to fay, your Vnckle brib'd me then.
 Edward. I do but fay mine Vnckle fav'd your life,
You know Count *Mansfield* your fellow Prifoner,
Was by the Duke of *Brunfchwig* put to death.
 Mentz. You are a Child my Lord, your words are wind.
 Edward. You are a Fox my Lord, and paft a Child.
 Bohem. My Lord of *Cornwall*, your great forwardnefs,

Crossing the Seas with aid of Englishmen,
Is more than we can any way requite;
But this your admirable patience,
In being pleas'd with our election,
Deserves far more than thanks can satisfie,
In any thing command the Emperours,
Who live to honour *Richard* Earl of *Cornwall*.

   Alpho. Our deeds shall make our Protestations
      good,
Mean while, brave Princes, let us leave this place,
And solace us with joy of this accord.

Enter Isabella *the Empress,* Hedewick *the Duke of*
   Saxon's *Daughter, apparelled like Fortune, drawn*
    on a Globe, with a Cup in her hand, wherein
     are Bay leaves, whereupon are written
      the lots. A train of Ladies follow-
       ing with Musick.

   Empress. To gratulate this unexpected Peace,
This glorious league confirm'd against all hope,
Joyful *Isabella* doth present this shew,
Of Fortunes triumph, as the custom is
At Coronation of our Emperours;
If therefore every party be well pleas'd,
And stand content with this arbitriment,
Then daign to do as your Progenitors,
And draw in sequence Lots for Offices.

   Alphon. This is an order here in *Germany,*
For Princes to disport themselves with all,
In sign their hearts so firmly are conjoyn'd,
That they will bear all fortunes equally,
And that the world may know I scorn no state,
Or course of life to do the Empire good,
I take my chance: My Fortune is to be the Forrester.

   Emp. If we want Venson either red or fallow,
Wild bore or bear, you must be sin'd my Lord.

   Bohem. The Emperour's Taster I.

   Emp. Your Majesty hath been tasted to so oft,

That you have need of fmall inftructions.
 Richard. I am the bowr, Sifter what is my charge?
 Emp. Tyr'd like a Carter, and a Clownifh Bowr,
To bring a load of Wood into the Kitchin.
Now for my felf, Faith I am Chamber Maid,
I know my charge : proceed unto the next.
 Alphon. Prince *Edward* ftandeth melancholy ftill,
Pleafe it your Grace, my Lord, to draw your lot.
 Emp. Nephew you muft be folemn with the fad,
And given to myrth in fportful Company,
The German Princes when they will be lufty,
Shake of all cares, and Clowns and they are Fellows.
 Edward. Sweet Aunt, I do not know the Country guife,
Yet would be glad to learn all fafhions.
Since I am next, good Fortune be my guide.
 Brand. A moft ingenuous countenance hath this Prince,
Worthy to be the King of *England*'s Heir.
 Edward. Be it no difparagement to you my Lords,
I am your Emperour.
 Alphon. Sound trumpets, God fave the Emperour.
 Collen. The world could never worfe have fitted me,
I am not old enough to be the Cook.
 Emprefs. If you be Cook, there is no remedy
But you muft drefs one Mefs of meat your felf.
 Branden. I am Phyfician.
 Trier. I am Secretary.
 Mentz. I am the Jefter.
 Edward. O excellent! is your Holinefs the Vice?
Fortune hath fitted you y'faith my Lord,
You'l play the Ambodexter cunningly.
 Mentz. Your Highnefs is to bitter in your Jefts.
 Alphon. Come hither *Alexander*, to comfort thee,
After the death of thy beloved Father,
Whofe life was deer unto his Emperour,
Thou fhalt make one in this folemnity,
Yet e're thou draw, my felf will honour thee,

Emperour of Germany. 217

And as the cuſtom is make thee a man.
Stand ſtiff Sir Boy, now com'ſt thou to thy tryal;
Take this, and that, and therewithall this Sword;
    He gives Alexander *Box on the ear or two.*
If while thou live, thou ever take the like,
Of me, or any man, I here pronounce
Thou art a ſchelm, otherwiſe a man.
Now draw thy lot, and Fortune be thy ſpeed.
  Edward. Vnckle I pray why did he box the fellow?
Foul lubber as he is, to take ſuch blows.
  Richard. Thus do the Princes make their Pages men.
  Edward. But that is ſtrange to make a man with blows.
We ſay in *England* that he is a man,
That like a man dare meet his enemy,
And in my judgement 'tis the ſounder tryal.
  Alex. Fortune hath made me Marſhall of the tryumphs.
  Alphon. Now what remains?
  Emperefs. That Fortune draw her lot.
  She opens it, and gives it to the Emperefs to read.
  Emprefs. Sound trumpets, Fortune is your Emperefs.
  Alphon. This happens right; for Fortune will be Queen.
Now Emperour you muſt unmask her face,
And tell us how you like your Emperefs,
In my opinion *England* breeds no fairer.
  Bohe. Fair *Hedewick* the Duke of *Saxons* daughter,
Young Prince of *England*, you are bravely match'd.
  Edward. Tell me ſweet Aunt, is that this *Saxon* Princefs,
Whoſe beauties fame made *Edward* croſs the Seas?
  Emperefs. Nephew, it is; hath fame been prodigal,
Or over ſparing in the Princefs praife?
  Edward. Fame I accuſe thee, thou did'ſt niggardize,
And faintly found my loves perfeƈtions.

Great Lady Fortune, and fair Emperefs,
Whom chance this day hath thrown into my arms,
More welcome than the Roman Emperefs. [*Edward
kiſſes her.*

Hede. **See doþh, daſs iſt hier kein geb=
rauch,
Mein Got iſt daſs dir Engliſch manier,
daſs dich.**
 Edward. What meaneth this? why chafes my
  Emperefs?
 Alphon. Now by my troth, I did expect this jeſt,
Prince *Edward* us'd his Country faſhion.
 Edward. I am an Engliſhman, why ſhould I not?
 Emp. Fy Nephew *Edward*, here in *Germany*
To kifs a Maid, a fault intollerable.
 Edward. Why ſhould not *German* Maids be kiſt
afwell as others?
 Richard. Nephew, becaufe you did not know the
  faſhion,
And want the language to excufe your felf,
I'l be your fpokes-man to your Emperefs.
 Edward. Excufe it thus: I like the firſt fo well,
That tell her, ſhe ſhall chide me twice as much
For fuch an other; nay tell her more than fo,
I'l double kifs on kifs, and give her leave
To chide and braul, and cry ten thoufand **daſs dich**,
And make her weary of her fretting humour,
E're I be weary of my kiſſing vein,
Daſs dich a Jungfraw angry for a kifs.
 Emprefs. Nephew, ſhe thinks you mock her in her
  mirth.
 Edward. I think the Princes make a fcorn of me.
If any do, I'l prove it with my Sword,
That Engliſh Courtſhip leaves it from the world.
 Bohem. The pleafant'ſt accident that I have feen.
 Bran. Me thinks the Prince is chaf'd as well as
  ſhe.

Emperour of Germany. 219

Rich. **Gnediges frawlin.**
Hede. **Dafs dich, muft ich arme kindt zu schanden gemacht werden.**
Edward. **Dafs dich** I have kift as good as you,
Pray Unckle tell her; if fhe miflike the kifs,
I'l take it off agen with fuch an other.
Rich. **Ey Lirbes frawlin nim es all fur gutti**
Es ift die Englifch manier Und gebrauche.
Hede. **Ewer gnaden weiffts woll es ift mir ein groffe fchande.**
Edward. Good Aunt teach me fo much Dutch to ask her pardon.
Emprefs. Say fo: **Gnediges frawlin bergebet mirs, ich wills nimmermehr thuen,**
Then kifs your hand three times **upfy** Dutch.
Edward, **Ich wills nimmermehr thuen,**
if I underftand it, right,
That's as much to fay, as I'l do fo no more.
Empr. True Nephew.
Edward. Nay Aunt pardon me I pray, I hope to kifs her many thoufand times,
And fhall I go to her like a great Boy, and fay I'l do fo no more.
Emprefs. I pray Cofin fay as I tell you.
Edward. **Gnediges frawlin bergebet mirfs ich wills nimmermehr thuen.**
Alphon. **Uorwahr knw fchandt.**
Hedew. **Gnediger hochgeborner Furft vndt herr**

ALPHONSUS

Wan ich konte so viel englisch sprechen ich
    wolt ewer Gnaden.
Fur wahr ein filtz geben, ich hoffe aber ich
    soll einmahl
So viel lernen dass Die mich verstehen soll.
   Edward. What fays fhe?
   Alphon. O excellent young Prince look to your
    felf,
She fwears fhe'l learn fome Englifh for your fake,
To make you underftand her when fhe chides.
   Edward. I'l teach her Englifh, fhe fhall teach me
    Dutch,
Gnediges frawlin, &c.
   Bohem. It is great pitty that the Duke of *Saxon*,
Is abfent at this joyful accident,
I fee no reafon if his Grace were here,
But that the Marriage might be folemniz'd,
I think the Prince of *Wales* were well content.
   Edward. I left fweet *England* to none other end;
And though the Prince her Father be not here,
This Royal prefence knows his mind in this.
   Emp. Since you do come fo roundly to the pur-
    pofe,
'Tis time for me to fpeak, the Maid is mine,
Giv'n freely by her Father unto me,
And to the end thefe broyls may have an end,
I give the Father's intereft and mine own,
Unto my Nephew *Edward* Prince of *Wales*.
   Edward. A Jewel of incomparable price,
Your Majefty hath here beftowed on me,
How fhall I ask her if fhe be content?
   Empr. Say thus, ist ewer gnaden woll hie=
    mit zufrieden.
   Edward. Ist ewer Gnaden woll hiemit
    zufrieden.

Emperour of Germany.

Hede. Waß ihr Durleichtigkeit daß will
daß will mein batter bndt
Waß mein batter will darmit muß ich
zufrieden fein.

Alphon. It is enough, fhe doth confirm the match;
We will difpatch a Poft unto her Father,
On Sunday fhall the Revels and the Wedding,
Be both folemnized with mutual joy.
Sound trumpets, each one look unto his charge,
For preparation of the Feftivals. *Exeunt.*

Manent Alphonfus *and* Alexander.

Alphon. Come hither *Alexander*, thy Fathers joy.
If tears and fighs, and deep-fetcht deadly groans,
Could ferve t' evert inexorable fate,
Divine *Lorenzo*, whom in life my heart,
In death my foul and better part adores,
Had to thy comfort and his Prince's honour,
Surviv'd, and drawn this day this breath of life.
  Alexan. Dread *Cæfar*, proftrate on my bended
    Knee,
I thank your Majefty for all favours fhewn
To my deceafed Father and my felf.
I muft confefs, I fpend but bootlefs tears,
Yet cannot bridle nature, I muft weep,
Or heart will break with burden of my thoughts;
Nor am I yet fo young or fond withall,
Cauflefs to fpend my gall, and fret my heart,
'Tis not that he is dead, for all muft dye;
But that I live to hear his lives reproach.
O facred Emperour, thefe ears have heard,
What no Sons ears can unrevenged hear,
The Princes all of them, but fpecially,
The Prince Eleftor Archbifhop of *Collen*,
Revil'd him by the names of murderer,
Arch villain, robber of the Empires fame,

And *Cæfars* tutor in all wickednefs,
And with a general voice applaus'd his death,
As for a fpecial good to Chriftendome.
 Alphon. Have they not reafon to applaud the deed
Which they themfelves have plotted ? ah my Boy,
Thou art too young to dive into their drifts.
 Alex. Yet old enough I hope to be reveng'd.
 Alphon. What wilt thou do, or whither wilt thou run ?
 Alex. Headlong to bring them death, then dye my felf.
 Alphon. Firft hear the reafon why I do miftruft them.
 Alex. They had no reafon for my Father's death,
And I fcorn reafon till they all be dead.
 Alphon. Thou wilt not fcorn my Counfel in revenge?
 Alex. My rage admits no Counfel but revenge.
 Alphon. Firft let me tell thee whom I do miftruft.
 Alex. Your highnefs faid you did miftruft them all.
 Alpho. Yea *Alexander*, all of them, and more than all,
My moft efpeciall neereft deareft friends.
 Alex. Alls one to me, for know thou Emperour,
Were it thy Father, Brother, or thine Emprefs,
Yea were't thy felf, that did'ft confpire his death,
This fatal hand fhould take away thy life.
 Alphon. Spoke like a Son, worthy fo dear a Father.
Be ftill and hearken, I will tell thee all,
The Duke of *Saxon*—
 Alex. O, I thought no lefs.
 Alphon. Suppref thy choler, hearken to the reft.
Saxon I fay fo wrought with flattering *Mentz*,
Mentz with *Bohemia*, *Trier*, and *Brandenburg*,
For *Collen* and the *Palfgrave* of the *Rhein*
Were principals with *Saxon* in the Plot,
That in a general meeting to that purpofe,
The feven felected Emperours electors,
Moft hainoufly concluded of the murder ;

The reason why they doom'd him unto death,
Was his deep wisdom and sound policy;
Knowing while he did live my state was firm,
He being dead my hope must dye with him.
Now *Alexander* will we be reveng'd
Upon this wicked whore of *Babylon*,
This hideous monster with the seven-fold head:
We must with cunning level at the heart,
With pierc'd and perisht all the body dyes:
Or strike we off her heads by one and one,
Behoveth us to use dexterity,
Lest she do trample us under her feet,
And tryumph in our honours overthrow.

  Alex. Mad and amaz'd to hear this tragick doom,
I do subscribe unto your sound advice.

  Alphon. Then hear the rest; these seven gave but the sentence
A neerer hand put it in execution,
And but I lov'd *Lorenzo* as my life,
I never would betray my dearest Wife.

  Alex. What? what the Empress accessary to?

  Alphon. What cannot kindred do? her Brother *Richard*,
Hoping thereby to be an Emperour,
Gave her a dram that sent him to his grave.

  Alex. O my poor Father, wert thou such an eye-sore,
That 9. the greatest Princes of the earth
Must be confederate in thy tragedy?
But why do I respect their mightiness,
Who did not once respect my Fathers life?
Your Majesty may take it as you please,
I'l be reveng'd upon your Emperess,
On English *Richard*, *Saxon*, and the Palsgrave,
On *Bohem*, *Collen*, *Mentz*, *Trier*, and *Brandenburg*,
If that the Pope of *Rome* himself were one
In this confederacy, undaunted I,
Amidst the College of his Cardinals,
Would press, and stab him in St. *Peters* chair,

Though clad in all his *Pontificalibus*.
  Alphon. Why *Alexander*? do'ſt thou ſpeak to me
As if thou didſt miſtruſt my forwardneſs?
No, thou ſhalt know my love to him was ſuch,
And in my heart I have proſcrib'd them all,
That had to do in this conſpiracy.
The bands of Wedlock ſhall not ſerve her turn,
Her fatal lot is caſt among the reſt,
And to conclude, my ſoul doth live in Hell
Till I have ſet my foot upon their necks,
That gave this ſpur of ſorrow to my heart;
But with advice it muſt be managed,
Not with a head-long rage as thou intend'ſt,
Nor in a moment can it be perform'd,
This work requires long time, diſſembling looks,
Commixt with undermining actions,
Watching advantages to execute.
Our foes are mighty, and their number great,
It therefore follows that our Stratagems
Muſt branch forth into manifold deceits,
Endleſs devices, bottomleſs concluſions.
  Alexan. What by your Majeſty is preſcrib'd to me,
That will I execute or dye the death.
I am content to ſuck my ſorrows up,
And with dull patience will attend the time,
Gaping for every opportunity
That may preſent the leaſt occaſion;
Although each minute multiply mine anguiſh,
And to my view preſent a thouſand forms
Of ſenſeleſs bodies in my Fathers ſhape,
Yelling with open throat for juſt revenge.
  Alphon. Content thy ſelf, he ſhall not cry in vain,
I have already plotted *Richards* death.
  Alex. That hath my Fathers ſacred Ghoſt inſpir'd,
O tell me, ſhall I ſtab him ſuddainly?
The time ſeems long, till I be ſet a work.
  Alphon. Thou knoweſt in griping at our lots to day,
It was Prince *Richard*'s hap to be the bowr;

Emperour of Germany.

So that his Office is to drive the Cart,
And bring a load of Wood into the Kitchin.
   Alex. O excellent, your Grace being Forefter,
As in the thicket he doth load the Cart,
May fhoot him dead, as if he were a Deer.
   Alphon. No *Alexander*, that device were fhallow,
Thus it muft be, there are two very bowrs
Appointed for to help him in the Wood,
Thefe muft be brib'd or cunningly feduc'd,
Inftead of helping him to murder him.
   Ale. *Verbum fatis fapienti*, it is enough,
Fortune hath made me Marfhal of the fports
I hope to Marfhal them to th' Devils Feaft.
Plot you the reft, this will I execute,
Dutch bowrs as towfandt fchelms and gold to tempt them.
   Alphon. 'Tis right, about it then, but cunningly.
   Alex. Elfe let me lofe that good opinion
Which by your Highnefs I defire to hold,
By Letters which I'l ftrew within the Wood,
I'l undermine the bowrs to murder him,
Nor fhall they know who fet them fo a work,
Like a familiar will I fly about,
And nimbly haunt their Ghofts in every nook.
             Exit. Manet Alphonfus.
   Alphon. This one nayl helps to drive the other out,
I flew the Father, and bewitch the Son,
With power of words to be the inftrument
To rid my foes with danger of his life.
How eafily can fubtil age intice,
Such credulous young novices to their death ?
Huge wonders will *Alphonfus* bring to pafs,
By the mad mind of this enraged Boy ;
Even they which think themfelves my greateft friends,
Shall fall by this deceit, yea my Arch-enemies
Shall turn to be my chief confederates.
My follitary walks may breed fufpect,
I'le therefore give my felf to Companie,
As I intended nothing but thefe fports,

                               P

Yet hope to fend moſt actors in this Pageant,
To Revel it with *Rhadamant* in Hell. *Exit.*

Enter Richard *Earl of* Cornwall *like a Clown.*

Richard. How far is *Richard* now unlike the man
That croſt the Seas to win an Emperie?
But as I plod it like a plumper Bowr,
To fetch in Fewel for the Kitchin fire,
So every one in his vocation,
Labours to make the paſtimes plauſible;
My Nephew *Edward* jets it through the Court,
With Princeſs *Hedewick* Empreſs of his Fortune,
The demy *Cæſar* in his hunters ſuit,
Makes all the Court to Ring with Horns and Hounds,
Collen the Cook beſtirs him in the Kitchin;
But that which joyes me moſt in all theſe ſports,
Is *Mentz*, to ſee how he is made an Aſs?
The common ſcorn and by-word of the Court;
And every one to be the ſame he ſeems,
Seems to forget to be the ſame he is.
Yet to my roabs I cannot ſuit my mind,
Nor with my habit ſhake diſhonour off.
The ſeven Electors promis'd me the Empire,
The perjur'd Biſhop *Mentz* did ſwear no leſs,
Yet I have ſeen it ſhar'd before my face,
While my beſt friends do hide their heads for ſhame;
I bear a ſhew of outward full content,
But grief thereof hath almoſt kill'd my heart.
Here reſt thee *Richard*, think upon a mean,
To end thy life, or to repair thine honour,
And vow never to ſee fair *Englands* bounds,
Till thou in *Aix* be Crowned Emperour.

Enter two Bowrs.

Holla, me thinks there cometh Company,
The Bowrs I troe that come to hew the Wood,
Which I muſt carry to the Kitchen Fire,
I'le lye a while and liſten to their talk.

Emperour of Germany.

Enter Hans *and* Jerick *two Dutch Bowrs.*

Je. Kom hier hans wore bist dow, warumb bist dow so trawrick? bis frolick kan wel gelt verdienen, wir wil ihn bey potts tawsandt todt schlagen.

Hans. Lat mich die brieffe sehen.

Rich. Me thinks they talk of murdering some body, I'l listen more.

Reads the Letter.

Hans vnd Jerick, mein liebe freinde, ich bitte lasset es bey euch bleiben in geheim, vnd schlaget den Engellander zu todt.

Rich. What's that? *Hans* vnd *Jerick* my good friend, I pray be secret and murder the Englishman.

Jerick *reads.*

Hear weiter, den er ist kein bowre nicht, er ist ein Juncker, vnd hatt viel gelt vnd kleinothen bey sich.

Rich. For he is no Bowre but a Gentleman, and hath store of Gold and Jewels by him.

Jeric. Noch weiter: ihr solt solche gelegenheit nicht versahmen, vnd wan ihr gethan habet, ich will euch sagen, was ich fur ein guter Karl bin, der euch raht gegeben habe.

Rich. Slip not this opportunity, and when you have done, I will discover who gave you the Counsel.

Jerick. Wat sagst dow, wilt dow es thun?

Hans. Wat will ich nich fur gelt thun? see potts tausendt, dar ist er.

Jerick. Ja, bey potts tausends flapperment, er ists, holla guter morgen, gluck zu Juncker.

Hans. Juncker, der dibell he is ein bowre!

Rich. Dow bist ein schelm, weich von mir.

Jerick. Holla, holla, bist dow so hoffertick? Juncker bowre, kompt hier, oder dieser vnd jenner selleuch holen.

Rich. Ich bien ein Furst, bried mich nicht ihr schelms, ihr verrahters.

Bath. Sla to, sla to, wir will yow furstlick tractieren.

Richard having nothing in his hand but his whip, defends himself a while and then fall's down as if he were dead:

Rich. O Got, nimb meine seele in deine hande.

Jerick. O excellent, hurtick he is todt, he is todt.

Lat vns see, wat he hat for gelt bey sich, holla hier is all enough, all satt, dor is for dich, and dor is for mich, vnd ditt will ich darto haben:

Jerick puts the chain about his neck.

Hans. How so Hans Narhals, geue mir die kette hier.

Jerick. Ja ein dreck, dit kett stehet hupsch vmb mein hals, ditt will ich tragen.

Hans. Dat dich potts velten leßden dat soltu nimmermehr thun dow schelm.

Jerick. Wat solt dow mich schelm heiten, nimb dat.

Hans. Dat dich hundert tonnen divells, harr ich will dich lernen.

Jerick. Wiltud hawen oder stechen?

Hans. Ich will redlich hawen;

Jerick. Nun wollan, dar ist mein ruck, sla to.

They muſt have axes made for the nonſt to fight withall, and while one ſtrikes, the other holds his back without defence.

Hans. Nimb dow das, vnd dar hast mein ruck.

Jerick. Noch amahl: O excellent, ligst dow dar, nun will ich alles haben, gelt vnd kett, vnd alle mit einander, O hurtig,

frisch-up lustig, nun bin ich ein hurtig Juncker.

Richard rises up again and snatcheth up the fellows hatchet that was slain.

Rich. *Nè Hercules contra duos,* yet pollicy hath gone beyond them both.

Du hudler schelm, morder, kehre dich, seestu mich? gebe mir die kett vnd gelt wieder;

Jerick. **Wat bistu wieder labendig worden, so mus ich meren, wat wiltu stechen oder hawen?**

Richard. **So will ich machen du schelm.**

Jerick. **Harr, harr, bistu ein redlich karle, so fight redlich, O ich sterb, ich sterb, lat mich leben!**

Richard. **Sagt mir dan wer hatt die brieffe geschrieben? Lie nicht sondern sagt die warheit:**

Jerick. **O mein fromer, guter, edler, gestrenger Juncker, dar ist dat gelt vnd kett wieder, pow soll alles haben, aber wer hatt die brieffe geschrieben, dat wet ich bey meiner seele nicht.**

Rich. **Lig dor still, still ich sag.**
The villain swears, and deeply doth protest
He knows not who incited them to this,
And as it seems the scrowl imports no less.

So sterb du mir schelm.

Emperour of Germany.

Jerick. **O ich sterb, awe, awe, awe dat dich der dibell hole!**

As Richard *kils the Bowr. Enter* Saxon *and the* Palsgrave.

Saxon. **Sy dich an loser schelm, hastu dein gesellen todt geschlagen?**
Palsgr. **Last bs den schelmen angreiffen.**
  Richard. Call you me **schelme** how dare you then
Being Princes offer to lay hands on me?
That is the Hangmans Office here in Dutch-land.
  Saxon. But this is ſtrange, our Bours can ſpeak no
    Engliſh,
What biſtum more than a damn'd murderer?
That thou art ſo much we are witneſſes.
  Rich. Can then this habit alter me ſo much,
That I am call'd a villain by my friends?
Or ſhall I dare once to ſuſpect your graces,
That for you could not make me Emperour,
Pittying my ſorrow through mine honour loſt,
You ſet theſe ſlaves to rid me of my life,
Yet far be ſuch a thought from *Richard*'s heart.
  Palſ. How now? what do I hear Prince *Richard*
    ſpeak?
  Rich. The ſame: but wonder that he lives to
    ſpeak.
And had not policy helpt above ſtrength,
Theſe ſturdy ſwains had rid me of my life.
  Sax. Far be it from your Grace for to ſuſpect us.
  Rich. Alas, I know not whom I ſhould ſuſpect;
But yet my heart cannot miſdoubt your Graces?
  Saxon. How came your Highneſs into this apparrel?
  Rich. We as the manner is drew lots for Offices,
My hap was hardeſt to be made a Carter,
And by this letter which ſome villain wrote,

I was betray'd, here to be murdered;
But Heav'n which doth defend the Innocent,
Arm'd me with strength and policy together,
That I escap'd out of their treacherous snare.
    Palf. Were it well founded, I dare lay my life,
The Spanish tyrant knew of this conspiracie;
Therefore the better to dive into the depth
Of this most devillish murderous complot,
As also secretly to be beholders,
Of the long-wisht for wedding of your daughter,
We will disrobe these bowrs of their apparrel,
Clapping their rustick cases on our backs,
And help your Highness for to drive the Cart.
T" may be the traytor that did write these lines,
Mistaking us for them will shew himself.
    Richard. Prince *Palatine* this plot doth please me well,
I make no doubt if we deal cunningly,
But we shall find the writer of this scroul.
    Saxon. And in that hope I will disrobe this slave.
Come Princes in the neighbouring thicket here,
We may disguise our selves, and talk at pleasure;
Fye on him heavy lubber how he weighs.
    Richard. The sin of murder hangs upon his soul,
It is no mervail then if he be heavy.
                                    Exeunt.

ACT. III.

Enter to the Revels.

Edward *with an Imperial Crown.* Hedewig *the Emprefs.* Bohemia *the Tafter.* Alphonfus *the Forrefter.* Mentz *the Gefter. Emprefs the Chambermaid.* Brandenburg *Phyfician.* Tryer *Secretarie.* Alexander *the Marfhal, with his Marfhals ftaff, and all the reft in their proper apparrel, and Attendants and Pages.*

Alex. Princes and Princes Superiors, Lords and Lords fellows, Gentlemen and Gentlemens Mafters, and all the reft of the States here affembled, as well Mafculine as Feminine, be it known unto you by thefe prefence, that I *Alexander de Toledo*, Fortunes chief Marfhal, do will and command you, by the authority of my faid Office, to take your places in manner and form following, Firft the Emperour and the Emprefs, then the Tafter, the Secretary, the Forrefter, the Phyfician, as for the Chambermaid and my felf, we will take our places at the neither end, the Jefter is to wait up, and live by the crums that fall from the Emperours trencher, But now I have Marfhal'd you to the table, what remains?

Mentz. Every fool can tell that, when men are fet to dinner they commonly expect meat.

Edward. That's the beft Jeft the fool made fince he came into his Office. Marfhal walk into the Kitchin, and fee now the *Churfurft* of *Collen* beftirs himfelf.

Exit. Alex.

Mentz. Shall I go with him too? I love to be imploy'd in the Kitchin.
Edward. I prethee go, that we may be rid of thy wicked Jefts.
Mentz. Have with thee Marfhal, the fool rides thee. *Exit. on Alex. back.*
Alphon. Now by mine honour, my Lord of *Mentz* plays the fool the worft that ever I faw.
Edward. He do's all by contraries; for I am fure he playd the wifeman like a fool, and now he plays the fool wifely.
Alphon. Princes and *Churfurfts* let us frolick now,
This is a joyful day to Chriftendome,
When Chriftian Princes joyn in amity,
Schinck bowls of Reinfal and the pureft Wine,
We'l fpend this evening luftie upfie Dutch,
In honour of this unexpected league.
Emprefs. Nay gentle Forrefter, there you range amifs,
His looks are fitly fuited to his thoughts,
His glorious Emprefs makes his heart tryumph,
And hearts tryumphing makes his countenance ftai'd,
In contemplation of his lives delight.
Edward. Good Aunt let me excufe my felf in this,
I am an Emperour but for a day,
She Emprefs of my heart while life doth laft;
Then give me leave to ufe Imperial looks,
Nay if I be an Emperour I'l take leave,
And here I do pronounce it openly,
What I have lately whifper'd in her ears,
I love mine Emprefs more than Empery,
I love her looks above my fortunes hope.
Alphon. Saving your looks dread Emperour es gelt a bowl,
Unto the health of your fair Bride and Emprefs.
Edward. Sam Got es foll mir en liebe

Emperour of Germany.   235

Drunk fein, fo much Dutch have I learnt fince I came into *Germany*.
 Bran. When you have drunk a dozen of thefe bowls,
So can your Majefty with a full mouth,
Trowl out high Dutch, till then it founds not right,

Drauff es gelt noch eins ihr Majeſtat.
Edward. **Sam Got lafs lauffen.**
 Bohem. My Lord of *Brandenburg* fpoken like a good Dutch Brother;
But moft unlike a good Phyfician,
You fhould confider what he has to do,
His Bride will give you little thanks to night.
 Alphon. Ha, ha my Lord, now give me leave to laugh,
He need not therefore fhun one Beaker full.
In *Saxon* Land you know it is the ufe,
That the firft night the Bridegroom fpares the Bride.
 Bohem. 'Tis true indeed, that had I quite forgotten.
 Edward. How underftand I that ?
 Alphon. That the firft night,
The Bride and Bridegroom never fleep together.
 Edward. That may well be, perchance they wake together.
 Bohem. Nay without fallace they have feveral Beds.
 Edward. I in one Chamber, that is moft Princely.
 Alphon. Not onely feveral Beds, but feveral Chambers,
Lockt foundly too, with Iron Bolts and Bars.
 Empr. Beleeve me Nephew, that's the cuftom here.
 Edward. O my good Aunt, the world is now grown new,
Old cuftoms are but fuperftitions.
I'm fure this day, this prefence all can witnefs,
The high and mighty Prince th' Archbifhop of *Collen*,
Who now is bufie in the skullery,
Joyn'd us together in St. *Peters* Church,

And he that would disjoyn us two to night,
'Twixt jeſt and earneſt be it proudly ſpoken,
Shall eat a piece of ill-digeſting Iron.

Bride wilt dow dis nicht ben mee ſchlapen.
Hede. Da behute mich Gott fur, Ich hoffe
Eure maieſtat wills von mir miſt, bege=
rau.

 Edward. What ſays ſhe behute mich Got fur?
 Alphon. She ſays God bleſs her from ſuch a deed.
 Edward. Tuſh Empreſs, clap thy hands upon thy
  head,
And God will bleſs thee, I have a *Jacobs* ſtaff,
Shall take the Elevation of the Pole ;
For I have heard it ſayd, the Dutch North ſtar,
Is a degree or two higher than ours.
 Bohem. Nay though we talk lets drink, and Em-
  perour,
I'l tell you plainly what you muſt truſt unto,
Can they deceive you of your Bride to night,
They'll ſurely do't, therefore look to your ſelf.
 Edward. If ſhe deceive me not, let all do their
  worſt.
 Alphon. Aſſure you Emperour ſhe'l do her beſt.
 Edward. I think the Maids in *Germany* are mad,
E're they be marryed they will not kiſs,
And being marryed will not go to Bed.
We drink about, let's talk no more of this,
Well warn'd half arm'd our Engliſh proverb ſay
 Alphon. Holla Marſhal, what ſays the Cook?

Enter Alexander.

Belike he thinks we have fed ſo well already,
That we diſdain his ſimple Cookery.
 Alex. Faith the Cook ſays ſo, that his Office was
to dreſs a meſs of meat with that Wood which the
Engliſh Prince ſhould bring in, but he hath neither

Emperour of Germany.

feen Dutch Wood nor Englifh Prince, therefore he defires you hold him excus'd.
 Alphon. I wonder where Prince *Richard* ftays fo long.
 Alex. An't, pleafe your Majefty, he's come at length,
And with him has he brought a crew of Bowrs,
A hipfe bowr maikins frefh as Flow'rs in *May*,
With whom they mean to dance a *Saxon* round,
In honour of the Bridegroom and his Bride.
 Edward. So has he made amends for his long tarrying.
I prethee Marfhall them into the prefence.
 Alphon. Lives *Richard* then? I had thought th' had'ft made him fure.
 Alex. O, I could tear my flefh to think upon 't,
He lives and fecretly hath brought with him,
The *Palfgrave* and the Duke of *Saxonie*,
Clad like two Bowrs, even in the fame apparrel.
That *Hans* and *Jerick* wore when they went out to murder him,
It now behooves us to be circumfpect.
 Alphon. It likes me not; Away Marfhal bring them.
          Exit. Alexander.
I long to fee this fports conclufion.
 Bohem. I'ft not a lovely fight to fee this couple
Sit fweetly billing like two Turtle Doves.
 Alphon. I promife you it fets my Teeth an Edge,
That I muft take mine Emprefs in mine arms.
Come hither *Ifabel*, though thy roabs be homely,
Thy face and countenance holds colour ftill.

Enter Alexander, Collen, Mentz, Richard, Saxony, Palſgrave, Collen Cook, *with a gamon of raw bacon, and links or puddings in a platter,* Richard, Palſgrave, Saxon, Mentz, *like Clowns with each of them a Miter with Corances on their heads.*

Collen. Dread Emperour and Empereſs for to day,
I Your appointed Cook untill to morrow,
Have by the Marſhal ſent my iuſt excuſe,
And hope your Highneſs is therewith content,
Our Carter here for whom I now do ſpeak,
Says that his Axletree broke by the way,
That is his anſwer, and for you ſhall not famiſh,
He and his fellow bowrs of the next dorp,
Haue brought a ſchinkel of good raw Bacon,
And that's a common meat with us, unſod,
Deſiring you, you would not ſcorn the fare ;
'Twil make a cup of Wine taſte nippitate.
    Edward. Welcome good fellows, we thank you for your preſent.
    Richard. So ſpell freſh up, and let us rommer daunſen.
    Alex. Pleaſe it your Highneſs to dance with your Bride?
    Edward. Alas I cannot dance your *German* dances.
    Bohem. I do beſeech your Highneſs mock us not,
We *Germans* have no changes in our dances,
An Almain and an upſpring that is all,
So dance the Princes, Burgers, and the Bowrs.
    Brand. So daunc'd our Aunceſtors for thouſand years.
    Edw. It is a ſign the Dutch are not new fangled.
I'le follow in the meaſure ; Marſhal lead.

Emperour of Germany.

Alexander *and* Mentz *have the fore dance with each of them a glafs of Wine in their hands, then* Edward *and* Hedewick, Palfgrave *and* Emprefs, *and two other couple, after Drum and Trumpet.*

The Palfgrave *whiſpers with the* Emprefs.

Alphon. I think the Bowr is amorous of my Emprefs ; **Fort bowr** and **leffel morgen,** when thou com'ft to houfe.
Collen. Now is your Graces time to fteal away, Look to't or elfe you'l lie alone to night.

Edward fteals away the Bride.

Alex. (Drinketh to the Palfgrave.) **Skelt bowre.**
Palfgrave. **Sam Gott.**

The Palfgrave *requefts the* Emprefs.

**Ey Jungfraw helpe mich doch ein Jung=
fraw drunck
Es gelt guter freundt ein frolocken drink.**
Alphon. **Sain Gott mein frundt ich
will gern befcheidt thun**
(Alphonfus *takes the Cup of the* Palfgrave, *and drinks to the King of* Bohemia, *and after he hath drunk puts poyfon into the Beaker.*)
Half this I drinke unto your Highnefs health,
It is the firft fince we were joynd in Office.
Bohem. I thank your Maiefty, I'le pledge you half.
(*As* Bohem *is a drinking, e're he hath drunk it all out,* Alphonfus *pulls the Beaker from his mouth*).
Alphon. Hold, hold, your Maiefty, drink not too much.
Bohem. What means your Highnefs.

Alphon. Methinks that fomething grates between my teeth,
Pray God there be not poyfon in the bowl.
Bohem. Marry God forbid.
Alex. So were I pepper'd.
Alphon. I highly do miftruft this fchelmifh bowr,
Lay hands on him, I'le make him drink the reft.

Whas ift whas ift wat will you mit mee machen

Alphon. Drink out, drink out **oder der dibell foll dich holen.**

Palf. **Ey geb you to frieden ich will gern drink.**

Saxon. Drink not Prince *Pallatine,* throw it on the ground,
It is not good to truft his Spanifh flies.
Bohem. *Saxon* and *Palfgrave,* this cannot be good.
Alphon. 'Twas not for nought my mind mifgave me fo ;
This hath Prince *Richard* done t'entrap our lives.
Richard. No *Alphonfus,* I difdain to be a traytor.
Emprefs. O fheath your fwords, forbear thefe needlefs broyls.
Alphon. Away, I do miftruft thee as the reft.
Bohem. Lord's hear me fpeak, to pacify thefe broyls ;
For my part I feel no diftemperature,
How do you feel your felf ?
Alphon. I can not tell, not ill, and yet methinks I am not well.
Bohem. Were it a poyfon 'twould begin to work.
Alphon. Not fo, all poyfons do not work alike.
Palf. If there were poyfon in, which God forbid,
The Emprefs and my felf and *Alexander,*
Have caufe to fear as well as any other.
Alphon. Why didft thou throw the Wine upon the earth ?

Emperour of Germany.

Hadſt thou but drunk, thou hadſt ſatisfied our minds.
Palſ. I will not be enforc't by Spaniſh hands.
Alphon. If all be well with us, that ſchuce ſhall ſerve
If not, the Spaniards blood will be reveng'd.
Rich. Your Maieſty is more afraid than hurt.
Bohem. For me I do not fear my ſelf a whit,
Let all be friends, and forward with our mirth.

Enter Edward *in his night-gown and his ſhirt.*

Richard. Nephew, how now? is all well with you?
Bohem. I lay my life the Prince has loſt his bride.
Edward. I hope not ſo, ſhe is but ſtray'd a little.
Alphon. Your Grace muſt not be angry though we laugh.
Edward. If it had hapned by default of mine,
You might have worthily laught me to ſcorn;
But to be ſo deceiv'd, ſo over reach'd,
Even as I meant to claſp her in mine arms,
The grief is intollerable, not to be gueſt,
Or comprehended by the thought of any,
But by a man that hath been ſo deceiv'd,
And that's by no man living but my ſelf.
Saxon. My Princely Son-in-Law God give you joy.
Edward. Of what my Princely Father?
Saxon. O' my Daughter.
Your new betroathed Wife and Bed-fellow.
Edward. I thank you Father, indeed I muſt confeſs
She is my Wife, but not my Bed-fellow.
Saxon. How ſo young Prince? I ſaw you ſteal her hence,
And as me thought ſhe went full willingly.
Edward. 'Tis true, I ſtole her finely from amongſt you,
And by the Arch-Biſhop of *Collens* help,
Got her alone in to the Bride-Chamber,
Where having lockt the Door, thought all was well.

I could not fpeak but pointed to the Bed,
She anfwered **Ja** and gan for to unlace her;
I feeing that fufpected no deceit,
But ftraight untruft my points, uncas'd my felf,
And in a moment flipt between the Sheets;
There lying in deep contemplation,
The Princefs of her felf drew neer to me,
Gave me her hand, fpake prettily in Dutch
I know not what, and kift me lovingly,
And as I fhrank out of my luke warm place
To make her room, fhe clapt thrice with her feet,
And through a trap-door funck out of my fight;
Knew I but her Confederates in the deed——
I fay no more.
 Emprefs. Tufh Cofin, be content;
So many Lands, fo many fafhions,
It is the *German* ufe, be not impatient,
She will be fo much welcomer to morrow.
 Rich. Come Nephew, we'l be Bed-fellows to-night.
 Edward. Nay if I find her not, I'le lye alone,
I have good hope to ferret out her Bed,
And fo good night fweet Princefs all at once.
 Alphon. Godnight to all; Marfhal difcharge the
  train.
 Alex. To Bed, to Bed the Marfhal crys 'tis time.
Exeunt.

Flourifh Cornets, Manent Saxon, Richard, Palfgrave,
  Collen, Emprefs.

 Saxon. Now Princes it is time that we advife,
Now we are all faft in the Fowlers gin,
Not to efcape his fubtle fnares alive,
Unlefs by force we break the Nets afunder.
When he begins to cavil and pick quarrels,
I will not truft him in the leaft degree.
 Emprefs. It may befeem me evill to miftruft
My Lord and Emperour of fo foul a fact;
But love unto his honour and your lives,

Emperour of Germany.

Makes me with tears intreat your Excellencies
To fly with speed out of his dangerous reach,
His cloudy brow foretells a suddain storm
Of blood not natural but prodigious.
    Rich. The Castle gates are shut, how should we fly;
But were they open, I would lose my life,
E're I would leave my Nephew to the slaughter;
He and his Bride were sure to bear the brunt.
    Saxon. Could I get out of doors, I'ld venture that,
And yet I hold their persons dear enough,
I would not doubt, but e're the morning Sun,
Should half way run his course into the South,
To compass and begirt him in his Fort,
With *Saxon* lansknights and brunt-bearing *Switzers*,
Who lye in Ambuscado not far hence,
That he should come to Composition,
And with safe conduct bring into our tents,
Both Bride and Bridegroom, and all other friends.
    Empress. My Chamber Window stands upon the Wall,
And thence with ease you may escape away.
    Saxon. Prince *Richard*, will you bear me Company?
    Richard. I will my Lord.
    Saxon. And you Prince *Pallatine*?
    Pals. The Spanish Tyrant hath me in suspect
Of poysoning him, I'l therefore stay it out,
To fly upon't were to accuse my self.
    Empress. If need require, I'le hide the *Pallatine*.
Untill to morrow, if you stay no longer.
    Saxon. If God be with us, e're to morrow noon
We'll be with Ensigns spread before the Walls;
We leave dear pledges of our quick return.
    Emp. May the Heavens prosper your just intents.
                                            Exeunt.

                   Enter Alphonsus.

    Alphon. This dangerous plot was happily over-heard,

Here didſt thou liſten in a bleſſed howr.
Alexander, where do'ſt thou hide thy ſelf ?
I've fought thee in each Corner of the Court,
And now or never muſt thou play the man.
   Alex. And now or never muſt your Highneſs ſtir.
Treaſon hath round encompaſſed your life.
   Alphon. I have no leaſure now to hear thy talk.
Seeſt thou this Key ?
   Alex. Intends your Majeſty, that I ſhould ſteal into
     the Princes Chambers,
And ſleeping ſtab them in their Beds to night ?
That cannot be.
   Alphon. Wilt thou not hear me ſpeak ?
   Alex. The Prince of *England*, *Saxon*, and of *Collen*,
Are in the Empreſs chamber privily.
   Alphon. All this is nothing, they would mur-
     der me,
I come not there to night; ſeeſt thou this Key ?
   Alex. They mean to fly out at the Chamber Window,
And raiſe an Army to beſeege your Grace ;
Now may your Highneſs take them with the deed.
   Alphon. The Prince of *Wales* I hope is none of
     them.
   Alex. Him and his Bride by force they will recover.
   Alphon. What makes the curſed *Palſgrave* of the
     Rhein ?
   Alex. Him hath the Empreſs taken to her charge,
And in her Cloſet means to hide him ſafe.
   Alphon. To hide him in her Cloſet ? of bold deeds,
The deareſt charge that e're ſhe undertook,
Well let them bring their Complots to an end,
I'le undermine to meet them in their works,
   Alex. Will not your Grace ſurprize them e're they
     fly ?
   Alphon. No, let them bring their purpoſe to effect,
I'le fall upon them at my beſt advantage,
Seeſt thou this Key ? there take it *Alexander* ;
Yet take it not unleſs thou be reſolv'd ;
Tuſh I am fond to make a doubt of thee ;

Take it I fay, it doth command all Doors,
And will make open way to dire revenge.
    Alex. I know not what your Majefty doth mean.
    Alphon. Hie thee with fpeed into the inner Chamber,
Next to the Chappel, and there fhalt thou find
The danty trembling Bride coutcht in her Bed,
Having beguil'd her Bridegroom of his hopes,
Taking her farewel of Virginity,
Which fhe to morrow night expects to lofe,
By night all Cats are gray, and in the dark,
She will imbrace thee for the Prince of *Wales*,
Thinking that he hath found her Chamber out,
Fall to thy bufinefs and make few words,
And having pleas'd thy fenfes with delight,
And fild thy beating vains with ftealing joy,
Make thence agen before the break of day,
What ftrange events will follow this device,
We need not ftudy on, our foes fhall find.
How now? how ftandft thou? haft thou not the heart?
    Alex. Should I not have the heart to do this deed,
I were a Baftard villain and no man;
Her fweetnefs, and the fweetnefs of revenge,
Tickles my fenfes in a double fenfe,
And fo I wifh your Majefty good night.
    Alphon. God night, fweet *Venus* profper thy attempt.
    Alex. Sweet *Venus* and grim *Ate* I implore,
Stand both of you to me aufpicious. *Exit.* Alexander.
    Alphon. It had been pitty of his Fathers life,
Whofe death hath made him fuch a perfect villain.
What murder, wrack, and caufelefs enmity,
'Twixt deareft friends that are my ftrongeft foes,
Will follow fuddainly upon this rape,
I hope to live to fee, and laugh thereat,
And yet this peece of practice is not all.
The King of *Bohem* though he little feel it,
Becaufe in twenty hours it will not work,
Hath from my Knives point fuck'd his deadly bane,
Whereof I will be leaft of all fufpected;

For I will feign my felf as fick as he,
And blind mine enemies eyes with deadly groans;
Upon the *Palfgrave* and mine Emperefs,
Heavy fufpect fhall light to bruze their bones;
Though *Saxon* would not fuffer him to tafte,
The deadly potion provided for him,
He cannot fave him from the Sword of Iuftice,
When all the world fhall think that like a villain,
He hath poyfon'd two great Emperours with one
    draught;
That deed is done, and by this time I hope,
The other is a doing, *Alexander*
I doubt it not will do it thorowly.
While thefe things are a brewing I'l not fleep,
But fudainly break ope the Chamber doors,
And rufh upon my Emprefs and the *Palfgrave*,
Holla wher's the Captain of the Guard?

Enter Captain, and Souldiers.

  Cap. What would you Majefty?
  Alphon. Take fix travants well arm'd and followe.
They break with violence into the Chamber, and Alphon-
    fus *trayles the Emprefs by the hair.*

Enter Alphonfus, *Emprefs, Souldiers, &c.*

  Alphon. Come forth thou damned Witch, adulterous
    Whore,
Foul fcandal to thy name, thy fex, thy blood.
  Emp. O Emperour, gentle Husband, pitty me.
  Alphon. Canft thou deny thou wert confederate,
With my arch enemies that fought my blood?
And like a Strumpet through thy Chamber Window,
Haft with thine own hands helpt to let them down,
With an intent that they fhould gather arms,
Befiege my Court, and take away my life?
  Emp. Ah my *Alphonfus.*
  Alphon. Thy *Alphonfus* Whore?
  Emp. O pierce my heart, trail me not by my hair

Emperour of Germany.   247

What I have done, I did it for the beſt.
  Alphon. So for the beſt advantage of thy luſt,
Haſt thou in ſecret *Clytemneſtra* like,
Hid thy *Ægeſtus* thy adulterous love.
  Emp. Heav'n be the record 'twixt my Lord and
    me,
How pure and ſacred I do hold thy Bed.
  Alphon. Art thou ſo impudent to bely the deed,
Is not the *Palſgrave* hidden in thy Chamber ?
  Empe. That I have hid the *Palſgrave* I confeſs ;
But to no ill intent your conſcience knows.
  Alphon. Thy treaſons, murders, inceſts, ſorceries,
Are all committed to a good intent ;
Thou know'ſt he was my deadly enemy.
  Emp. By this device I hop'd to make your friends :
  Alphon. Then bring him forth, we'l reconcile our
    ſelves.
  Emp. Should I betray ſo great a Prince's life ?
  Alphon. Thou holdſt his life far dearer than thy
    Lords,
This very night haſt thou betrayd my blood,
But thus, and thus, will I revenge my ſelf,
And but thou ſpeedily deliver him,
I'le trail thee through the Kennels of the Street,
And cut the Noſe from thy bewitching face,
And into *England* ſend thee like a Strumpet.
  Emp. Pull every hair from off my head,
Drag me at Horſes tayls, cut off my noſe
My Princely tongue ſhall not betray a Prince.
  Alph. That will I try.
  Emp. O Heav'n revenge my ſhame.

Enter Palſgrave.

  Pal. Is *Cæſar* now become a torturer,
A Hangman of his Wife, turn'd murderer ?
Here is the *Pallatine*, what wouldſt thou more ?
  Alphon. Upon him Souldiers, ſtrike him to the
    ground.

Emp. Ah Souldiers, ſpare the Princely *Pallatine.*
Alphon. Down with the damn'd adulterous murderer.
Kill him I ſay, his blood be on my head.

They kill the Pallatine.

Run to the Tow'r, and Ring the Larum Bell,
That fore the world I may excuſe my ſelf,
And tell the reaſon of this bloody deed.

Enter Edward *in his night gown and ſhirt.*

Edw. How now? what means this ſudain ſtrange Allarm?
What wretched dame is this with blubbered cheeks,
And rent diſhevel'd hair?
Emp. O my dear Nephew,
Fly, fly the Shambles, for thy turn is next.
Edward. What, my Imperial Aunt? then break my heart.
Alphon. Brave Prince be ſtill; as I am nobly born,
There is no ill intended to thy perſon.

Enter Mentz, Tryer, Branden. Bohem.

Mentz. Where is my Page? bring me my two hand Sword.
Tryer. What is the matter? is the Court a fire
Bran. Whoſe that? the Emperour with his weapon drawn?
Bohem. Though deadly ſick yet am I forc'd to riſe,
To know the reaſon of this hurley burley.
Alphon. Princes be ſilent, I will tell the cauſe,
Though ſudainly a griping at my heart
Forbids my tongue his wonted courſe of ſpeech.
See you this Harlot, traytreſs to my life,
See you this murderer, ſtain to mine honour,
Theſe twain I found together in my Bed,
Shamefullly committing lewd Adultery,
And hainouſly conſpiring all your deaths,

Emperour of Germany.

I mean your deaths, that are not dead already;
As for the King of *Boheme* and my felf,
We are not of this world, we have our tranfports
Giv'n in the bowl by this adulterous Prince,
And leaft the poyfon work too ftrong with me,
Before that I have warnd you of your harms,
I will be brief in the relation.
That he hath ftaind my Bed, thefe eyes have feen,
That he hath murder'd two Imperial Kings,
Our fpeedy deaths will be too fudain proof;
That he and fhe have bought and fold your lives,
To *Saxon, Collen,* and the Englifh Prince,
Their Enfigns fpread before the Walls to morrow
Will all too fudainly bid you defiance.
Now tell me Princes have I not juft caufe,
To flay the murderer of fo many fouls?
And have not all caufe to applaud the deed?
More would I utter, but the poyfons force
Forbids my fpeech, you can conceive the reft.
 Bohem. Your Majefty reach me your dying hand,
With thoufand thanks for this fo juft revenge.
O, how the poyfons force begins to work!
 Mentz. The world may pitty and applaud the deed.
 Brand. Did never age bring forth fuch hainous
  acts.
 Edward. My fenfes are confounded and amaz'd.
 Emp. The God of Heav'n knows my unguiltinefs.
    Enter Meffenger.
 Mef. Arm, arm my Lords, we have defcry'd a far,
An Army of ten thoufand men at arms.
 Alphon. Some run unto the Walls, fome draw up
  the Sluce,
Some fpeedily let the Purcullefs down.
 Mentz. Now may we fee the Emperours words are
  true.
To prifon with the wicked murderous Whore. *Exeunt.*

ACT. IV.

Enter Saxon *and* Richard *with Souldiers.*

Saxon. My Lord of *Cornwall,* let us march before,
To fpeedy refcue of our deareft friends,
The rereward with the armed Legions,
Committed to the Prince of *Collen's* charge,
Cannot fo lightly pafs the mountain tops.
　Richard. Let's fummon fudainly unto a Parly,
I do not doubt but e're we need their helps,
Collen with all his forces will be here.

Enter Collen *with Drums and an Army.*

　Richard. Your Holinefs hath made good haft to day,
And like a beaten Souldier lead your troops.
　Collen. In time of peace I am an Arch-Bifhop,
And like a Church-man can both fing and fay;
But when the innocent do fuffer wrong,
I caft my rocket off upon the Altar,
And like a Prince betake my felf to arms.

Enter above Mentz, Tryer, *and* Brandenburg.

　Mentz. Great Prince of *Saxonie,* what mean thefe arms?
Richard of *Cornwall,* what may this intend?
Brother of *Collen* no more Churchman now,
Inftead of Miter, and a Croffier Staff,
Have you betane you to your Helme and Targe?
Were you fo merry yefterday as friends,

Emperour of Germany.

Cloaking your treafon in your Clowns attire ?
  Saxon. *Mentz,* we return the traytor in thy face.
To fave our lives, and to releafe our friends,
Out of the Spaniards deadly trapping Snares,
Without intent of ill, this power is rais'd ;
Therefore grave Prince Marquefs of *Brandenburg,*
My loving Cofin, as indifferent Judge,
To you an aged Peace-maker we fpeak,
Deliver with fafe conduct in our tents,
Prince *Edward* and his Bride, the *Pallatine,*
With every one of high or low degree,
That are fufpicious of the King of *Spain,*
So fhall you fee that in the felf fame howr
We marched to the Walls with colours fpread,
We will cafhier our troups, and part good friends.
  Brand. Alas my Lord, crave you the *Pallatine* ?
  Rich. If craving will not ferve, we will command.
  Brand. Ah me, fince your departure, good my Lords,
Strange accidents of bloud and death are hapned.
  Saxon. My mind mifgave a maffacre this night.
  Rich. How do's Prince *Edward* then ?
  Sax. How do's my Daughter ?
  Collen. How goes it with the *Palfgrave* of the *Rhein* ?
  Brand. Prince *Edward* and his Bride do live in health,
And fhall be brought unto you when you pleafe.
  Saxon. Let them be prefently deliver'd ?
  Coll. Lives not the *Palfgrave* too ?
  Mentz. In Heaven or Hell he lives, and reaps the merrit of his deeds.
  Coll. What damned hand hath butchered the Prince ?
  Saxon. O that demand is needlefs, who but he,
That feeks to be the Butcher of us all ;
But vengeance and revenge fhall light on him.
  Bran. Be patient noble Princes, hear the reft.
The two great Kings of *Bohem* and *Caftile,*

God comfort them, lie now at point of death,
Both poyſon'd by the *Palſgrave* yeſterday.
  Rich. How is that poſſible ? ſo muſt my Siſter,
The *Pallatine* himſelf, and *Alexander*,
Who drunk out of the bowl, be poyſoned too.
  Mentz. Nor is that hainous deed alone the cauſe,
Though cauſe enough to ruin Monarchies ;
He hath defil'd with luſt th' Imperial Bed,
And by the Emperour in the faƈt was ſlain.
  Collen. O worthy guiltleſs Prince ; O had he fled.
  Rich. But ſay where is the Empreſs, where's my Siſter.
  Mentz. Not burnt to aſhes yet, but ſhall be ſhortly.
  Rich. I hope her Majeſty will live to ſee
A hundred thouſand flattering turncoat ſlaves,
Such as your Holineſs, dye a ſhameful death.
  Brand. She is in priſon, and attends her tryal.
  Sax. O ſtrange heart-breaking miſchievous intents,
Give me my children if you love your lives,
No ſafety is in this enchanted Fort.
O ſee in happy hour there comes my Daughter,
And loving ſon, ſcapt from the Maſſacre.

Enter Edward *and* Hedewick.

  Edward. My body lives, although my heart be ſlain,
O Princes this hath been the diſmall'ſt night,
That ever eye of ſorrow did behold,
Here lay the *Palſgrave* weltring in his bloud,
Dying *Alphonſus* ſtanding over him,
Upon the other hand the King of *Bohem*,
Still looking when his poyſon'd bulk would break ;
But that which pierc'd my ſoul with natures touch
Was my tormented Aunt with blubberd cheeks,
Torn bloody Garments, and diſheveld' hair,
Waiting for death ; deſervedly or no,
That knows the ſearcher of all humane thoughts ;
For theſe devices are beyond my reach.

Emperour of Germany.

Saxon. **Saſt doch liebes doiſter who wart dow dieſelbienaß.**

Hede. **Als who who ſolt ich ſein ich war in bette.**

Saxon. **Wert dow allein ſo wart dow gar vorſchrocken.**

Hede. **Ich ha miſt audes gemeint dam das ich wolt allein geſchlaffne haben, abur umb mitternaiſt kam meiner bridegroom bunnðt ſchlaffet bey mir, bis wir mit dem getummel erwacht waren.**

Edward. What fays fhe ? came her Bridegroom to to her at midnight ?

Rich. Nephew, I fee you were not over-reach'd; Although fhe flipt out of your arms at firſt, You ceiz'd her furely, e're you left the chace.

Saxon. But left your Grace your Bride alone in Bed ?
Or did fhe run together in the Larum ?

Edward. Alas my Lords, this is no time to jeſt; I lay full fadly in my Bed alone, Not able for my life to fleep a wink, Till that the Larum Bell began to Ring, And then I ſtarted from my weary couch.

Saxon. How now? this rimes not with my daughters fpeech,
She fays you found her Bed, and lay with her.

Edward. Not I, your Highnefs did miſtake her words.

Collen. Deny it not Prince *Edward*, 'tis an honour.

Edward. My Lords I know no reaſon to deny it; T'have found her Bed, I would have given a million.

Saxon. **Hedewick der Furſt ſagt er hatt nicht be dir ſchlaſin.**

Hede. **Es gefelt ihm alſo zum ſagun aber ich habes woll gerfület.**
   Rich. She ſay's you are diſpos'd to jeſt with her;
But yeſternight ſhe felt it in good earneſt.
   Edward. Unckle theſe jeſts are too unſavorie,
Ill ſuited to theſe times, and pleaſe me not,
Lab ich bin you **geſhlapen** yeſternight.
   Hede. **I leff, warum ſult ihrs fragen.**
   Saxon. *Edward*, I tell thee 'tis no jeſting matter,
Say plainly, wa'ſt thou by her I or no?
   Edward. As I am Prince, true heir to *Englands* Crown,
I never toucht her body in a Bed.
   Hede. **Das hatte gethan order holle mich der dibell.**
   Rich. Nephew, take heed, you hear the Princeſs words.
   Edward. It is not ſhe, nor you, nor all the world,
Shall make me ſay I did anothers deed.
   Saxon. Anothers deed? 'what, think'ſt thou her a whore?

Saxon *ſtrikes* Edward.

   Edward. She may be Whore, and thou a villain too.
Strook me the Emperor I will ſtrike again.
   Collen. Content you Princes, buffet not like boys.
   Richard. Hold you the one, and I will hold the other.
   Hede. **O her got, help, help, oich arms kindt.**
   Saxon. Souldiers lay hands upon the Prince of *Wales*,
Convey him ſpeedily unto a priſon,
And load his Legs with grievous bolts of Iron;

Emperour of Germany.   255

Some bring the Whore my Daughter from my fight;
And thou fmooth Englifhman to thee I fpeak,
My hate extends to all thy Nation,
Pack thee out of my fight, and that with fpeed
Your Englifh practifes have all to long,
Muffled our *German* eyes, pack, pack I fay.
   Richard. Although your Grace have reafon for your rage,
Yet be not like a madman to your friends.
   Saxon. My friends? I fcorn the friendfhip of fuch mates,
That feek my Daughters fpoil, and my difhonour;
But I will teach the Boy another leffon,
His head fhall pay the ranfom of his fault.
   Richard. His head?
   Saxon. And thy head too, O how my heart doth fwell!
Was there no other Prince to mock but me?
Firft woo, then marry her, then lye with her,
And having had the pleafure of her Bed,
Call her a Whore in open audieuce,
None but a villain and a flave would do it,
My Lords of *Mentz*, of *Tryer*, and *Brandenburg*,
Make ope the Gates, receive me as a friend,
I'le be a fcourge unto the Englifh Nation.
   Mentz. Your Grace fhall be the welcom'ft gueft alive,
   Collen. None but a madman would do fuch a deed.
   Saxon. Then *Collen* count me mad, for I will do it.
I'le fet my life and Land upon the hazard,
But I will thoroughly found this deceit.
What will your Grace leave me or follow me?
   Collen. No *Saxon* know I will not follow thee.
And leave Prince *Richard* in fo great extreams.
   Saxon. Then I defy you both, and fo farwell.
   Rich. Yet *Saxon* hear me fpeak before thou go,
Look to the Princes life as to thine own,
Each perifht hair that falleth from his head

By thy default, fhall coft a *Saxon* City,
Henry of *England* will not lofe his heir,
And fo farwel and think upon my words.
　　Saxon.　Away, I do difdain to anfwer thee.
Pack thee with fhame again into thy Countrie,
I'le have a Cock-boat at my proper charge,
And fend th' Imperial Crown which thou haft won,
To *England* by Prince *Edward* after thee.　　*Exeunt.*
　　　　　　　　　　　　　　Man. Rich. and *Coll.*
　　Collen.　Anfwer him not Prince *Richard*, he is
　　　mad,
Choler and grief have rob'd him of his fenfes.
Like accident to this was never heard.
　　Rich.　Break heart and dye, flie hence my troubled
　　　fpirit,
I am not able for to underbear
The weight of forrow which doth bruze my foul,
O *Edward*, O fweet *Edward*, O my life.
O noble *Collen* laft of all my hopes,
The only friend in my extremities,
If thou doeft love me, as I know thou doeft,
Unfheath thy fword, and rid me of this forrow.
　　Collen.　Away with abject thoughts, fie Princely
　　　Richard,
Rouze up thy felf, and call thy fenfes home,
Shake of this bafe pufillanimitie,
And caft about to remedie thefe wrongs,
　　Richard.　Alas I fee no means of temedie.
　　Collen.　Then hearken to my Counfel and advice,
We will Intrench our felves not far from hence,
With thofe fmall pow'rs we have, and fend for more,
If they do make affault, we will defend ;
If violence be offer'd to the Prince,
We'l refcue him with venture of our lives ;
Let us with patience attend advantage,
Time may reveal the author of thefe treafons,
For why undoubtedly the fweet young Princefs,
Fowly beguild by night with cunning fhew,
Hath to fome villain loft her Maiden-head.

Emperour of Germany.

Rich. O that I knew the foul inceſtuous wretch,
Thus would I tear him with my teeth and nails.
Had *Saxon* ſenſe he would conceave ſo much,
And not revenge on guiltleſs *Edwards* life.
 Collen. Perſwade your ſelf he will be twice advis'd,
Before he offer wrong unto the Prince.
 Rich. In that good hope I will have patience.
Come gentle Prince whoſe pitty to a ſtranger
Is rare and admirable, not to be ſpoken.
England cannot requite this gentleneſs.
 Collen. Tuſh talk not of requital, let us go,
To fortifie our ſelves within our trench.   *Exeunt.*

Enter Alphonſo (*carried in the Couch*) Saxony, Mentz,
 Tryer, Brandenburg, Alexander.

 Alphon. O moſt exceſſive pain, O raging Fire!
Is burning *Cancer* or the *Scorpion*,
Deſcended from the Heavenly Zodiack,
To parch mine Entrals with a quenchleſs flame?
Drink, drink I ſay, give drink or I ſhall dye.
Fill a thouſand bowls of Wine, Water I ſay
Water from forth the cold *Tartarian* hils.
I feel th' aſcending flame lick up my blood,
Mine Entrals ſhrink together like a ſcrowl
Of burning parchment, and my Marrow fries,
Bring hugie Cakes of Ice, and Flakes of Snow.
That I may drink of them being diſſolved.
 Saxon. We do beſeech your Majeſtie have
  patience,
 Alphon. Had I but drunk an ordinary poyſon,
The ſight of thee great Duke of *Saxony*,
My friend in death, in life my greateſt foe,
Might both allay the venom and the torment;
But that adulterous *Palſgrave* and my Wife,
Upon whoſe life and ſoul I vengeance cry,
Gave me a mineral not to be digeſted,
Which burning eats, and eating burns my heart.
My Lord of *Tryer*, run to the King of *Bohem*,

R

Commend me to him, ask him how he fares,
None but my felf can rightly pitty him ;
For none but we have fympathie of pains.
Tell him when he is dead, my time's not long,
And when I dye bid him prepare to follow.
Exit Tryer.
Now, now it works a frefh ; are you my friends ?
Then throw me on the cold fwift running *Rhyn*,
And let me bath there for an hour or two,
I cannot bear this pain.
　　Mentz. O would th' unpartial fates afflict on me,
Thefe deadly pains, and eafe my Emperour,
How willing would I bear them for his fake.
　　Alphon. O *Mentz*, I would not wifh unto a Dog,
The leaft of thoufand torments that afflict me,
Much lefs unto your Princely holinefs.
See, fee my Lord of *Mentz*, he points at you.
　　Mentz. It is your fantafie and nothing elfe ;
But were death here, I would difpute with him,
And tell him to his teeth he doth unjuftice,
To take your Majefty in the prime of youth ;
Such wither'd rotten branches as my felf,
Should firft be lopt, had he not partial hands ;
And here I do proteft upon my Knee,
I would as willingly now leave my life,
To fave my King and Emperour alive,
As erft my mother brought me to the world.
　　Brand. My Lord of *Mentz*, this flattery is too grofs,
A Prince of your experience and calling,
Should not fo fondly call the Heavens to witnefs.
　　Mentz. Think you my Lord, I would not hold my word ?
　　Brand. You know my Lord, death is a bitter gueft.
　　Mentz. To eafe his pain and fave my Emperour,
I fweetly would embrace that bitternefs.
　　Alex. If I were death, I knew what I would do.
　　Mentz. But fee, his Majefty is faln a fleep,

Ah me, I fear it is a dying flumber.
 Alphon. My Lord of *Saxonie* do you hear this
   jeft.
 Saxon. What fhould I hear my Lord?
 Alphon. Do you not hear
How loudly death proclames it in mine ears,
Swearing by trophies, Tombs and deadmens Graves,
If I have any friend fo dear to me,
That to excufe my life will lofe his own,
I fhall be prefently reftor'd to health.

Enter Tryer.

Mentz. I would he durft make good his promifes.
 Alphon. My Lord of *Tryer*, how fares my fellow
   Emperour?
 Tryer. His Majefty is eas'd of all his pains.
 Alphon. O happy news, now I have hope of health.
 Mentz. My joyful heart doth fpring within my
   bodie,
To hear thofe words,
Comfort your Majeftie I will excufe you,
Or at the leaft will bear you Company.
 Alphon. My hope is vain, now, now my heart will
   break,
My Lord of *Tryer* you did but flatter me,
Tell me the truth, how fares his Majeftie.
 Tryer. I told your Highnefs, eas'd of all his pain.
 Alphon. I underftand thee now, he's eas'd by
   death,
And now I feel an alteration;
Farewel fweet Lords, farewel my Lord of *Mentz,*
The trueft friend that ever earth did bear,
Live long in happinefs to revenge my death,
Upon my Wife and all the Englifh brood.
My Lord of *Saxonie* your Grace hath caufe.
 Mentz. I dare thee death to take away my life.
Some charitable hand that loves his Prince.
And hath the heart, draw forth his Sword and rid me
   of my life.

Alex. I love my Prince, and have the heart to do it.
Mentz. O ſtay a while.
Alex. Nay now it is to late.
Bran. Villain what haſt thou done ? th'aſt ſlain a Prince.
Alex. I did no more than he intreated me,
Alphon. How now, what make I in my Couch ſo late ?
Princes why ſtand you ſo gazing about me ?
Or who is that lies ſlain before my face ?
O I have wrong, my ſoul was half in Heaven,
His holineſs did know the joys above,
And therefore is aſcended in my ſtead.
Come Princes let us bear the body hence ;
I'le ſpend a Million to embalm the ſame.
Let all the Bels within the Empire Ring,
Let Maſs be ſaid in every Church and Chappel,
And that I may perform my lateſt vow,
I will procure ſo much by Gold or friends,
That my ſweet *Mentz* ſhall be Canonized,
And numbred in the Bed-role of the Saints,
I hope the Pope will not deny it me,
I'le build a Church in honour of thy name,
Within the antient famous Citie *Mentz,*
Fairer than any one in *Germany,*
There ſhalt thou be interrd with Kingly Pomp,
Over thy Tomb ſhall hang a ſacred Lamp,
Which till the day of doom ſhall ever burn,
Yea after ages ſhall ſpeak of thy renown,
And go a Pilgrimage to thy ſacred Tomb.
Grief ſtops my voice, who loves his Emperour,
Lay to his helping hand and bear him hence,
Sweet Father and redeemer of my life. *Exeunt.*

Manet *Alexander.*

Alex. Now is my Lord ſole Emperour of *Rome,*
And three Conſpirators of my Fathers death,

Emperour of Germany.

Are cunningly fent unto Heaven or Hell;
Like fubtilty to this was never feen.
Alas poor *Mentz* I pittying thy prayers,
Could do no lefs than lend a helping hand,
Thou wert a famous flatterer in thy life,
And now haft reapt the fruits thereof in death;
But thou fhalt be rewarded like a Saint,
With Maffes, Bels, dirges and burning Lamps,
'Tis good, I envie not thy happinefs:
But ah the fweet remembrance of that night,
That night I mean of fweetnefs and of ftealth,
When for a Prince, a Princefs did imbrace me,
Paying the firft fruits of her Marriage Bed,
Makes me forget all other accidents.
O *Saxon* I would willingly forgive,
The deadly trefpafs of my Fathers death,
So I might have thy Daughter to my Wife,
And to be plain, I have beft right unto her,
And love her beft, and have deferv'd her beft;
But thou art fond to think on fuch a match;
Thou muft imagin nothing but revenge,
And if my computation fail me not.
Ere long I fhall be thorowly reveng'd. *Exit.*

Enter the Duke of Saxon, and Hedewick with the Child.

Saxon. Come forth thou perfect map of miferie,
Defolate Daughter and diftreffed Mother,
In whom the Father and the Son are curft;
Thus once again we will affay the Prince.
'T may be the fight of his own flefh and blood
Will now at laft pierce his obdurate heart.
Jailor how fares it with thy prifoner?
Let him appear upon the battlements.

Hede. 𝕺 mein deere vatter, ich habe in dis lang lang 30. weeken, welche mich duncket fein 40. jahr gewefen, ein litte

𝕰𝖓𝖌𝖑𝖎𝖘𝖈𝖍 𝖌𝖊𝖑𝖊𝖗𝖓𝖊𝖙, 𝖇𝖓𝖉 𝖎𝖈𝖍 𝖍𝖔𝖕𝖊, 𝖍𝖊 𝖜𝖎𝖑𝖑 𝖒𝖊 𝖇𝖊𝖗𝖘𝖙𝖔𝖍𝖓, 𝖇𝖓𝖉 𝖘𝖍𝖊𝖜 𝖒𝖊 𝖆 𝖑𝖎𝖙𝖙𝖊 𝖕𝖎𝖙𝖙𝖎𝖊.

Enter Edward *on the Walls and Jailor.*

Saxon. Good morrow to your grace *Edward of Wales,*
Son and immediate Heir to *Henry* the third,
King of *England* and Lord of *Ireland,*
Thy Fathers comfort, and the peoples hope ;
'Tis not in mockage nor at unawares,
That I am ceremonious to repeat
Thy high defcent joynd with thy Kingly might ;
But therewithall to intimate unto thee
What God expecteth from the higher powers,
Juftice, and mercie, truth, fobrietie,
Relenting hearts, hands innocent of blood.
Princes are Gods chief fubftitutes on earth,
And fhould be Lamps unto the common fort.
But you will fay I am become a Preacher,
No, Prince, I am an humble fuppliant,
And to prepare thine ears make this exordium,
To pierce thine eyes and heart, behold this fpectacle,
Three Generations of the *Saxon* blood,
Defcended lineallie from forth my Loyns,
Kneeling and crying to thy mightinefs ;
Firft look on me, and think what I have been,
For nowI think my felf of no account,
Next *Cæfar,* greateft man in *Germanie,*
Neerly a lyed, and ever friend to *England* ;
But Womens fighs move more in manly hearts,
O fee the hands fhe elevates to Heaven,
Behold thofe eyes that whilome were thy joyes,
Uttering domb eloquence in Chriftal tears ;
If thefe exclames and fights be ordinarie,
Then look with pittie on thy other felf,
This is thy flefh, and blood, bone of thy bone,
A goodly Boy the Image of his fire.

Turn'ſt thou away ? O were thy Father here,
He would, as I do, take him in his arms,
And ſweetly kiſs his Grand-child in the face.
O *Edward* too young in experience,
That canſt not look into the grievous wrack,
Enſuing this thy obſtinate deniall ;
O *Edward* too young in experience,
That canſt not ſee into the future good,
Enſuing thy moſt juſt acknowledgement ;
Hear me thy trueſt friend, I will repeat them ;
For good thou haſt an Heir indubitate,
Whoſe eyes already ſparckle Majeſty,
Born in true Wedlock of a Princely Mother,
And all the *German* Princes to thy friends ;
Where on the contrary thine eyes ſhall ſee,
The ſpeedy Tragedie of thee and thine ;
Like *Athamas* firſt will I ceize upon
Thy young unchriſtened and deſpiſed Son,
And with his guiltleſs brains bepaint the Stones ;
Then like *Virginius* will I kill my Child,
Unto thine eyes a pleaſing ſpectacle ;
Yet ſhall it be a momentarie pleaſure,
Henry of *England* ſhall mourn with me ;
For thou thy ſelf *Edward* ſhall make the third,
And be an actor in this bloody Scean.

Hede. Ah myne ſeete Edouart, mein herzkin, myne ſcherzkin, mein herziges, einiges herz, mein allerleibeſt husband, I preedee mein leeſe ſee me friendlich one, good ſeete harte tell de trut: and at leſt to me, and dyne allerleefeſt ſchild ſhew pitty! dan ich bin dyne, und dow biſt myne, dow haſt me geben ein kindelein ; O Edouart, ſeete, Edouart erbarmet ſein!

Edw. O Hedewick peace, thy speeches pierce my soul.

Hede. Hedewick doe yow excellencie hight me Hedewick leete Edouart yow sweete ich bin yowr allerlieueste wife.

Edward. The Priest I must confess made thee my Wife,
Curst be the damned villanous adulterer,
That with so fowl a blot divorc'd our love.

Hede. O mein allerliebesser, hieborne Furst bnd Herr, dinck dat unser Herr Gott sitts in himmells trone, and sees dat hart bnd will my cause woll recken:

Saxon. Edward hold me not up with long delays;
But quickly say, wilt thou confess the truth?

Edward. As true as I am born of Kingly Linage,
And am the best *Plantagenet* next my Father,
I never carnallie did touch her body.

Saxon. Edward this answer had we long ago,
Seest thou this brat? speak quickly or he dyes.

Edward. His death will be more piercing to thine eyes,
Than unto mine, he is not of my kin.

Hede. O Father, O myne Uatter spare myne kindt
O Edouart O Prince Edouart spreak now oder nimmermehr die kindt ist mein, it soll nicht sterben:

Saxon. Have I dishonoured my self so much,
To bow my Knee to thee, which never bow'd
But to my God, and am I thus rewarded?
Is he not thine? speak murderous-minded Prince.

Edward. O *Saxon*, *Saxon* mitigate thy rage.

Emperour of Germany.

First thy exceeding great humilitie,
When to thy captive prisoner thou didst kneel,
Had almost made my lying tongue confess,
The deed which I protest I never did;
But thy not causeless furious madding humour,
Together with thy Daughters pitious cryes,
Whom as my life and soul I dearly love,
Had thorowly almost perswaded me,
To save her honour and belie my self,
And were I not a Prince of so high blood,
And Bastards have no scepter-bearing hands,
I would in silence smother up this blot,
And in compassion of thy Daughters wrong,
Be counted Father to an others Child;
For why my soul knows her unguiltiness.

 Saxon. Smooth words in bitter sense; is thine answer?

Hede. **Ey batter geue mir mein kindt, die kind ist mein.**

 Saxon. **Das weis ich woll, er sagt es ist nicht sein;** therefore it dyes.

     He dashes out the Childs brains.

Hede. **O Got in seinem trone, O mein kindt mein kindt.**

 Saxon. There murderer take his head, and breathless lymbs,
Ther's flesh enough, bury it in thy bowels,
Eat that, or dye for hunger, I protest,
Thou getst no other food till that be spent.
And now to thee lewd Whore, dishonour'd strumpet,
Thy turn is next, therefore prepare to dye.

 Edward. O mighty Duke of *Saxon,* spare thy Child.

 Sax. She is thy Wife *Edward,* and thou shouldst spare her.

One Gracious word of thine will save her life.

Edward. I do confefs *Saxon* fhe is mine own,
As I have marryed her, I will live with her,
Comfort thy felf fweet *Hedewick* and fweet Wife.

Hede. Ach, ach vnd wehe, warumb fagt your Excellence nicht fo before, now ist to late, vnfer arme kindt ist kilt.

Edward. Though thou be mine, and I do pittie thee,
I would not Nurfe a Baftard for a Son.

Hede. O Edouard now ich mark your mennng ich fholdt be your whore, mein Vatter ich begehr upon meine knee, faft mich lieber fterben, ade falce Edouart, falce Prince, ich begehrs nicht.

Saxon. Unprincely thoughts do hammer in thy head,
I'ft not enough that thou haft fham'd her once,
And feen the Baftard torn before thy face;
But thou wouldft get more brats for Butcherie?
No *Hedewick* thou fhalt not live the day.

Hede. O Herr Gott, nimb meine feele in deiner henden.

Saxon. It is thy hand that gives this deadly ftroak.

Hede. O Herr Sabote, das mein vnfchuldt an tag kommen mocht.

Edward. Her blood be on that wretched villains head,
That is the caufe of all this mifery.

Saxon. Now murderous-minded Prince, haft thou beheld
Vpon my Child and Childs Child, thy defire,
Swear to thy felf, that here I firmly fwear,
That thou fhall furely follow her to morrow,
In Company of thy adulterous Aunt,

Emperour of Germany.

Jaylor convey him to his Dungeon,
If he be hungrie, I have thrown him meat,
If thirſtie let him ſuck the newly born lymbs.
  Edward. O Heavens and Heavenly powers, if you be juſt,
Reward the author of this wickedneſs.
                              Exit Edw. *&* Jaoler.

             Enter Alexander.

  Alex. To arms great Duke of *Saxonie*, to arms,
My Lord of *Collen*, and the Earl of *Cornwall*,
In reſcue of Prince *Edward* and the Empreſs,
Have levy'd freſh supplies, and preſently
Will bid you battail in the open Field.
  Sax. They never could have come in fitter time ;
Thirſt they for blood ? and they ſhall quench their thirſt.
  Alex. O piteous ſpectacle ! poor Princeſs *Hedewick*.
  Sax. Stand not to pittie, lend a helping hand.
  Alex. What ſlave hath murdered this guiltleſs Child ?
  Sax. What ? dar'ſt thou call me ſlave unto my face ?
I tell thee villain, I have done this deed.
And ſeeing the Father and the Grand ſires heart,
Can give conſent and execute their own,
Wherefore ſhould ſuch a raſcal as thy ſelf
Preſume to pittie them, whom we have ſlain ?
  Alex. Pardon me, if it be preſumption
To pittie them, I will preſume no more.
  Sax. Then help, I long to be amidſt my foes.
                                    Exeunt.

Alarum and Retreat.   ACT. V.

Enter Richard *and* Collen *with Drums and Souldiers.*

 Richard. What means your Excellence to found retreat?
This is the day of doom unto our Friends;
Before Sun set, my Sister, and my Nephew,
Vnless we rescue them must lose their lives:
The cause admits no dalliance nor delay.
He that so tyrant-like hath slain his own,
Will take no pittie on a strangers blood.
 Collen. At my entreaty e're we strike the battail,
Let's summon out our enemies to a parle.
Words spoken in time, have vertue, power, and price,
And mildness may prevail and take effect,
When dynt of Sword perhaps will aggravate.
 Rich. Then found a Parly to fulfill your mind,
Although I know no good can follow it.   *A Parley.*

Enter Alphonso, *Empress*, Saxon, Edward *prisoner*, Tryer, Brandenburg, Alexander *and Souldiers.*

 Alphon. Why now now Emperour that should have been,
Are these the English Generals bravado's?
Make you assault so hotly at the first,
And in the self same moment found retreat?
To let you know, that neither War nor words,
Hove power for to divert their fatall doom,
Thus are we both resolv'd; if we tryumph,
And by the right and justice of our cause
Obtain the victorie, as I doubt it not,
Then both of you shall bear them Company,
And e're Sun set we will perform our oaths,
With just effusion of their guilty bloods;

If you be Conquerours, and we overcome,
Carry not that conceit to refcue them,
My felf will be the Executioner,
And with thefe Poynards fruftrate all your hopes,
Making you tryumph in a bloodie Field.
 Saxon. To put you out of doubt that we intend it,
Pleafe it your Majefty to take your Seate,
And make a demonftration of your meaning.
 Alphon. Firft on my right hand bind the Englifh
  Whore,
That venemous Serpent nurft within my breaft
To fuck the vitall bloud out of my veins,
My Emprefs muft have fome preheminence,
Efpecially at fuch a bloodie Banquet,
Her State, and love to me deferves no lefs.
 Saxon. That to Prince *Edward* I may fhew my love,
And do the lateft honour to his State,
Thefe hands of mine that never chained any,
Shall faften him in fetters to the Chair.
Now Princes are you ready for the battail?
 Collen. Now art thou right the picture of thy felf,
Seated in height of all thy Tyrannie;
But tell us what intends this fpectacle.
 Alphon. To make the certaintie of their deaths
  more plain,
And Cancel all your hopes to fave their lives,
While *Saxon* leads the troups into the Field,
Thus will I vex their fouls, with fight of death,
Loudly exclaming in their half dead ears;
That if we win they fhall have companie,
Viz. The Englifh Emperour,
And you my Lord Archbifhop of *Collen*,
If we be vanquifht, then they muft expect
Speedy difpatch from thefe two Daggers points.
 Collen. What canft thou tyrant then expect but
  death?
 Alphon. Tufh hear me out, that hand which fhed
  their blood,
Can do the like to rid me out of bonds.

Rich. But that's a damned refolution.
Alphon. So muft this defperate difeafe be cur'd.
Rich. O *Saxon* I'le yield my felf and all my power,
To fave my Nephew, though my Sifter dye.
Sax. Thy Brothers Kingdom fhall not fave his life.
Edward. Uncle, you fee thefe favage minded men.
Will have no other ranfome but my blood,
England hath Heirs, though I be never King,
And hearts and hands to fcourge this tyrannie,
And fo farewel.
Emp. A thoufand times farewel,
Sweet Brother *Richard* and brave Prince of *Collen.*
Sax. What *Richard*, hath this object pierc'd thy heart?
By this imagine how it went with me,
When yefterday I flew my Children.
Rich. O *Saxon* I entreat thee on my Knees.
Sax. Thou fhalt obtain like mercy with thy kneeling,
As lately I obtained at *Edward's* hands.
Rich. Pitty the tears I powr before thy feet.
Sax. Pitty thofe tears? why I fhed bloudie tears.
Rich. I'le do the like to fave Prince *Edwards* life.
Sax. Then like a Warrior fpill it in the Field,
My griefull anger cannot be appeaz'd,
By facrifice of any but himfelf.
Thou haft difhonour'd me, and thou fhalt dye;
Therefore alarum, alarum to the fight,
That thoufands more may bear thee company.
Rich. Nephew and Sifter now farewell for ever.
Ed. Heaven and the Right prevail, and let me die;
Uncle farewell.
Emp. Brother farewell untill wee meet in Heaven.
Exeunt. Manent Alphon. Edw. Emp. Alex.
Alphon. Here's farewell Brother, Nephew, Vncle, Aunt,
As if in thoufand years you fhould not meet;
Good Nephew, and good Aunt content your felves,
The Sword of *Saxon* and thefe Daggers-points,

Emperour of Germany.

Before the Evening-Star doth ſhew it ſelf,
Will take ſufficient order for your meeting.
But *Alexander*, my truſtie *Alexander*,
Run to the Watch-Tow'r as I pointed thee,
And by thy life I charge thee look unto it
Thou be the firſt to bring me certain word
If we be Conquerors, or Conquered.
   Alex. With carefull ſpeed I will perform this charge.
Exit.
   Alphon. Now have I leaſure yet to talk with you.
Fair *Iſabel.* the *Palſgrave*'s Paramour,
Wherein was he a better man than I?
Or wherfore ſhould thy love to him, effect
Such deadly hate unto thy Emperour?
Yet welfare wenches that can love Good fellows,
And not mix Murder with Adulterie.
   Emp. Great Emperor, I dare not call you Husband,
Your Conſcience knows my hearts unguiltineſs.
   Alpho. Didſt thou not poiſon or conſent to poiſon us?
   Emp. Should any but your Highneſs tell me ſo,
I ſhould forget my patience at my death,
And call him Villain, Liar, Murderer.
   Alphon. She that doth ſo miſcall me at her end,
Edward I prethee ſpeak thy Conſcience,
Thinkſt thou not that in her proſperitie
Sh'hath vext my Soul with bitter Words and Deeds?
O Prince of *England* I do count thee wiſe
That thou wilt not be cumber'd with a wife,
When thou hadſt ſtoln her daintie roſe Corance,
And pluck'd the flow'r of her virginitie.
   Edw. Tyrant of *Spain* thou lieſt in thy throat.
   Alpho. Good words, thou feeſt thy life is in our hands.
   Edw. I ſee thou art become a common Hangman,
An Office farre more fitting to thy mind
Than princelie to the Imperiall dignitie.
   Alphon. I do not exerciſe on common perſons,

Your Highnefs is a Prince, and fhe an Emprefs,
I therefore count not of a dignitie.
Hark *Edward* how they labour all in vain,
With lofs of many a valiant Soldiers life,
To refcue them whom Heaven and we have doom'd
Doft thou not tremble when thou think'ft upon't ?
 Edw. Let guiltie minds tremble at fight of Death,
My heart is of the nature of the Palm,
Not to be broken, till the higheft Bud
Be bent and ti'd unto the loweft Root;
I rather wonder that thy Tyrants heart
Can give confent that thofe thy Butcherous hands
Should offer violence to thy Flefh and Blood.
See how her guiltlefs innocence doth plead
In filent Oratorie of her chafteft tears.
 Alphon. Thofe tears proceed from Fury and curft
 heart.
I know the ftomach of your Englifh Dames.
 Emp. No Emperour, thefe tears proceed from
 grief.
 Alphon. Grief that thou canft not be reveng'd
of Vs.
 Emp. Grief that your Highnefs is fo ill advis'd,
To offer violence to my Nephew *Edward*;
Since then there muft be facrifice of Blood,
Let my heart-blood fave both your bloods unfpilt,
For of his death, thy Heart muft pay the guilt.
 Edw. No Aunt, I will not buy my life fo dear:
Therefore *Alphonfo* if thou beeft a man
Shed manly blood, and let me end this ftrife.
 Alphon. Here's ftraining curt'fie at a bitter Feaft,
Content thee Emprefs for thou art my Wife,
Thou fhalt obtain thy Boon and die the death,
And for it were unprincely to deny
So flight requeft unto fo great a Lord,
Edward fhall bear thee company in Death. *A Retreat.*
But hark the heat of battail hath an end;
One fide or other hath the victory, *Enter Alxeander.*
And fee where *Alexander* fweating comes;

Emperour of Germany.

Speak man what newes fpeak, fhall I die or live?
Shall I ftab fure, or els prolong their lives
To grievous Torments? fpeak, am I Conquerour?
What, hath thy haft bereft thee of thy fpeech?
Haft thou not breath to fpeak one fillable?
O fpeak, thy dalliance kills me, wonn or loft? *Amaz'd*
    Alex. Loft.   *lets fall the*
    Alphon. Ah me my Senfes fail! my fight *Daggers.*
is gon.
    Alex. Will not your Grace difpatch the Strumpet
    Queen?
Shall fhe then live, and we be doom'd to death?
Is your Heart faint, or is your Hand too weak?
Shall fervill fear break your fo facred Oaths?
Me thinks an Emperour fhould hold his word;
Give me the Weapons I will foon difpatch them,
My Fathers yelling Ghoft cries for revenge,
His Blood within my Veins boyls for revenge;
O give me leave *Cæfar* to take revenge.
    Alphon. Vpon condition that thou wilt proteft
To take revenge upon the Murtherers,
Without refpect of dignity, or State,
Afflicted, fpeedy, pittilefs Revenge,
I will commit this Dagger to thy truft,
And give thee leave to execute thy Will.
    Alex. What need I here reiterate the Deeds
Which deadly forrow made me perpetrate?
How neer did I entrap Prince *Richard's* life?
How fure fet I the Knife to *Mentz* his heart?
How cunninglie was *Palfgrave* doom'd to death?
How fubtilly was *Bohem* poifoned?
How flily did I fatisfie my luft
Commixing dulcet Love with deadly Hate,
When Princeffe *Hedwick* loft her Maidenhead,
Sweetly embracing me for *Englands* Heir?
    Edw. O execrable deeds!
    Emp. O falvage mind!
    Alex. Edward, I give thee leave to hear of this,
But will forbid the blabbing of your tongue.

ALPHONSUS

Now gratious Lord and facred Emperour,
Your highnefs knowing thefe and many more,
Which fearles pregnancie hath wrought in me,
You do me wrong to doubt that I will dive
Into their hearts that have not fpar'd their betters,
Be therefore fuddain left we die our felves.
I know the Conquerour hafts to refcue them.

Alphon. Thy Reafons are effectuall, take this Dagger;
Yet pawfe a while.

Emp. Sweet Nephew now farewell.

Alphon. They are moft dear to me whom thou muft kill.

Edward. Hark Aunt he now begins to pittie you.

Alex. But they confented to my Fathers death.

Alphon. More then confented, they did execute.

Emp. I will not make his Majeftie a Lyar,
I kill'd thy Father, therefore let me die,
But fave the life of this unguilty Prince.

Edward. I kill'd thy Father, therefore let me die,
But fave the life of this unguiltie Emprefs.

Alphon. Hark thou to me, and think their words as wind.
I kill'd thy Father, therfore let me die,
And fave the lives of thefe two guiltlefs Princes.
Art thou amaz'd to hear what I have faid?
There, take the weapon, now revenge at full
Thy Fathers death, and thofe my dire deceits
That made thee murtherer of fo many Souls.

Alex. O Emperour, how cunningly wouldft thou entrap
My fimple youth to credit Fictions?
Thou kill my Father, no, no Emperour,
Cæfar did love *Lorentzo* all to dearly:
Seeing thy Forces now are vanquifhed,
Fruftrate thy hopes, thy Highnefs like to fall
Into the cruel and revengefull hands
Of mercilefs incenfed Enemies,
Like *Caius Caffius* wearie of thy life,

Now wouldſt thou make thy Page an inſtrument
By ſuddain ſtroak to rid thee of thy bonds.
 Alphon. Haſt thou forgotten how that very night
Thy Father dy'd, I took the Maſter-Key,
And with a lighted Torch walk'd through the Courts.
 Alex. I muſt remember that, for to my death
I never ſhall forget the ſlighteſt deed,
Which on that diſmall Night or Day I did.
 Alphon. Thou waſt no ſooner in thy reſtfull Bed,
But I diſturb'd thy Father of his reſt,
And to be ſhort, not that I hated him,
But for he knew my deepeſt Secrets,
With cunning Poiſon I did end his life:
Art thou his Son? expreſs it with a Stabb,
And make account if I had proſpered,
Thy date was out, thou waſt already doom'd,
Thou knewſt too much of me to live with me.
 Alex. What wonders do I hear great Emperour?
Not that I do ſtedfaſtlie believe
That thou didſt murder my beloved Father;
But in meer pittie of thy vanquiſh'd ſtate
I undertake this execution:
Yet, for I fear the ſparkling Majeſtie
Which iſſues from thy moſt Imperial eyes
May ſtrike relenting Paſſion to my heart,
And after wound receiv'd from fainting hand,
Thou fall halfe dead among thine Enemies,
I crave thy Highneſs leave to bind thee firſt.
 Alphon. Then bind me quickly, uſe me as thou pleaſe
 Emp. O Villain, wilt thou kill thy Sovereign?
 Alex. Your Highneſs ſees that I am forc'd unto it.
 Alphon. Fair Empreſs, I ſhame to aſk thee pardon,
Whom I have wrong'd ſo many thouſand waies.
 Emp. Dread Lord and Huſband, leave theſe deſperat thoughts,
Doubt not the Princes may be reconcil'd.
 Alex. 'T may be the Princes will be reconcil'd,
But what is that to me? all Potentates on Earth

Can neuer reconcile my grieved Soul.
Thou flew'ft my Father, thou didft make this hand
Mad with Revenge to murther Innocents,
Now hear, how in the height of all thy pride
The rightfull Gods have powr'd their juftfull wrath
Upon thy Tyrants head, Devill as thou art.
And fav'd by miracle thefe Princes lives;
For know, thy fide hath got the Victory;
Saxon triumphs over his deareft friends;
Richard and *Collen*, both are Prifoners,
And every thing hath forted to thy wifh;
Only hath Heaven put it in my mind
(for he alone directed then my thoughts
Although my meaning was moft mifchievous)
To tell thee thou hadft loft, in certain hope
That fuddainly thou wouldft have flain them both,
For if the Princes came to talk about it,
I greatly feard their lives might be prolong'd.
Art thou not mad to think on this deceit?
Ile make the madder, with tormenting thee.
I tell thee Arch-Thief, Villain, Murtherer,
Thy Forces have obtaind the Victory,
Victory leads thy Foes in captive bands;
This Victory hath crown'd thee Emperour,
Only my felf have vanquifht Victory,
And triumph in the Victors overthrow.
   Alphon. O *Alexander* fpare thy Princes life.
   Alex. Even now thou didft entreat the contrary.
   Alphon. Think what I am that begg my life of thee.
   Alex. Think what he was whom thou haft doom'd to death.
But leaft the Princes do furprize us here
Before I have perform'd my ftrange revenge,
I will be fuddain in the execution.
   Alphon. I will accept any condition.
   Alex. Then in the prefence of the Emperefs,
The captive Prince of *England*, and my felf,
Forfwear the joyes of Heaven, the fight of God,

Emperour of Germany. 277

Thy Souls falvation, and thy Saviour Chrift,
Damning thy Soul to endlefs pains of Hell.
Do this or die upon my Rapiers point.
   Emp. Sweet Lord and Husband, fpit in's face.
Die like a man, and live not like a Devill.
   Alex. What ? wilt thou fave thy life, and damn thy Soul ?
   Alph. O hold thy hand, *Alphonfus* doth renounce.
   Edward. Aunt ftop your ears, hear not this Blafphemy.
   Empr. Sweet Husband think that Chrift did dy for thee.
   Alphon. Alphonfus doth renounce the joyes of Heaven,
The fight of Angells and his Saviours blood,
And gives his Soul unto the Devills power.
   Alex. Thus will I make delivery of the Deed,
Die and be damn'd, now am I fatisfied.
   Edward. O damned Mifcreant, what haft thou done ?
   Alex. When I have leafure I will anfwer thee:
Mean while I'le take my heels and fave my felf.
If I be ever call'd in queftion,
I hope your Majefties will fave my life,
You have fo happily preferved yours;
Did I not think it, both of you fhould die.
                                             Exit Alex.

Enter Saxon, Branden. Tryer, (Richard *and* Collen *as prifoners*) *and Soldiers.*

   Saxon. Bring forth thefe daring Champions to the Block,
Comfort your felves you fhall have company.
Great Emperor, where is his Majeftie ?
What bloody fpectacle do I behold ?
   Emp. Revenge, revenge, O *Saxon, Brandenburg,*
My Lord is flain, *Cæfar* is doom'd to death.

Edward. Princes make haste, follow the murtherer.

Saxon. Is *Cæsar* slain?

Edward. Follow the Murtherer.

Emp. Why stand you gasing on an other thus? Follow the Murtherer.

Saxon. What Murtherer?

Edward. The villain *Alexander* hath slain his Lord,
Make after him with speed, so shall you hear
Such villanie as you have never heard.

Brand. My Lord of *Tryer*, we both with our light Horse
Will scoure the Coasts and quickly bring him in.

Saxon. That can your Excellence alone perform,
Stay you my Lord, and guard the Prisoners,
While I, alas, unhappiest Prince alive,
Over his Trunk consume my self in Tears.
Hath *Alexander* done this damned deed?
That cannot be, why should he slay his Lord?
O cruel Fate, O miserable me!
Me thinks I now present *Mark Antony*,
Folding dead *Julius Cæsar* in mine arms.
No, no, I rather will present *Achilles*,
And on *Patroclus* Tomb do sacrifise.
Let me be spurn'd and hated as a Dogg,
But I perform more direfull bloody Rites
Than *Thetis* Son for *Menetiades*.

Edward. Leave mourning for thy Foes, pitty thy Friends.

Sax. Friends have I none, and that which grieves my Soul,
Is want of Foes to work my wreak upon;
But were you Traitors 4, four hundred thousand,
Then might I satisfie my self with Blood.

Enter Brandenb. Alexand. *and Soldiers.*

Saxon. See *Alexander* where *Cæsar* lieth slain,
The guilt whereof the Traitors cast on thee;

Emperour of Germany. 279

Speak, canſt thou tell who ſlew thy Soveraign ?
   Alexan. Why who but I? how ſhould I curſe my
ſelf
If any but my ſelf had done this deed?
This happy hand, bleſt be my hand therefore,
Reveng'd my Fathers death upon his Soul:
And *Saxon* thou haſt cauſe to curſe and bann
That he is dead, before thou didſt inflict
Torments on him that ſo hath torn thy heart.
   Saxon. What Myſteries are theſe?
   Bran. Princes, can you inform us of the Truth?
   Edward. The Deed's ſo heinous that my faltering
tongue
Abhorres the utterance. Yet I muſt tell it.
   Alex. Your Highneſs ſhall not need to take the
pains,
What you abhorr to tell, I joy to tell,
Therefore be ſilent and give audience.
You mighty men, and Rulers of the Earth,
Prepare your Ears to hear of Stratagems
Whoſe dire effects have gaul'd your princely hearts,
Confounded your conceits, muffled your eyes:
Firſt to begin this villanous Fiend of Hell
Murther'd my Father, ſleeping in his Chair,
The reaſon why, becauſe he only knew
All Plotts, and complots of his villanie;
His death was made the Baſis and the Ground
Of every miſchief that hath troubled you.
   Saxon. If thou, thy Father and thy Progenie
Were hang'd and burnt, and broken on the Wheel,
How could their deaths heap miſchief on our
heads?
   Alex. And if you will not hear the Reaſon
chuſe.
I tell thee I have ſlain an Emperour,
And thereby think my ſelf as good a man
As thou, or any man in Chriſtendom,
Thou ſhalt entreat me ere I tell thee more.
   Brand. Proceed.

Alex. Not I.

Saxon. I prethe now proceed.

Alex. Since you intreat you then, I will proceed.
This murtherous Devill having flain my Father,
Buz'd cunningly into my credulous ears,
That by a General Councell of the States,
And as it were by Act of Parlement,
The feven Electors had fet down his death,
And made the Emprefs Executioner,
Transferring all the guilt from him to you.
This I believ'd, and firft did fet upon
The life of Princely *Richard*, by the Boors,
But how my purpofe faild in that, his Grace beft knows;
Next, by a double intricate deceit,
Midft all his Mirth was *Bohem* poyfoned,
And good old *Mentz* to fave *Alphonfo's* life,
(Who at that inftant was in perfect health)
Twixt jeft and earneft was made a Sacrifice;
As for the *Palatine*, your Graces knew
His Highnefs and the Queens unguiltines;
But now my Lord of *Saxon* hark to me,
Father of *Saxon* fhould I rather call you,
Twas I that made your Grace a Grandfather:
Prince *Edward* plow'd the ground, I fow'd the Seed,
Poor *Hedewick* bore the moft unhappy fruit,
Created in a moft unluckie hour,
To a moft violent and untimely death.

Sax. O loathfome Villain, O detefted deeds,
O guiltlefs Prince, O me moft miferable.

Brand. But tell us who reveal'd to thee at laft
This fhamefull guilt, and our unguiltinefs?

Alex. Why that's the wonder Lords, and thus it was:
When like a tyrant he had tane his feat,
And that the furie of the Fight began,

Emperour of Germany.

Upon the higheſt Watch-Tow'r of the Fort,
It was my office to behold alofft
The Warres event, and having ſeen the end,
I ſaw how Victory with equal wings
Hang hovering 'twixt the Battails here and there,
Till at the laſt, the Engliſh Lyons fled,
And *Saxon*'s ſide obtain'd the Victory;
Which ſeen, I poſted from the turrets top,
More furiouſly than ere *Laocoon* ran,
When Trojan hands drew in *Troy's* overthrow,
But yet as fatally as he or any.
The tyrant ſeeing me, ſtar'd in my face,
And ſuddainly demanded whats the newes,
I, as the Fates would have it, hoping that he
Even in a twinkling would have ſlain 'em both,
For ſo he ſwore before the Fight began,
Cri'd bitterly that he had loſt the day,
The ſound whereof did kill his daſtard heart,
And made the Villain deſperatly confeſs
The murther of my Father, praying me,
With dire revenge, to ridd him of his life;
Short tale to make, I bound him cunningly,
Told him of the deceit, triumphing over him,
And laſtly with my Rapier ſlew him dead.
    Sax. O Heavens! juſtly have you tane revenge.
But thou, thou murtherous adulterous ſlave,
What Bull of *Phalaris*, what ſtrange device,
Shall we invent to take away thy life?
    Alex. If *Edward* and the Empreſs, whom I fav'd,
Will not requite it now, and ſave my life,
Then let me die, contentedly I die,
Having at laſt reveng'd my Fathers death.
    Sax. Villain, not all the world ſhall ſave thy life.
    Edw. Hadſt thou not been Author of my *Hedewicks* death,

I would have certainly fav'd thee from death ;
But if my Sentence now may take effect,
I would adjudge the Villain to be hang'd
As here the Jewes are hang'd in *Germany.*
    Sax. Young Prince it fhall be fo; go dragg the Slave
Unto the place of execution :
There let the *Judas*, on a Jewifh Gallowes,
Hang by the heels between two Englifh Maftives,
There feed on Doggs, let Doggs there feed on thee,
And by all means prolong his miferie.
    Alex. O might thy felf and all thefe Englifh Currs,
Inftead of Maftive-Doggs hang by my fide,
How fweetly would I tugg upon your Flefh.
                                Exit Alex.
    Sax. Away with him, fuffer him not to fpeak.
And now my lords, *Collen*, *Tryer*, and *Brandenburg*,
Whofe Hearts are bruz'd to think upon thefe woes,
Though no man hath fuch reafon as my felf,
We of the feven Electors that remain,
After fo many bloody Maffacres,
Kneeling upon our Knees, humbly intreat
Your Excellence to be our Emperour.
The Royalties of the Coronation
Shall be, at *Aix*, fhortly folemnized.
    Cullen. Brave Princely *Richard* now refufe it not,
Though the Election be made in Tears,
Joy fhall attend thy Coronation.
    Richard. It ftands not with mine Honour to deny it,
Yet by mine Honour, fain I would refufe it.
    Edward. Uncle, the weight of all thefe Miferies
Maketh my heart as heavy as your own,
But an Imperial Crown would lighten it,
Let this one reafon make you take the Crown.

Richard. What's that sweet nephew?
Edward. Sweet Uncle, this it is,
Was never Englishman yet Emperour,
Therefore to honour *England* and your self,
Let private sorrow yield to publike Fame,
That once an Englishman bare *Cæsar's* name.
 Richard. Nephew, thou hast prevail'd; Princes stand up,
We humbly do accept your sacred offer.
 Cullen. Then sound the Trumpets, and cry *Vivat Cæsar.*
 All. *Vivat Cæsar.*
 Cullen. Richardus Dei gratia Romanorum Imperator, semper Augustus, Comes Cornubiæ.
 Richard. Sweet Sister now let *Cæsar* comfort you,
And all the rest that yet are comfortless;
Let them expect from English *Cæsar's* hands
Peace, and abundance of all earthly Joy.

FINIS

REVENGE,
FOR
HONOUR.
A
TRAGEDIE,
BY
GEORGE CHAPMAN.

LONDON,
Printed for *Richard Marriot,* in *S. Dunstan's*
Church-yard, Fleetstreet. 1654.

The Perſons Acting.

Almanzor Caliph of Arabia.
Abilqualit his eldeſt Son.
Abrahen his Son by a ſecond Wife.
   Brother to *Abilqualit*.
Tarifa an old General, Conqueror of
   Spain, Tutor to *Abilqualit*.
Mura a rough Lord, a Souldier, Kinſ-
   man by his Mother, to *Abrahen*.
Simanthes a Court Lord, allyed to
   Abrahen.
Selinthus an honeſt, merrie Court
   Lord.
Meſithes a Court Eunuch, Attendant
   on *Abilqualit*.
Ofman a Captain to *Tarifa*.
Gafelles another Captain.
Caropia Wife to *Mura*, firſt beloved of
   Abrahen, then of *Abilqualit*.
Perilinda her Woman.

   Souldiers,   Guard.
   Muts.   Attendants.

PROLOGUE.

Ovr *Author thinks 'tis not i'th power of Wit,*
Invention, Art, nor Industrie, to fit
The several phantasies which in this age
With a predominant humour rule the Stage.
Some men cry out for Satyr, others chuse
Meerly to story to confine each Muse;
Most like no Play, but such as gives large birth
To that which they judiciously term mirth.
Nor wil the best works with their liking crown,
Except 't be grac'd with part of foole or clown.
Hard and severe the task is then to write,
So as may please each various appetite.
Our Author hopes wel though, that in this Play,
He has endeavour'd so, he justly may
Gain liking from you all, unlesse those few
Who wil dislike, be't ne're so good, so new;
Whe rather Gentlemen, he hopes, cause I
Am a mean Actor in this Tragedie:
You've grac'd me sometimes in another Sphear,
And I do hope you'l not dislike me here.

REVENGE

FOR HONOUR.

Actus Primus. Scena I.

Enter Selinthus, Gafelles, and Ofman.

Sel. NO murmurings, Noble Captains.
Gaf. Murmurings, Cofen ?
this Peace is worfe to men of war and action
then fafting in the face o'th' fo, or lodging
on the cold earth. Give me the Camp, fay I,
where in the Sutlers palace on pay-day
we may the precious liquor quaff, and kiffe
his buxome wife ; who though fhe be not clad
in Perfian Silks, or coftly Tyrian Purples,
has a clean fkin, foft thighes, and wholfome corps,
fit for the trayler of the puiffant Pike,
to follace in delight with.
Of. Here in your lewd Citie,

T

the Harlots do avoid us fons o'th' Sword
worfe then a fevere Officer. Befides,
here men o'th' Shop can gorge their muftie maws
with the delicious Capon, and fat limbs
of Mutton large enough to be held fhoulders
o' th' Ram ancouge the 12 Signes, while for pure want
Your fouldier oft dines at the charge o' th' dead,
'mong tombs in the great Mofque.
  Sel. 'Tis beleev'd Coz,
and by the wifeft few too, that i' th' Camp
you do not feed on pleafant poults ; a fallad,
and without oyl or vinegar, appeafes
fometimes your guts, although they keep more noife
then a large pool ful of ingendring frogs.
Then for accoutrements, you wear the Buff,
as you believ'd it herefie to change
for linnen : Surely moft of yours is fpent
in lint, to make long tents for your green wounds
after an onflaught.
  Gaf. Coz. thefe are fad truths,
incident to fraile mortals !
  Sel. You yet crie
out with more eagerneffe ftil for new wars,
then women for new fafhions.
  Cf. 'Tis confefs'd,
Peace is more oppofite to my nature, then
the running ach in the rich Ufurers feet,
when he roars out, as if he were in hel
before his time. Why, I love mifchief, Coz,
when one may do't fecurely ; to cut throats
with a licencious pleafure ; when good men
and true o' th Jurie, with their froftie beards
fhall not have power to give the noble wefand,
which has the fteele defied, to th' hanging mercy
of the ungracious cord.
  Sel. Gentlemen both,
and Cozens mine, I do believe't much pity,
to ftrive to reconvert you from the faith

you have been bred in : though your large difcourfe
and praife, wherein you magnifie your Miftrifs,
Warr, fhall fcarce drive me from my quiet fheets,
to fleep upon a turfe. But pray fay, Cozens,
How do you like your General, Prince,
is he a right Mars?
   Gaf. As if his Nurfe had lapt him
in fwadling clouts of fteele; a very *Hector*
and *Alcibiades.*
   Sel. It feems he does not relifh
thefe boafted fweets of warre : for all his triumphs,
he is reported melencholy.
   Of. Want of exercife
renders all men of actions, dul as dormife ;
your Souldier only can dance to the Drum,
and fing a Hymn of joy to the fweet Trumpet :
there's no mufick like it.

Enter Abrahen, Mura, and Simanthes.

   Ab. I'll know the caufe,
he fhall deny me hardly elfe.
   Mu. His melancholy
known whence it rifes once, 't may much conduce
to help our purpofe.
   Gaf. Pray Coz. what Lords are thefe?
they feem as ful of plot, as Generals
are in Siege, they're very ferious.
   Sel. That young Stripling
is our great Emperors fon, by his laft wife :
that in the rich Imbroidery's, the Count *Hermes* ;
one that has hatcht more projects, then the ovens
in Egypt chickens ; the other, though they cal
friends, his meer oppofite Planet *Mars,*
one that does put on a referv'd gravitie,
which fome call wifdom, the rough Souldier *Mura,*
Governour i' th' *Moroccos.*
   Of. Him we've heard of
before : but Cozen, fhal that man of truft,

thy tailor, furnish us with new accoutrements?
haft thou tane order for them?
  Sel. Yes, yes, you shal
flourish in fresh habiliments; but you must
promise me not to ingage your corporal oathes
you wil see't satisfied at the next press,
out of the profits that arise from ransome
of those rich yeomans heires, that dare not look
the fierce foe in the face.
  Gaf. Doubt not our truths,
though we be given much to contradictions,
we wil not pawn oaths of that nature.
  Sel. Well then, this note does fetch the garments:
meet me Cozens anon at Supper. *Exeunt. Gaf. Of.*
  Of. Honourable Coz. we wil come give our
    thanks.   *Enter Abilqualit.*
  Ab. My gracious brother,
make us not such a stranger to your thoughts,
to confume all your honors in close retirements;
perhaps since you from *Spain* return'd a victor,
with (the worlds conqueror) *Alexander*, you greive
Nature ordain'd no other earths to vanquish;
if't be so, Princely brother, we'le bear part
in your heroique melancholy.
  Abil. Gentle youth,
press me no farther, I stil hold my temper
free and unshaken, only some fond thoughts
of trivial moment, cal my faculties
to private meditations
  Sim. Howsoe're your Highnesse
does please to term them, 'tis meer melancholy,
which next to sin, is the greatest maladie
than can opprefs mans soul.
  Sel. They say right:
and that your Grace may see what a meer madnesse,
a very mid-summer frenzy, 'tis to be
melancholy, for any man that wants no monie,
I (with your pardon) wil discusse unto you
All sorts, all sizes, persons and conditions,

that are infected with it ; and the reasons
why it in each arises.
    Ab. Learned *Selinthus*,
Let's tast of thy Philosophie.
    Mu. Pish, 'Tis unwelcome
to any of judgment, this fond prate :
I marvel that our Emperor dos permit
fools to abound ith' Court !
    Sel. What makes your grave Lordship
in it, I do beseech you ? But Sir, mark me,
the Kernel of the text enucleated,
I shall confute, refute, repel, refel,
explode, exterminate, expunge, extinguish
like a rush candle, this same heresie,
that is shot up like a pernicious Mushroom,
to poison true humanitie.
    Ab. You shall stay and hear a lecture read
on your disease ; you shal, as I love virtue.
    Sel. First the cause then
from whence this *flatus Hypocondriacus*
this glimmering of the gizard (for in wild fowl,
'tis term'd so by *Hypocrates*) arises,
is as *Averroes* and *Avicen*,
with *Abenbucar*, *Baruch* and *Aboflii*,
and all the Arabick writers have affirm'd,
a meer defect, that is as we interpret, a want of——
    Abil. Of what, *Selinthus* ?
    Sel. Of wit, and please your Highnesse,
That is the cause in gen'ral, for particular
and special causes, they are all deriv'd
from severall wants ; yet they must be considerd,
pondred, perpended, or premeditated.
    Sim. My Lord, y'ad best be brief,
your Patient will be wearie else.
    Sel. I cannot play the fool rightly, I mean, the
      Physician
without I have licence to expalcat
on the disease. But (my good Lord) more briefly,
I shall declare to you like a man of wisdom

and no Phyſician, who deal all in ſimples,
why men are melancholy. Firſt, for your Courtier.
   Sim. It concerns us all to be attentive, Sir.
   Sel. Your ſage and ſerious Courtier, who does walk
with a State face, as he had dreſt himſelf
ith' Emperors glaſſe, and had his beard turn'd up
by the' irons Roial, he will be as penſive
as Stallion after Catum, when he wants ſuits,
begging ſuits, I mean. Me thinks, (my Lord)
you are grown ſomething ſolemn on the ſudden;
ſince your Monopolies and Patents, which
made your purſe ſwell like a wet ſpunge, have been
reduc'd to th' laſt gaſp. Troth, it is far better
to confeſſe here, then in a worſer place.
Is it not ſo indeed ?
   Abil. What ere he does
by mine, I'me ſure h'as hit the cauſe from whence
your grief ſprings, Lord *Simanthes.*
   Sel. No *Egyptian* Soothſayer
has truer inſpirations, then your ſinall Courtiers
from cauſes and wants manifold ; as when
the Emperors count'nance with propitious noiſe
does not cry chink in pocket, no repute is
with Mercer, nor with Tailor ; nay ſometimes too
the humor's pregnant in him, when repulſe
is given him by a Beautie : I can ſpeak this
though from no Memphian Prieſt, or ſage Caldean,
from the beſt Miſtris (Gentlemen) an Experience.
Laſt night I had a mind t'a comly Semſtreſs,
who did refuſe me, and behold, ere ſince
how like an Aſs I look.

Enter Tarifa.

   Tar. What, at your Counſels, Lords ? the great *Almanzor*
requires your preſence, *Mura* ; has decree'd
the Warr for *Perſia.* You (my gracious Lord)

Prince *Abilqualet*, are appointed Chief :
And you, brave ſpirited *Abrahen*, an Aſſiſtant
to your victorious Brother : You, Lord *Mura*,
deſtin'd Lieutenant General.
  Abil. And muſt I march againſt the foe, without
thy company ? I reliſh not th' imployment.
  Tar. Alas, my Lord,
Tarifa's head's grown white beneath his helmet ;
and your good Father thought it charity
to ſpare mine age from travel : though this eaſe
will be more irkſome to me then the toil
of war in a ſharp winter.
  Abr. It arrives juſt to our wiſh. My gracious
    brother, I
anon ſhall wait on you : mean time, valiant *Mura*,
let us attend my Father.
                    Exeunt Ab. Mura, Sim.
  Abil. Good *Selinthus*,
vouchſafe a while your abſence, I ſhall have
imployment ſhortly for your truſt.
  Sel. Your Grace ſhall have as much power to com-
    mand
Selinthus, as his beſt fanci'd Miſtreſs. I am your crea-
    ture.   *Exit.*
  Tar. Now, my Lord,
I hope y'are cloath'd with all thoſe reſolutions
that uſher glorious minds to brave atchievements.
The happy genius on your youth attendant
declares it built for Victories and Triumphs ;
and the proud *Perſian* Monarchie, the ſole
emulous oppoſer of the Arabique Greatneſſe,
courts (like a fair Bride) your Imperial Arms,
waiting t'inveſt You Soveraigne of her beauties.
Why are you dull (my Lord ?) Your cheerful looks
ſhould with a proſp'rous augury preſage
a certain Victory : when you droop already,
as if the foe had raviſh'd from your Creſt
the noble Palm. For ſhame (Sir) be more ſprightly ;

your fad appearance, fhould they thus behold you,
would half unfoul your Army.

 Abil. 'Tis no matter,
Such looks beft fute my fortune. Know (*Tarifa*)
I'm undifpos'd to manage this great Voiage,
and muft not undertake it.

 Tar. Muft not, Sir !
Is't poffible a love-fick youth, whofe hopes
are fixt on marriage, on his bridal night
fhould in foft flumbers languifh ? that your Arms
fhould ruft in eafe, now when you hear the charge,
and fee before you the triumphant Prize
deftin'd t'adorn your Valour ? You fhould rather
be furnifh'd with a power above thefe paffions ;
and being invok'd by the mighty charm of Honour,
flie to atchieve this war, not undeitake it.
I'd rather you had faid, *Tarifa* ly'd,
then utter'd fuch a found, harfh and 'unwelcome.

 Abil. I know thou lov'ft me truly, and durft I
to any born of woman, fpeak my intentions,
the fatal caufe which does withdraw my courage
from this imployment, which like health I covet,
thou fhouldft enjoy it fully. But (*Tarifa*)
the faid difcov'ry of it is not fit
for me to utter, much leffe for thy vertue
to be acquainted with.

 Tar. Why (my Lord ?)
my loyaltie can merit no fufpicion
from you of falfhood : whatfoere the caufe be
or good, or wicked, 't-meets a truftie filence,
and my beft care and honeft counfel fhall
indeavour to reclaim, or to affift you
if it be good, if ill, from your bad purpofe.

 Abil. Why, that I know *Tarifa*. 'Tis the love
thou bear'ft to honour, renders thee unapt
to be partaker of thofe refolutions
that by compulfion keep me from this Voiage :
For they with fuch inevitable fweetneffe
invade my fenfe, that though in their performance

my Fame and Vertue even to death do languifh,
I muft attempt, and bring them unto act,
or perifh i' th' purfuance.
 Tar. Heaven avert
a mifchief fo prodigious. Though I would not
with over-fawcie boldneffe preffe your counfels;
yet pardon (Sir) my Loialtie, which timorous
of your lov'd welfare, muft intreat, befeech you
with ardent love and reverence, to difclofe
the hidden caufe that can eftrange your courage
from its own *Mars,* with-hold you from this Action
fo much ally'd to honour : Pray reveal it :
By all your hopes of what you hold moft precious,
I do implore it; for my faith in breeding
your youth in warrs great rudiments, relieve
Tarifa's fears, that wander into ftrange
unwelcome doubts, left fome ambitious frenzy
'gainft your imperial fathers dignitie
has late feduc'd your goodnefs.
 Abr. No, *Tarifa,*
I ne're durft aim at that unholy height
in viperous wickedneffe ; a finleffe, harmleffe
(ift can be truly term'd one) 'tis my foul
labours even to difpaire with : 't faine would out,
did not my blufhes interdict my language :
'tis unchaft love, *Tarifa* ; nay, tak't all,
and when thou haft it, pity my misfortunes,
to fair *Caropia,* the chaft, vertuous wife
to furly *Mura.*
 Tar. What a fool Defire is !
with Giant ftrengths it makes us court the knowledg
of hidden myfteries, which once reveal'd,
far more inconftant then the air, it fleets
into new wifhes, that the coveted fecret
had flept ftill in oblivion.
 Abil. I was certaine
'twould fright thy innocence, and look to be
befieged with ftrong diffwafions from my purpofe :
but be affur'd, that I have tir'd my thoughts

with all the rules that teach men moral goodneſſe,
ſo to reclaime them from this love-ſick looſeneſs;
but they (like wholeſome medicines miſaplied)
fac'd their beſt operation, fond and fruitleſſe.
Though I as wel may hope to kiſs the Sun-beams
'cauſe they ſhine on me, as from her to gaine
one glance of comfort; yet my mind, that pities
it ſelf with conſtant tenderneſſe, muſt needs
revolve the cauſe of its calamity,
and melt i' th' pleaſure of ſo ſweet a ſadneſs.

  Tar. Then y'are undone for ever; Sir, undon
beyond the help of councel or repentance.
'Tis moſt ignoble, that a mind unſhaken
by fear, ſhould by a vain deſire be broken;
or that thoſe powers no labour e're could vanquiſh,
ſhould be orecome and thral'd by ſordid pleaſure.
Pray (Sir) conſider, that in glorious war,
which makes Ambition (by baſe men termed ſin)
a big and gallant Virtue, y'ave been nurs'd,
lull'd (as it were) into your infant ſleeps
by th' ſurly noiſe o' th' trumpet, which now ſummons
you to victorious uſe of your indowments:
and ſhall a Miſtriſſe ſtay you! ſuch a one too,
as to attempt, then war it ſelf's more dangerous!

  Abil. All theſe perſwaſions are to as much purpoſe,
as you ſhould ſtrive to reinveſt with peace,
and all the ioyes of health and life, a foul
condemn'd to perpetuity of torments.
No (my *Tarifa*) though through all diſgraces,
loſſe of my honour, fame, nay hope for Empire,
I ſhould be forc'd to wade to obtain her love;
thoſe ſeas of miſchief would be pleaſing ſtreams,
which I would haſt to bath in, and paſſe through them
with that delight thou would'ſt to victory,
or ſlaves long chain'd to' th' oare, to ſudden freedome.

  Tar. Were you not *Abilqualit*, from this time then
our friendſhips (like two rivers from one head
riſing) ſhould wander a diſſever'd courſe,
and never meet againe, unleſſe to quarrel.

Revenge for Honour.

Nay, old and ſtiffe, now as my iron garments,
were you my ſon, my ſword ſhould teach your wildneſs
a ſwift way to repentance   Y'are my Prince,
on whom all hopes depend ; think on your Father,
that lively Image of majeſtick goodneſs,
who never yet wrong'd Matron in his luſt,
or man in his diſpleaſure.   Pray conjecture
your Father, Countrie, Army, by my mouth
beſeech your pietie to an early pittie
of your yet unſlain Innocence.   No attention !
Farwel : my praiers ſhall wait you, though my Counſels
be thus deſpiſ'd.   Farwel Prince !   *Exit.*
   Abil. 'Las good man, he weeps.
Such tears I've ſeen fall from his manly eyes
once when ye loſt a battel.   Why ſhould I
put off my Reaſon, Valor, Honour, Virtue,
in hopes to gain a Beautie, whoſe poſſeſſion
renders me more uncapable of peace,
then I am now I want it ?   Like a ſweet,
much coveted banquet, 'tis no ſooner taſted,
but it's delicious luxury's forgotten.
Beſides, it is unlawful.   Idle fool,
there is no law, but what's preſcribed by Love,
Natures firſt moving Organ ; nor can ought
what Nature dictates to us be held vicious.
On then, my ſoul, and deſtitute of fears,
like an adventrous Mariner, that knows
ſtorms muſt attend him, yet dares court his peril,
ſtrive to obtain this happy Port.   *Meſithes*
(Loves cunning Advocate) does for me beſiege
(with gifts and vows) her Chaſtitie.   She is
compaſs'd with fleſh, that's not invulnerable,
and may by Love's ſharp darts be pierc'd.   They ſtand
firm, whom no art can bring to Love's command.
                              Enter Abrahen.
   Abr. My gracious brother !
   Abil. Deareſt *Abrahen*, welcome.
Tis certainly decreed by our dread Father,
we muſt both march againſt th' inſulting foe.

How does thy youth, yet uninur'd to travel,
relish the Imploiment?

Abr. War is sweet to those
that neuer have experienc'd it. My youth
cannot desire in that big Art a nobler
Tutor then you (my Brother:) Like an Eglet
following her dam, I shall your honour'd steps
trace through all dangers, and be proud to borrow
a branch, when your head's coverd ore with Lawrel,
to deck my humbler temples.

Abil. I do know thee
of valiant active soul; and though a youth,
thy forward spirit merits the Command
of Chief, rather then Second in an Armie.
Would heaven our Roial Father had bestow'd
On thee the Charge of General.

Abr. On me, Sir!
Alas, 'tis fit I first should know those Arts
that do distinguish Valour from wild rashness.
A Gen'ral (Brother) must have abler nerves
of Judgment, then in my youth can be hop'd for.
Your self already like a flourishing Spring
teeming with early Victories, the Souldier
expects should lead them to new Triumphs, as
if you had vanquisht fortune.

Abil. I am not so
ambitious (*Abrahen*) of particular glories,
but I would have those whom I love partake them.
This *Persian* war, the last of the whole East
left to be managed, if I can perswade
the great *Almanzor*, shall be the trophee
of thy yet maiden Valour. I have done
enough already to inform Succession,
that *Abilqualit* durst on fiercest foes
    run to fetch Conquest home, and would have thy name
as great as mine in Arms, that Historie
might register, our Familie abounded
with Heroes, born for Victorie.

Abr. Tis an honour,
which, though it be above my powers, committed
to my direction, I would feek to manage
with care above my years, and courage equal
to his, that dares the horrid'ſt face of danger:
But 'tis your noble courtefie would thruſt
this mafc'line honor (far above his merits)
on your regardlefs Brother; for my Father,
he has no thought tending to your intentions;
nor though your goodnefs fhould defire, would hardly
be won to yeild confent to them.
   Abil. Why, my *Abrahen*,
w'are both his fons, and fhould be both alike
dear to's affections; and though birth hath given me
the larger hopes and Titles, 'twere unnatural,
fhould he not ſtrive t' indow thee with a portion
apted to the magnificence of his Off-fpring.
But thou perhaps art timorous, leſt thy firſt
effayes of valour fhould meet fate difaſtrous.
The bold are Fortunes darlings. If thou haſt
courage to venture on this great imploiment,
doubt not, I fhall prevail upon our Father
t' ordain thee Chief in this brave hopefull Voiage.
   Abr. You imagine me
beyond all thought of gratitude; and doubt not
that I'll deceive your truſt. The glorious Enfignes
waving i' th' air once, like fo many Comets,
fhall fpeak the Perfians funerals, on whofe ruines
we'l build to Fame and Victorie new temples,
which fhall like Pyramids preferve our memories,
when we are chang'd to afhes.
   Abil. Be fure, continue
in this brave minde; I'll inſtantly folicite
our Father to confirm thee in the Charge
of General. I'll about it.   *Exit.*
   Abr. Farewell gracious Brother.
This haps above my hopes. 'Las, good dull fool,
I fee through thy intents, clear, as thy foul
were as tranfparent as thin air or Criſtal.

He would have me remov'd, march with the Armie,
that he mean time might make a fure defeat
on our aged fathers life and Empire: 'tmuſt
be certain as the light. Why ſhould not his
with equall heat, be like my thoughts, ambitious?
Be they as harmleſs as the prai'rs of Virgins,
I'll work his ruine out of his intentions.
He like a thick cloud ſtands 'twixt me and Greatneſſe:
Greatneſſe, the wife mans true felicity,
Honour's direct inheritance. My youth
wil quit fuſpicion of my fubtil practice:
then have I furly *Mura* and *Simanthes*,
my allyes by my dead Mothers bloud, my affiſtants,
his Eunuch too *Meſithes* at my fervice.
Simanthes ſhall inform the King, the people
defire Prince *Abilqualit's* ſtay; and *Mura*
whoſe blunt demeanour renders him oraculous,
make a ſhrewd inference out of it. He is my half
    Brother,
th' other's my Father; names, meer airie titles!
Soveraigntie's onely ſacred, Greatneſſe goodneſſe,
true ſelf-affection Juſtice, every thing
righteous that's helpfull to create a King.

           Enter Mura, Simanthes.

  Abr. My truſtie friends, y'are welcome:
our fate's above our wiſhes; *Abilqualit*
by whatſo'ere pow'r mov'd to his own ruine,
would fain inforce his charge of General on me,
and ſtay at home.
  Sim. Why, how can this conduce
t' advance our purpoſe?
  Abr. Tis the maineſt engine
could ever move to ruine him. *Simanthes*,
you ſhall inform our Father, tis the people
out of their tender love defires his ſtay.
You (*Mura*) ſhall infer my Brothers greatneſſe
with people; out of it, how nice it is and dangerous.

The air is open here; come, wee'll difcourfe
with more fecure privacie our purpofe.
Nothing's unjuft, unfacred, tends to advance
us to a Kingdom; that's the height of chance.

ACTUS SECUNDUS. Scena 1.

Enter Almanzor, Mura, and Simanthes.

Al. How? not go, *Simanthes*?
Sim. My dread Soveraign,
I fpeak but what the well affected people
out of their loyal care and pious duty
injoyn'd me utter: they do look upon him
as on your eldeft Son, and next Succeffor,
and would be loth the *Perfian* War fhould rob
their eies of light, their fouls of joy and comfort,
this flourifhing Empire leave as it were widow'd
of its lov'd Spoufe: They humbly do befeech
your Maiefty would therefore deftine fome
more fitting General, whofe lofs (as heaven
avert fuch a misfortune) fhould it happen,
might leffe concern the State.
   Al. 'Tis not the leaft
among the bleffings Heaven has fhowr'd upon us,
that we are happie in fuch loving Subjects,
to govern whom, when we in peace are afhes,
we leave them a Succeffor whom they truly reverence:
A loving people and a loving Soveraign
makes Kingdoms truly fortunate and flourifhing.
But I beleeve (*Simanthes*) their intents,
though we confirm them, will fcarce take effect:

My *Abilqualit* (like a Princely Lion,
in view of's prey (wil fcarcely be orecom
to leave the honour of the *Perfian* War,
in's hopes already vanquifh'd by his valour,
and reft in lazy quiet, while that Triumph
is ravifh'd by another.

Sim. With the pardon
of your moft facred Majeftie, 'tis fit then
your great commands forbid the Princes Voyage :
boldneffe inforces youth to hard atchievements
before their time, makes them run forth like Lapwings
from their warm neft, part of the fhel yet flicking
unto their downie heads. Sir, good fucceffe
is oft more fatal far then bad ; one winning
caft from a flatt'ring Die tempting a Gamefter
to hazard his whole fortunes.

Mur.   This is dull,
fruitlefs Philofophy, he that falls nobly
winns as much honour by his lófs, as conqueft.

Sim. This rule may hold wel among common men,
but not 'mong Princes. Such a prince as ours is,
who knows as wel to conquer mens affeftions
as he does enemies, fhould not be expof'd
to every new caufe, honourable danger.
Prince *Abilqualit's* fair and winning carriage
has ftolne poffeffion of the peoples hearts,
they doate on him fince his late Spanifh conqueft,
as new made brides on their much coveted husbands ;
and they would pine like melancholy turtles,
fhould they fo foone lofe the invalued objeft
both of their love and reverence : Howfoe're,
what ere your awful wil (Sir) fhall determine,
as heaven, is by their ftrift obedience
held facred and religious.

Al.   Good *Simanthes*, let them receive our thanks
for their true care of our dear *Abilqualit*.
Wee'l confider of their requeft, fay.

Sim. Your highneffe humbleft creature.   *Exit.*

Mu. I do not like this.

Al. Like what? Valiant *Mura*,
we know thy counſels ſo ſupremely wiſe,
and thy true heart ſo excellently faithful,
that whatſoere diſpleaſes thy ſage Judgment,
Almanzor's wiſdome muſt account diſtaſtful.
What is't diſlikes thee?
 Mu. Your Majeſtie knows me
a downright Souldier, I affect not words;
but to be brief, I reliſh not your ſon
ſhould (as if you were in your tomb already)
ingroſs ſo much the giddie peoples favours.
'Tis neither fit for him, nor ſafe for you
to ſuffer it.
 Al. Why, how can they, *Mura*,
Give a more ſerious teſtimony of reverence
to me, then by conferring their affections,
their pious wiſhes, zealous contemplations
on him that fits the neareſt to my heart,
my *Abilqualit*, in whoſe hopeful virtues
my age more glories then in all my conqueſts?
 Mu. May you prove fortunate in your pious care
of the Prince *Abilqualit*. But (my Lord)
Mura is not ſo prone to idle language
(the Paraſits beſt ornament) to utter
ought, but what (if you'l pleaſe to give him audience
hee'l ſhow you a blunt reaſon for.
 Al. Come, I ſee
into thy thoughts, good *Mura*; too much care
of us, informs thy loyal ſoul with fears
the Princes too much popularity
may breed our danger: baniſh thoſe ſuſpicions;
neither dare they who under my long raign
have been triumphant in ſo many bleſſings,
have the leaſt thought may tend to diſobedience:
or if they had, my *Abilqualit's* goodneſſe
would ne're conſent with them to become impious.
 Mu. 'Tis too ſecure a confidence betrays
minds valiant to irreparable dangers.
Not that I dare invade with a foule thought

the noble Princes loyalty ; but (my Lord)
when this fame many headed beaft (the people)
violent, and fo not conftant in affections,
fubject to love of novelty, the fickneffe
proper t'all humane fpecially light natures,
do magnifie with too immoderate praifes
the Princes actions, doate upon his prefence,
nay chaine their fouls to th' fhadow of his foot-fteps,
as all exceffes ought to be held dangerous,
efpecially when they do aim at Scepters,
their too much dotage fpeaks, you in their wifhes
are dead alreadie, that their darling hope
the Prince might have the Throne once.

 Al. 'Tis confefs'd, all this a ferious truth.

 Mu. Their mad applaufes
oth' noble Prince, though he be truly virtuous,
may force ambition into him, a mifchief
Seafing the foul with too much craft and fweetnefs,
as pride or luft do's minds unftay'd and wanton :
'tmakes men like poyfon'd rats, which when they'ave
  fwallow'd
the pleafing bane, reft not until they drink,
and can reft then much leffe, until they burft with't.

 Al. Thy words are ftil oraculous.

 Mu. Pray then think
with what an eafie toil the haughty Prince,
a demy God by th' popular acclamations,
nay, the world's Soveraign in the vulgar wifhes,
had he a refolution to be wicked,
might fnatch this diadem from your aged temples ?
What law fo holy, tye of blood fo mightie,
which for a Crown, minds fanctified and religious
have not prefum'd to violate ? How much more then
may the foul dazling glories of a Scepter
work in his youth, whofe conftitution's fierie,
as overheated air, and has to fan it
into a flame, the breath of love and praifes
blown by ftrong thought of his own worth and actions.

 Al. No more of this, good *Mura.*

Mu. They dare already limit your intentions,
demand (as 'twere) with cunning zeal (which rightly
interpreted, is infolence) the Princes
abode at home. I wil not fay it is,
but I guefs, 'tmay be their fubtle purpofe
while we abroad fight for new kingdomes purchafe
depriv'd by that means of our faithful fuccors,
they may deprive you of this crown, inforce
upon the prince this Diadem ; which however
he may be loth t'accept, being once poffeffed of't
and tafted the delights of fupreme greatnefs,
hee'l be more loath to part with. To prevent this,
not that I think it wil, but that may happen,
'tis fit the Prince march. I'ave obferved in him too
of late a fullen Melancholly, whence rifing
i'le not conjecture : only I fhould grieve, Sir,
beyond a moderate forrow, traitorous practife
fhould take that from you which with loyal blood
ours and your own victorious arms have purchas'd.
and now I have difcharg'd my honeft confcience
cenfure on't as you pleafe ; henceforth I'me filent.

Al. Would thou hadft been fo now, thy loyal fears
have made me fee how miferable a King is,
whofe rule depends on the vain people fuffrage.
Black now and horrid as the face of ftorms
appears al *Abilqualits* lovely vertues,
becaufe to me they only make him dangerous,
and with great terror fhall behold thofe actions
which with delight before we view'd, and dotage ;
like Mariners that blefs the peaceful feas,
which when fufpected to grow up tempeftuous,
they tremble at. Though he may ftil be virtuous,
'tis wifdome in us, to him no injuftice,
to keep a vigilant eie o're his proceedings
and the wild peoples purpofes.

Enter Abil.

Al. Abilqualit!
come to take your leave, I do conjecture.
Abil. Rather, Sir, to beg

your gracious licence, I may ſtil at home
attend your dread commands, and that you'd pleaſe
to nominate my hopeful brother *Abrahen*
(in lieu of me) chief of your now raiſed Forces
for th' *Perſian* expedition,
  Al. Dare you (Sir) preſume to make this ſuit to us?
  Abil. Why? (my roial Lord)
I hope this cannot pull your anger on
your moſt obedient Son : a true affection
to the young Prince my brother, did beget
this my requeſt ; I willingly would have
his youth adorn'd with glorie of this conqueſt.
No tree bears fruit in Autumn, 'leſs it bloſſome
firſt in the Spring : 'tis fit he were acquainted
in theſe ſoft years with military action,
that when grown perfect man, he may grow up too
perfect in warlike diſcipline.
  Al. Hereafter
we ſhall by your appointment guide our Counſels.
Why do you not intreat me to reſigne
my Crown, that you the peoples much lov'd minion
may with't impale your glorious brow ? Sir, henceforth
or know your duty better, or your pride
ſhall meet our juſt wak'd anger. To your Charge,
and march with ſpeed, or you ſhall know what 'tis
to diſobey our pleaſure. When y'are King,
learn to command your Subjects ; I will mine (Sir.)
You know your Charge, perform it.
                    Exit Alm. and *Mura.*
  Abil. I have done.
Our hopes (I ſee) reſemble much the Sun,
that riſing and declining caſt large ſhadows ;
but when his beams are dreſs'd in's midday brightneſſe,
yeelds none at all : when they are fartheſt from
ſucceſſe, their guilt reflection does diſplay
the largeſt ſhow of events fair and proſp'rous.
With what a ſetled confidence did I promiſe
my ſelf, my ſtay here, *Mura's* wiſh'd departure ?
when ſtead of theſe, I finde my fathers wrath

destroying mine intentions. Such a fool
is self-compaſſion, ſoothing us to faith
of what we wiſh ſhould hap, while vain deſire
of things we have not, makes us quite forget
thoſe w'are poſſeſs'd of.
Enter Abrahen.

Abr. Alone the engine works
beyond or hope or credit. How I hug
with vaſt delight, beyond that of ſtoln pleaſures
forbidden Lovers taſte, my darling Miſtriſs,
my active Brain! If I can be thus ſubtle
while a young Serpent, when grown up a Dragon
how glorious ſhall I be in cunning practiſe?
My gracious brother!

Abil. Gentle *Abrahen*, I
am griev'd my power cannot comply my promiſe:
my Father's ſo averſe from granting my
requeſt concerning thee, that with angrie frowns
he did expreſs rather a paſſionate rage
then a refuſall civil, or accuſtom'd
to his indulgent diſpoſition.

Abr. Hee's our Father,
and ſo the tyrant Cuſtome doth inforce us
to yeeld him that which fools call natural,
when wiſe men know 'tis more then ſervile duty,
a ſlaviſh, blind obedience to his pleaſure,
be it nor juſt, nor honourable.

Abil. O my *Abrahen*,
theſe ſounds are unharmonious, as unlookt for
from thy unblemiſh'd innocence: though he could
put off paternal pietie, 't gives no priviledg
for us to wander from our filial dutie:
though harſh, and to our natures much unwelcom
be his decrees, like thoſe of Heaven, we muſt not
preſume to queſtion them.

Abr. Not, if they concern
our lives and fortunes? 'Tis not for my ſelf
I urge theſe doubts; but 'tis for you, who are
my Brother, and I hope, muſt be my Soveraigne,

my fears grow on me almoſt to diſtraction :
Our Father's age betrayes him to a dotage,
which may be dang'rous to your future fafetie ;
he does fufpect your loyaltie.
    Abil. How, *Abrahen* ?
    Ab. I knew 'twould ſtart your innocence ; but 'tis
    truth,
a fad and ſerious truth ; nay his fuſpicion
almoſt arriv'd unto a fetled faith
that y'are ambitious.
    Abil. 'Tis impoſſible.
    Ab. The glorious ſhine of your illuſtrious vertues
are grown too bright and dazling for his eyes
to look on as he ought, with admiration ;
and he with fear beholds them, as it were,
through a perſpective, where each brave action
of yours furvey'd though at remoteſt diſtance,
appears far greater then it is. In brief,
that love which you have purchaſ'd from the people
that ſing glad Hymns to your victorious fortunes,
betraies you to his hate ; and in this Voiage
which he inforces you to undertake,
he has ſet fpies upon you.
    Abil. 'Tis fo : afflictions
do fal like hailſtones, one no ſooner drops,
but a whole Showre does follow. I obſerv'd
indeed, my *Abrahen*, that his looks and language
was dreſſ'd in unaccuſtom'd clouds, but did not
imagine they'd preſag'd fo fierce a tempeſt.
Ye gods, why do you give us gifts and graces,
ſhare your own attributes with men, your virtues,
when they betray them to worſe hate then vices ?
But *Abrahen*, prithee reconfirm my feares
by teſtimonial how this can be truth ;
for yet my innocence with too credulous truſt
fooths up my foul, our father ſhould not thus
put that off which does make him fo, his fweetneſſe,
to feed the irregular flames of falſe fuſpicions
and foul tormenting jealouſies.

Ab. Why, to me,
to me (my Lord) he did with ſtrong Injunctions
give a ſolicitous charge to overlook your actions.
My *Abrahen* (quoth he) I'me not ſo unhappie,
that like thy brother thou ſhouldſt be ambitious,
who does affect, 'fore thy ag'd Fathers aſhes,
with greedie luſt my Empire. Have a ſtrict
and cautious diligence to obſerve his carriage,
'twil be a pious care. Mov'd with the baſe
indignity, that he on 'me ſhould force
the office of a ſpy ; your ſpy, my noble
and much lov'd brother : my beſt manhood ſcarce
could keep my angry tears in ; I reſolv'd .
I was in duty bound to giue you early
intelligence of his unjuſt intentions,
that you in wiſedome might prevent all dangers
might fall upon you from them, like ſwift lightning,
killing 'cauſe they invade with ſudden fierceneſſe.
 Abil. In afflicting me, miſery is grown witty.
 Ab. Nay beſides (Sir)
the ſullen *Mura* has the ſelf ſame charge too
conſign'd and ſetled on him ; which his blind
duty will execute. O brother, your
ſoft paſſive nature, do's like jet on fire
when oyls caſt on't, extinguiſh : otherwiſe,
this baſe ſuſpicion would inflame your ſufferance,
nay make the pureſt loyalty rebellious.
However, though your too religious piety
forces you 'ndure this foul diſgrace with patience,
look to your ſafety, brother, that dear ſafety
which is not only yours, but your whole Empires :
for my part, if a faithfull brothers ſervice
may aught avail you, tho againſt our father,
ſince he can be ſo unnaturally ſuſpicious,
as your own thoughts, command it.

        Enter *Selinthus* and *Meſithes.*
 Sel. Come, I know,
although th' aſt loſt ſome implements of manhood

may make thee gracious in the fight of woman,
yet th' aſt a little engine, cal'd a tongue,
by which thou canſt orecome the niceſt female,
in the behalf of friend. Inſooth, you Eunuchs
may well be ſtil'd Pimps-royal, for the skill
you have in quaint procurement.
   Meſ. Your Lordſhip's merry,
and would inforce on me what has been your
office far oftner than the cunningſt Squire belonging
to the ſmock tranſitory. May't pleaſe your Highneſſe.
   Abil. Ha! *Meſithes.*
   Ab. His countenance varies ſtrangely, ſome affaire
the Eunuch gives him notice of, 't ſhould ſeem,
begets much pleaſure in him.
   Abil. Is this truth?
   Meſ. Elſe let me taſte your anger.
   Abil. My dear *Abrahen*,
wee'l march to night, prethee give ſpeedie Notice
to our Lieutenant *Mura*, to collect
the forces from their ſeveral quarters, and
draw them into Battalia on the plain
behind the Citie, lay a ſtrict command
he ſtir not from the Enſigns til our ſelf
arrive in perſon there. Be ſpeedie, brother,
a little haſtie buſineſs craves our preſence.
We wil anon be wiih you, my *Meſithes.*
                        Exeunt Abil. and Meſ.
   Sel. Can your grace imagine
whether his highneſs goes now?
   Ab. No, *Selinthus*;
canſt thou conjecture at the Eunuchs buſineſs?
what ere it was, his countenance ſeem'd much altred:
Il'd give a talent to have certain knowledg
what was *Meſithes* meſſage.
   Sel. I'll inform you
at a far eaſier rate. *Meſithes* buſineſſe
certes concern'd a limber petticoate,
and the ſmock ſoft and ſlipperie; on my honour,
has been providing for the Prince, ſome female

that he takes his leave of Ladies flefh
ere his departure.
 Ab. Not improbable, it may be fo.
 Sel. Nay, certain (Sir) it is fo :
and I believe, your little bodie earnes
after the fame fport. You were once reported
a wag would have had bufinefs of ingendring
with furly *Mura's* Lady : and men may
conjecture y'are no chafter then a vot'rie :
yet though fhe would not folace your defires,
there are as handfome Ladies wil be proud
to have your Grace inoculate their flocks
with your graft-royal.
 Ab. Thou art *Selinthus* flil,
and wilt not change thy humor. I muft go
and find out *Mura* ; fo farwel *Selinthus*,
thou art not for thefe warrs, I know.   *Exit.*
 Sel. No truly,
nor yet for any other, 'lefs 't be on
a naked yeilding enemie ; though there may
be as hot fervice upon fuch a foe
as on thofe clad in fteel : the little fquadron,
we civill men affault body to body,
oft carry wild-fire, about them privately,
that findges us ith' fervice from the crown
even to the fole, nay fometimes hair and all off.
But thefe are tranfitory perills.
      Enter Gafilles, Ofman.
Couzens,
I thought you had been dancing to the drum.
Your General has given order for a march
this night, I can affure you.
 Gaf. It is Couzen,
fomething of the fooneft ; but we are prepar'd
at all times for the journey.
 Sel. To morrow morning
may ferve the turn though. Hark you, Couzens mine;
if in this *Perfian* War you chance to take a
handfome fhe Captive, pray you be not unmindfull

of us your friends at home ; I will disburse
her ransome, Couzens, for I've a months mind
to try if strange flesh, or that of our own
Countrey has the compleater relish.
 Os. We will accomplish thy pleasure, noble Couzen.
 Sel. But pray do not
take the first say of her your selves. I do not
love to walk after any of my kindred
ith' path of copulation.
 Gas. The first fruits
shall be thy own, dear Couz. But shall we part
(never perhaps to meet agen) with dry
lips, my right honoured Coz?
 Sel. By no means,
though by the *Alcharon* wine be forbidden,
you Souldiers in that case make't not your faith.
Drink water in the Camp, when you can purchase
no other liquor; here you shall have plenty
of wine, old and delicious. I'le be your leader,
and bring you on, let who will bring you off.
To the encounter, come let us mareh, Couzens.
Exeunt Omnes.

    Song.

Scena Secunda.

Enter Abilqualit, Caropia, and Mesithes, Perilinda.

 Car. No more, my gracious Lord, where real love
  is
needlesse are all expressions ceremonious:
the amorous Turtles, that at first acquaintance
strive to expresse in murmuring notes their loves,
do when agreed on their affections change
their chirps to billing.
 Abil. And in feather'd arms
incompasse mutually their gawdy necks.
 Mes: How do you like

these love tricks, *Perilinda* ?
 Per. Very well ;
but one may fooner hope from a dead man
to receive kindnefs, than from thee, an Eunuch.
You are the coldeft creatures in the bodies,
no fnow-balls like you.
 Mef. We muft needs, who have not
that which like fire fhould warm our conftitutions,
the inftruments of copulation, girle,
our toyes to pleafe the Ladies.
 Abil. Caropia, in your well becoming pity
of my extream afflictions and ftern fufferings,
you've fhown that excellent mercy as muft render
what ever action you can fix on, virtuous.
But Lady, I till now have been your tempter,
one that defired hearing, the brave refiftance
you made my brother, when he woo'd your love,
only to boaft the glory of a conqueft
which feem'd impoffible, now I have gain'd it
by being vanquifher, I my felf am vanquifh'd
your everlafting Captive.
 Car. Then the thraldome
will be as profperqus as the pleafing bondage
of palms, that flourifh moft when bowd down fafteft ;
Conftraint makes fweet and eafie things laborious,
when love makes greateft miferies feem pleafures.
Yet 'twas ambition (Sir) join'd with affection
that gave me up a fpoil to your temptations.
I was refolv'd, if ever I did make
a breach on matrimonial faith, 't fhould be
with him that was the darling of kind fortune
as well as liberall nature ; who poffeff'd
the height of greatneffe to adorn his beauty ;
which fince they both confpire to make you happy,
I thought 't would be a greater fin to fuffer
your hopeful perfon, born to fway this Empire,
in loves hot flames to languifh, by refufal
to a confuming feaver, then t' infringe
a vow which ne're proceeded from my heart

when I unwillingly made it.
 Abil. And may break it with confidence, fecure from the
leaſt guilt, as if 't had only in an idle dream
been by your fancy plighted. Madam, there
can be no greater mifery in love,
than feparation from the object which
we affect; and fuch is our misfortune
we muſt ith' infancy of our defires
breath at unwelcome diſtance; ith' mean time,
lets make good ufe of the moſt precious minuts
we have to fpend together.
 Car. Elfe we were unworthy to be titled lovers; but
I fear loath'd *Mura* may with fwift approach
difturb our happineſſe.
 Abil. By my command hee's muſtring up our forces.
Yet *Mefithes*, go you to *Abrahen*, and with intimations
from us, ſtrengthen our charge. Come my *Caropia*,
love's wars are harmleſſe, for who ere do's yeild,
gains as much honor as who wins the field.

Actus Tertius Scena I.

*Enter Abilqualit and Caropia, as rifing from
bed, Abrahen without, Perilinda.*

Br. Open the door, I muſt and will have entrance
unto the Prince my brother, as you love
your life and fafety and that Ladies honor,

whom you are lodg'd in amorous twines with, do not
deny me entrance to you, I am *Abrahen,*
your loyal brother *Abrahen.*
    Abil. 'Tis his voice,
and there can be no danger in't, *Caropia,*
be not difmaid, though w'are to him difcover'd.
Your fame fhall tafte nq blemifh by't. Now brother,
'tis fomething rude in you, thus violently
to preffe upon our privacies.
    Abr. My affection
fhall be my Advocate, and plead my care
of your lov'd welfare, as you love your honour,
hafte from this place, or you'l betray the Lady
to ruin moft inevitable. Her husband
has notice of your being here, and's comming
on wings of jealoufie and defperate rage
to intercept you in your clofe delights.
In breif, I over heard a trufty Servant
of his ith' Camp come and declare your highneffe
was private with *Caropia*: at which tidings
the fea with greater hafte when vext with tempefts,
fo fudden and boyftrous, flies not towards the fhore,
then he intended homewards. He by this
needs muft have gain'd the City; for with all my
    power
I hafted hitherward, that by your abfence
you might prevent his veiw of you.
    Abil. Why? the flave
dare not invade my perfon, had he found me
in fair *Caropias* armes : 'twould be ignoble,
now I have cauf'd her danger, fhould I not
defend her from his violence. I'le ftay
though he come arm'd with thunder.
    Abr. That will be
a certain means to ruin her : To me'
count that cure, I'le ftand between the Lady,
and *Mura's* fury, when your very fight,
giving frefh fire to th' injury, will incenfe him
'gainft her beyond all patience.

Car. Nay, befides
his violent wrath breaking through his allegiance
may riot on your perfon. Dear my Lord
withdraw your felf, there may be fome excufe
when you are abfent thought on, to take off
Mura's fufpition : by our loves, depart
I do befeech you. Haplefs I was born
to be moft miferable.
 Abil. You fhall over-rule me.
Better it is for him with unhallowed hands
to act a facriledg on our Prophets tombe
then to profane this purity with the leaft
offer of injurie ; be careful *Abrahen*,
to thee I leave my heart. Farewell *Caropia*,
your tears inforce my abfence.   *Exit Abil.*
 Abr. Pray haft my Lord
left you fhould meet the inrag'd *Mura* : now Madam
where are the boafted glories of that virtue,
which like a faithful Fort withftood my batt'ries?
demolifh'd now, and ruin'd they appear ;
like a fair building toter'd from its bafe
by an unruly whirlewind, and are now
inftead of love the objects of my pitie.
 Car. I'me bound to thank you Sir, yet credit me ;
my fin's fo pleafing 't' cannot meet repentance.
Were *Mura* here, and arm'd with all the horrors
rage could inveft his powers with ; not forgiven
Hermits with greater peace fhal haft to death,
then I to be the Martyr of this caufe,
which I fo love and reverence.
 Abr. 'Tis a noble
and wel becoming conftancie, and merits
a lover of thofe Supreme eminent graces,
that do like ful winds fwel the glorious Sails
of *Abilqualit's* dignitie and beautie !
yet Madam, let me tell you, though I could not
envie my brothers happineffe, if he
could have enjoy'd your pricelefs love with fafetie,
free from difcoverie, I am afflicted

Revenge for Honour.

beyond a moderate forrow, that my youth
which with as true a zeal, courted your love,
fhould appear fo contemptible to receive
a killing fcorn from you : yet I forgive you,
and do fo much refpect your peace, I wifh
you had not fin'd fo carelefly to be
betray'd ith' firft fruitions of your wifhes
to your fufpicious husband.

    Car. 'Tis a fate Sir,
which I muft ftand, though it come drefs'd in flames,
killing as circular fire, and as prodigious
as death prefaging Comets: there's that ftrength
in love, can change the pitchie face of dangers
to pleafing formes, make ghaftly fears feeme beauteous;
and I'me refolv'd, fince the fweet Prince is free
from *Mura's* anger, which might have been fatal
if he fhould here have found him, unrefiftlefs
I dare his utmoft fury.

    Abr. 'Twil bring death with't
fure as ftifling dampe ; and 'twere much pitie
fo fweet a beautie fhould unpitied fall,
betrai'd to endleffe infamie ; your husband
knowes only that my brother in your chamber
was entertained ; the fervant that betrayed you,
curfe on his diligence, could not affirm
he faw you twin'd together: yet it is
death by the law, you know, for any Ladie
at fuch an hour, and in her husbands abfence ;
to entertain a ftranger.

    Car. 'Tis confidered Sir,
and fince I cannot live to enjoy his love,
I'le meet my death as willingly as I
met *Abilqualit's* dear embraces.

    Abr. That were too fevere a crueltie. Live *Caropia*,
til the kind deftinies take the loath'd *Mura*
to their eternal Manfions, til he fal
either in war a facrifice to fortune,
or elfe by ftratagem take his deftruction

from angry *Abilqualit*, whofe faire Empreffe
you were created for : there is a mean yet
to fave th' opinion of your honour fpotleffe,
as that of Virgin innocence, nay to preferve,
(though he doth know (as certainly he muft do)
my Brother have injoy'd thee) thee ftil precious
in his deluding fancie.

Car.   Let me adore you
if you can give effect to your good purpofe.
But tis impoffible.

Abr.   With as fecure an eafe
't fhal be accomplifh'd as the bleft defires
of uncrofs'd lovers : you fhal with one breath
diffolve thefe mifts that with contagious darkneffe
threaten the lights both of your life and honour.
Affirm my brother ravifh'd you.

Car.   How my Lord?

Abr.   Obtained by violence entry into your chamber
where his big luft feconded by force,
defpight of yours and your Maids weak refiftance
furpris'd your honor : when't fhall come to queftion,
my brother cannot fo put off the truth,
he owes his own affection and your whitenefs,
but to acknowledg it a rape.

Car.   And fo by faving mine, betray his fame and
  fafety,
to the lawes danger, and your fathers juftice,
which with impartial doome will moft feverely
fentence the Prince, although his fon.

Abr.   Your fears
and too affectionate tenderneffe wil ruine
all that my care has builded.   Sure, *Mefithes*
has (as my charge injoin'd him) made relation

Enter Mura.

to him of *Abilqualit's* action.   See your Husband,
refolve on't, or y'are miferable.

Mu.   Furies,
where is this luftful Prince, and this lafcivious
Strumpet? ha *Abrahen*, here?

Abr. Good Cozen *Mura*,
be not ſo paſſionate, it is your Prince
has wrought your injury; reſolve to bear
your croſſes like a man : the great'ſt afflictions
ſhould have the greateſt fortitude in their ſuff'rings
from minds reſolv'd and noble. 'Las poor Ladie,
'twas not her fault; his too unruly luſt
'tis, has deſtroi'd her puritie.
Mu. Ha, in tears !
Are theſe the liverie of your fears and penitence,
or of your ſorrows (minion) for being rob'd
ſo ſoon of your Adulterer ?
Abr. Fie, your paſſion
is too unmannerly; you look upon her
with eyes of rage, when you with grief and pitie
ought to ſurveigh her innocence. My Brother,
degenerate as he is from worth, and meerly
the beaſt of luſt, (what fiends would fear to violate)
has with rude inſolence deſtroyed her honor,
by him inhumane raviſhed.
Car. Good Sir be
ſo merciful as to ſet free a wretch
from loath'd mortalitie, whoſe lifes ſo great
and hateful burden now ſh'as loſt her honor :
'Twil be a friendly charitie to deliver
her from the torment of it.
Mu. That I could
contract the ſoul of univerſal rage
into this ſwelling heart, that it might be
as ful of poiſonous anger as a dragons
when in a toile inſnar'd. *Caropia* raviſhed !
Methinks the horror of the ſound ſhould fright
to everlaſting ruine, the whole world,
ſtart natures Genius.
Abr. Gentle Madam, pray
withdraw your ſelf, your ſight, til I have wrought
a cure upon his temper, wil but adde
to his affliction.
Car. You're as my good Angel,

I'll follow your directions. *Exit.*

Abr. Cozen *Mura,*
I thought a person of your masculine temper,
in dangers fostred, where perpetual terrors
have been your play-fellowes, would not have resented
with such effeminate passion a disgrace,
though ne're so huge and hideous.

Mu. I am tame,
collected now in all my faculties,
which are so much oppress'd with injuries,
they've lost the anguish of them: can you think, Sir,
when all the winds fight, the inrag'd billows
that use to imprint on the black lips of clouds
a thousand brinie kisses, can lie stil,
as in a lethargie? that when baths of oyl
are pour'd upon the wild irregular flames
in populous Cities, that they'll then extinguish?
Your mitigations adde but seas to seas,
give matter to my fires to increase their burning,
and I ere long enlightned by my anger
shall be my owne pile, and consume to ashes.

Abr. Why, then I see indeed your injuries
have ravished hence your reason and discourse,
and left you the meere prostitute of passion.
Can you repaire the ruins you lament so
with these exclaimes? was ever dead man call'd
to life again by fruitful sighs? or can
your rage reedifie *Caropias* honour,
slain and betrai'd by his foul lust? Your manhood,
that heretofore has thrown you on all dangers,
me thinks should prompt you to a noble vengance,
which you may safely prosecute with Justice,
to which this crime, although he be a Prince,
Renders him liable.

Mu. Yes, I'le have justice
or I'le awake the sleepy Deities,
or like ambitious Gyants wage new wars
with heaven it self, my wrongs shall steel my courage,
and on this vicious Prince like a fierce Sea-breach

my juſt wak'd rage ſhall riot till it ſink
in the remorceleſſe eddie, ſink where time
ſhall never find his name but with diſgrace
to taint his hatefull memory.

 Abr. This wildneſſe neither befit your wiſdom nor
  your courage,
which ſhould with ſetled and collected thoughts
walk on to noble vengeance. He before
was by our plots proſcrib'd to death and ruine
to advance me to the Empire ; now with eaſe
we may accompliſh our deſigns

 Mu. Would heaven
I nere had given conſent, o'recome by love
to you to have made a forfeit on my allegiance,
'tis a juſt puniſhment, I by him am wrong'd,
whom for your ſake I fearleſſe fought to ruin.

 Abr. Are you repentant grown, *Mura ?* this ſoft-
  neſe ?
ill ſuits a perſon of your great reſolves,
on whom my fortunes have ſuch firm dependance.
Come, let *Caropia's* fate invoke thy vengeance
to gain full maſtry o're all other paſſions,
leave not a corner in thy ſpacious heart
unfurniſh'd of a noble rage, which now
will be an attribute of glorious juſtice :
the law you know with loſs of fight doth puniſh
all rapes, though on mean perſons ; and our father
is ſo ſevere a Juſticer, not blood
can make a breach upon his faith to juſtice.
Beſides, we have already made him dangerous
in great *Almanzors* thoughts, and being delinquent
he needs muſt ſuffer what the meaneſt offender
merits for ſuch a treſpaſs.

 Mu. I'me awake now,
the lethargy of horror and amaze
that did obſcure my reaſon, like thoſe dul
and lazy vapors that o'reſhade the Sun,
vaniſh, and it reſumes its native brightneſs.
And now I would not but this devil Prince

had done this act upon *Caropia's* whitenefs,
fince't yeilds you free accefs unto the Empire,
The deprivall of's fight do's render him incapable
of future foveraignty.

   Abr. Thou'rt in the right,
and haft put on manly confiderations :
Caropia (fince fhee's in her will untainted)
ha's not forgon her honor : he difpatc'd once,
as we will have him fhortly, 't fhall go hard elfe,
a tenant to his marble, thou agen
wedded in peace maift be to her pure vertues,
and live their happy owner.

   Mu. I'le repair
to great *Almanzor* inftantly, and if
his partial piety do defcend to pitty,
I will awake the Executioner
of juftice, death, although in fleep more heavy
than he can borrow from his natural coldnefs ;
on this good fword I'le wear my caufes juftice
till he do fall its facrifice.

   Abr. But be fure
you do't with cunning fecrefie, perhaps,
fhould he have notice of your juft intentions,
he would repair to th' Army, from which fafegard
our beft force could not pluck him without danger
to the whole Empire.

   Mu. Doubt not but I'le manage
with a difcreet feverity my vengeance,
invoke *Almanzors* equity with fudden
and private hafte.

   Abr. Mean time
I will go put a new defign in practice
that may be much conducing to our purpofe.
Like clocks, one wheele another on muft drive,
affairs by diligent labor only thrive.   *Exeunt.*

Scena Secunda.

Enter *Selinthus, Gafelles, Ofman,* and *Souldiers.*

   Sel. No quarrelling good Couzens, left it be

with the glafs, 'caufe 'tis not of fize fufficient
to give you a magnificent draught.   You will
have fighting work enough when you're i' th' wars,
do not fall out among your felves.
    Of. Not pledg
my peerleffe Miftreffe health ? Souldier, thou'rt mor-
    tall,
if thou refufe it.
    Gaf. Come, come, he fhall pledg it,
and 'twere a Tun.   Why, w'are all as dull
as dormife in our liquor : Here's a health
to the Prince *Abilqualit.*
    Soul. Let go round :
I'ld drink't, were it an Ocean of warm bloud
flowing from th' enemie.   Pray, good my Lord
what news is ftirring ?
    Sel. It fhould feem, Souldier,
thou canft not read ; otherwife the learn'd Pamphlets
that flie about the ftreets, would fatisfie
thy curiofitie with news ; they'r true ones,
full of difcreet intelligence.
    Of. Cofens, fhal's have a Song ? here is a Souldier
in's time hath fung a dirge unto the foe
oft in the field.
    Soul. Captain, I have a new one,
the Souldiers Joy 'tis call'd.
    Sel. That is an harlot.
Preethee be muficall, and let us tafte
the fweetneffe of thy voice.   *A Song.*
    Gaf. Whift, give attention.
    Soul. How does your Lordfhip like it ?
    Sel. Very well.
And fo here's to thee.   There's no drum beats yet,
and 'tis cleer day ; fome hour hence 'twill be
                            Enter Abr. Mef.
time to break up the Watch.   Ha ! young Lord
    Abrahen,
and trim *Mefithes* with him ! what the divel
does he make up fo early ?   He has been

a bat-fowling all night after thofe Birds,
thofe Ladie-birds term'd wagtails; what ftrange bufi-
　　nefs
can he have here, tro?
　　Abr. "Twas wel done, *Mefithes*!
and truft me, I fhal find an apt reward,
both for thy care and cunning.　Prethee haft
to Lord *Simanthes*, and deliver this
note to him with beft diligence, my dear Eunuch;
thou'rt halfe the foul of *Abrahen*:
　　Mef. I was borne
to be intituled your moft humble vaffal;
I'll haft to the Lord *Simanthes*.　　　　　　　*Exit.*
　　Sel. How he cringes!
Thefe youths that want the inftruments of Manhood,
are very fupple in the hams.
　　Abr. Good morrow
to noble Lord *Selinthus*: what companions
have you got here thus early?
　　Sel. Blades of metal,
tall men of war, and't pleafe your Grace, of my
own blood and family, men who gather'd
a fallad on the enemies ground, and eaten it
in bold defiance of him;
and not a Souldier here but's an *Achylles*,
valiant as ftouteft *Mirmidon*.
　　Abr. And they
never had jufter caufe to fhow their valor;
the Prince my deareft brother, their Lord **General's**
became a forfeit to the ftern laws rigour;
and 'tis imagin'd, our impartial father,
will fentence him to lofe his eyes.
　　Gaf. Marry heaven
defend, for what, and 't like your Grace!
　　Abr For a fact
which the fevere law punifhes with lofs
of natures precious lights; my teares wil fcarce
permit me utter't: for a rape committed
on the fair wife of *Mura*.

Of. Was it for nothing elfe, and pleafe your Grace?
ere he fhal lofe an eie for fuch a trifle,
or have a haire diminifh'd, we wil
lofe our heads; what, hoodwink men like fullen hawks
for doing deeds of nature! I'me afham'd
the law is fuch an Afs.
   Sel. Some Eunuch Judg,
that could not be acquainted with the fweets
due to concupifcencial parts, invented
this law, I'll be hang'd elfe. 's Life, a Prince,
and fuch a hopeful one, to lofe his eyes,
for fatisfying the hunger of the ftomack
beneath the waft, is crueltie prodigious,
not to be fuffer'd in a common-wealth
of ought but geldings.
   Abr. 'Tis vain to footh
our hopes with thefe delufions, he wil fuffer
lefs he be reskued. I would have you therfore
if you ow any fervice to the Prince,
my much lamented brother, to attend
without leaft tumult 'bout the Court, and if
there be neceffity of your ayd, I'le give you
notice when to imploy it.
   Sel. Sweet Prince, wee'l fwim
in blood to do thee or thy brother fervice.
Each man provide their weapons.
   Abr. You will win
my brothers love for ever, nay my father,
though hee'l feem angry to behold his juftice
deluded, afterwards when his rage is paft,
will thank you for your loyalties: Pray be there
with all fpeed poffible, by this my brothers
commanded 'fore my father, Ile go learn
the truth, and give you notice: pray be fecret
and firm to your refolves.   *Exit.*
   Sel. For him that flinches
in fuch a caufe, I'le have no more mercy
on him. Heres *Tarifa*   *Enter Tarifa and Mura.*
the Princes fometimes Tutor, *Mura* with him

a walking towards the Court, let's take no notice
of them, left they difcover our intentions
by our grim looks.   March fair and foftly Couzens,
wee'l be at Court before them.
 Tar. You will not do this, *Mura* !
 Mu. How *Tarifa ?*
will you defend him in an act fo impious ?
Is't fit the drum fhould ceafe his furly language,
when the bold Souldiers marches, or that I
fhould paffe o're this affront in quiet filence,
which Gods and men invoke to fpeedy vengeance?
which I will have, or manhood fhall be tame
as Cowardice.
 Tar. It was a deed fo barbarous,
that truth it felf blufhes as well as juftice
to hear it mention'd : but confider *Mura,*
he is our Prince, the Empires hope, and pillar
of great *Almanzors* age.   How far a publick
regard fhould be prefer'd before your private
defire of vengeance ! which if you do purchace
from our impartial Emperors equity,
his lofs of fight, and fo of the fuccefsion,
will not reftore *Caropia* to the honor
he ravifh't from her.   But fo foule the caufe is,
I rather fhould lament the Princes folly
than plead in his behalf.
 Mur. 'Tis but vain,
there is your warrant, as you are high Marfhal,
to fummon him to make his fpeedy appearance
'fore the Tribunall of *Almanzor ;*
fo pray you execute your office.   *Exit.*
 Tar. How one vice
can like a fmall cloud when 't breaks forth in fhowers,
black the whole heaven of vertues ! O my Lord,
  Enter Abilqualit, Muts, whifpring, feem to make
    proteftations. Exeunt.
that face of yours which once with Angell brightneffe
cheer'd my faint fight, like a grim apparition
frights it with ghaftly terror : you have done

a deed that ftartles vertue till it fhakes
as it got a palfie. I'me commanded
to fummon you before your father, and
hope you'l obey his mandate.
 Abil. Willingly,
what's my offence, *Tarifa* ?
 Tar. Would you knew not,
I did prefage your too unruly paffions
would hurry you to fome difaft'rous act,
but ne're imagin'd you'd have been fo loft
to mafculine honor, to commit a rape
on that unhappy object of your love,
whom now y'ave made the fpoil of your foul luft,
the much wrong'd wife of *Mura.*
 Abil. Why, do's *Mura* charge me with his *Caropia's*
  rape ?
 Tar. This warrant fent by your angry father, tefti-
  fies
he means to appeach you of it.
 Abil. 'Tis my fortune, all natural motions when they
approach their end, haft to draw to't with accuftom'd
fwiftneffe. Rivers with greedier fpeed run neere
their out-falls, than at their fprings. But I'me refolv'd,
let what happen that will, I'le ftand it, and defend
Caropia's honor, though mine own I ruin;
Who dares not dye to juftifie his love,
deferves not to enjoy her. Come, *Tarifa,*
what e're befall, I'me refolute. He dies
glorious, that falls loves innocent facrifice. *Exeunt.*

Actus Quartus.   Scena I.

Enter Almanzor, Abilqualit, Tarifa and Mura.

Al. NO more *Tarifa*, you'l provoke our anger,
  if you appear in this caufe fo folicitous,
the act is too apparent : nor fhal you

need (injur'd *Mura*) to implore our juſtice,
which with impartial doome ſhall fal on him
more rigorouſly, then on a ſtrange offender.
O *Abilqualit*, (for the name of Son,
when thou forſookſt thy native virtue, left thee ;)
Were all thy blood, thy youth and fortunes glories
of no more value, then to be expos'd
to ruine for one vice ; at whoſe name only
the furies ſtart, and baſhful fronted juſtice
hides her amaz'd head ? But it is now bootleſs
to ſhew a fathers pitie, in my grief
for thy amiſs. As I'me to be thy Judg,
be reſolute, I'll take as little notice,
thou art my off-ſpring, as the wandring clouds
do of the ſhowers, which when they've bred to ripeneſſe,
they ſtraight diſperſe through the vaſt earth forgotten.

   Abil. I'me ſorrie Sir, that my unhappie chance
ſhould draw your anger on me ; my long ſilence
declares I have on that excelling ſweetneſſe,
that unexampled pattern of chaſt goodneſſe ;
Caropia acted violence. I confeſs,
I lov'd the Ladie, and when no perſwaſions
ſerv'd to prevail on her, too ſtubborn, incenſs'd,
by force I ſought my purpoſe and obtain'd it ;
nor do I yet (ſo much I prize the ſweetneſſe
of that unvalued purchaſe) find repentance
in any abject thought ; what ere fals on me
from your ſterne rigor in a cauſe ſo precious,
wil be a pleaſing puniſhment.

   Al. You are grown
a glorious malefactor, that dare brave thus
the awful rod of juſtice ! Loſt young man,
for thou'rt no child of mine ; doſt not conſider
to what a ſtate of deſperate deſtruction
thy wild luſt has betrai'd thee ! What rich bleſſings
(that I may make thee ſenſible of thy ſins
by ſhowing thee thy ſuffering) haſt thou loſt
by thy irregular folly ! Firſt my love,

which never more muſt meet thee, ſcarce in pitie ;
the glorie flowing from thy former actions
ſtopt up for ever ; and thoſe luſtful eies,
by whoſe deprival (thou'rt depriv'd of being
capable of this Empire) to the law,
which wil exact them, forfeited. Cal in there
a Surgeon, and our Mutts to execute this act
Enter Surg. Muts.
of juſtice on the unworthie traitor, upon whom
my juſt wak'd wrath ſhall have no more compaſſion,
then the incens'd flames have on periſhing wretches
that wilfully leap into them.

   Tar. O my Lord,
that which on others would be fitting juſtice,
on him your hopeful though offending ſon,
wil be exemplar crueltie ; his youth Sir,
that hath abounded with ſo many vertues,
is an excuſe ſufficient for one vice :
he is not yours only, hee's your Empires,
deſtin'd by nature and ſucceſſions priviledg,
when you in peace are ſhrowded in your marble,
to weild this Scepter after you. O do not,
by putting out his eies, deprive your Subjects
of light, and leave them to dul mournful darkneſſe.

   Al. 'Tis but in vain, I am inexorable.
If thoſe on which his eyes hang, were my heart ſtrings,
I'de cut them out rather then wound my Juſtice ;
nor dos't befit thy vertue intercede
for him in this cauſe horrid and prodigious ;
the crime 'gainſt me was acted ; 'twas a rape
upon my honour, more then on her whiteneſſe ;
his was from mine derivative, as each ſtream
is from its ſpring ; ſo that he has polluted
by his foul fact, my fame, my truth, my goodneſſe,
ſtrucken through my dignitie by his violence :
nay, ſtarted in their peaceful urnes, the aſhes
of all my glorious Anceſtors ; defil'd
the memorie of their ſtil deſcendent vertues ;
nay, with a killing froſt, nipt the fair bloſſomes,

that did prefage fuch goodly fruit arifing
from his own hopeful youth.
 Mur. I ask but juftice;
thofe eyes that led him to unlawful objects,
tis fit fhould fuffer for't a lafting blindneffe;
the Sun himfelf, when he darts rayes lafcivious,
fuch as ingender by too piercing fervence
intemperate and infectious heats, ftraight wears
obfcuritie from the clouds his own beams raifes.
I have been your Souldier Sir, and fought your battails;
for all my fervices, I beg but juftice,
which is the Subjects beft prerogative,
the Princes greateft attribute; and for a fact,
then which, none can be held more black and hideous,
which has betrai'd to an eclipfe the brighteft
ftar in th' heaven of vertues: the juft law
does for't ordain a punifhment, which I hope
you the laws righteous guider, wil accordiug
to equitie fee executed.
 Tar. Why! that law
was only made for common malefactors,
but has no force to extend unto the Prince,
to whom the law it felf muft become fubject.
This hopeful Prince, look on him, great *Almanzor*;
and in his eyes, thofe volumes of all graces,
which you like erring Meteors would extinguifh:
read your own lively figure, the beft ftorie
of your youths nobleft vigor; let not wrath (Sir)
o'recome your pietie, nay your humane pity.
'Tis in your breft, my Lord, yet to fhew mercie;
that precious attribute of heavens true goodneffe,
even to your felf, your fon! me thinks that name
fhould have a power to interdict your Juftice
in its too rigorous progrefs.
 Abil. Dear *Tarifa,*
I'me more afflicted at the interceffions,
then at the view of my approaching torments,
which I wil meet with fortitude and boldnefs,

Revenge for Honour.

too bafe to fhake now at one perfonal danger,
when I've incountred thoufand perils fearlefs;
Nor do I blame my gracious fathers Juftice,
though it precede his nature. I'ld not have him
(for my fake) forfeit that for which hee's famous,
his incorrupted equitie, nor repine
I at my deftinie; my eies have had
delights fufficient in *Caropia's* beauties,
to ferve my thoughts for after contemplations;
nor can I ever covet a new object,
fince they can ne're hope to incounter any
of equal worth and fweetnefs.
Yet hark *Tarifa*, to thy fecrefie
I wil impart my deareft, inmoft counfels;
if I fhould perifh, as 'tis probable
I may, under the hands of thefe tormentors;
thou maift unto fucceffion fhow my innocence;
Caropia yeilded without leaft conftraint,
and I injoy'd her freely.
 Tar. How my Lord?
 Abil. No words on't,
as you refpect my honour! I'ld not lofe
the glorie I fhall gain by thefe my fufferings;
come grim fures, and execute your office. I wil ftand
  you,
unmov'd as hills at whirlewinds, and amidft
the torments you inflict, retain my courage.
 Al. Be fpeedie villaines.
 Tar. O ftay your cruel hands,
you dumb minifters of injur'd Juftice,
and let me fpeak his innocence ere you further
afflict his precious eye-fight.
 Al. What does this mean, *Tarifa*!
 Tar. O my Lord,
the too much braverie of the Princes fpirit
'tis has undone his fame, and pul'd upon him
this fatal punifhment; 'twas but to fave
the Ladies honour, that he has affum'd
her rape upon him, when with her confent

the deed of shame was acted.

Mur. Tis his fears
makes him traduce her innocence : he who did not
stick to commit a riot on her person,
can make no conscience to destroy her fame
by his untrue suggestions.

Al. 'Tis a baseneffe
beyond thy other villanie (had shee yeilded)
thus to betraie for transitorie torture,
her honour, which thou wert ingag'd to safeguard
even with thy life. A son of mine could never
show this ignoble cowardize : Proceed
to execution, I'll not hear him speak,
he his made up of treacheries and falshoods.

Tar. Wil you then
be to the Prince so tyrannous ? Why, to me
just now he did confefs his only motive
to undergoe this torment, was to save
Caropia's honour blamelefs.

Abil. I am more troubled
Sir, with his untimely frenzie,
then with my punishment ; his too much love
to me, has spoild his temperate reafon. I
confefs *Caropia* yeilded ! Not the light
is half so innocent as her spotleffe virtue.
'Twas not wel done, *Tarifa*, to betray
the fecret of your friend thus, though Shee yeilded,
the terror of ten thousand deaths shall never
force me to confefs it.

Tar. Agen, my Lord, even now
he does confefs, she yeilded, and protests
that death shall never make him say shee's guiltie :
the breath scarce pafs'd his lips yet.

Abil. Hapleffe man,
to run into this lunacie !
Fie *Tarifa*,
so treacherous to your Friend !

Tar. Agen, agen.
Wil no man give me credit ?

Revenge for Honour.

Enter Abrahen.

Abr. Where is our roial father ? where our brother ?
As you refpect your life and Empires fafetie,
difmifs thefe tyrannous inftruments of death
and crueltie unexemplified. O Brother,
that I fhould ever live to enjoy my eie-fight,
and fee one halfe of your dear lights indanger'd.
My Lord, you've done an act, which my juft fears
tels me, wil fhake your Scepter ! O for heavens fake,
look to your future fafetie; the rough Souldier
hearing their much lov'd General, My good Brother
was by the law betrai'd to fome fad danger,
have in their pietie befet the pallace ;
think on fome means to appeafe them, ere their furie
grow to its ful unbridled height ; they threaten
your life, dear Sir : pray fend my brother to them,
his fight can only pacifie them.

Al. Have you your Champions !
We wil prevent their infolence, you fhal not
boaft, you have got the Empire by our ruine.
Muts, Strangle him immediately.

Abr. Avert
fuch a prodigious mifchief, heaven, Hark, hark
Enter, Enter.
they're entred into th' Court ; defift you monfters,
my life fhal ftand betwixt his and this violence,
or I with him wil perifh. Faithful Souldiers,
haft to defend your Prince, curfe on your flowneffe.
Hee's dead ; my fathers turn is next. O horror,
would I might fink into forgetfulneffe !
What has your furie urg'd you to ?

Al. To that
which whofo murmurs at, is a faithleffe traitor
Enter Simanthes.
to our tranquilitie. Now Sir, your bufinefs ?

Sim. My Lord, the Citie
is up in arms, in refcue of the Prince ;
the whole Court throngs with Souldiers.

Al. 'Twas high time

to cut this viper off, that would have eat his paſſage
through our very bowels to our Empire.
Nay, we wil ſtand their furies, and with terror
of Majeſtie ſtrike dead theſe inſurrections.
                                         Enter Souldiers.
Traitors, what means this violence?
   Abr. O dear Souldiers,
your honeſt love's in vain ; my Brother's dead,
ſtrangled by great *Almanzor's* dire command,
ere your arrival. I do hope they'l kill him
in their hot zeal.
   Al. Why do you ſtare ſo, traitors ?
'twas I your Emp'ror that have done this act,
which who repines at, treads the ſelf ſame ſteps
of death that he has done. Withdraw and leave us,
wee'ld be alone. No motion ! Are you ſtatues ?
Stay you, *Tarifa* here. For your part, *Mura,*
you cannot now complain but you have juſtice ;
ſo quit our preſence.
   Oſ. Faces about, Gentleman.   *Exeunt.*
   Abr. It has happ'ned
above our wiſhes, we ſhall have no need now
to imploy your handkercher. Yet give it me.
You'r ſure 'tis right, *Simanthes.*
   Al. *Tarifa,*
I know the love thou bearſt Prince *Abilqualit*
makes thy big heart ſwell as 't had drunk the fome
of angry Dragons. Speak thy free intentions,
Deſerv'd he not this fate ?
   Tar. No : You're a Tyrant,
one that delights to feed on your own bowels,
and were not worthie of a Son ſo vertuous.
Now you have tane his, add to your injuſtice,
and take *Tarifa's* life, who in his death,
ſhould it come flying on the wings of torments,
would ſpeak it out as an apparant truth :
the Prince to me declar'd his innocence,
and that *Caropia* yeelded.
   Al. Riſe *Tarifa ;*

we do command thee, rife : a fudden chilneffe,
fuch as the hand of winter cafts on brooks,
thrils our ag'd heart. I'll not have thee ingrofs
forrow alone for *Abilqualit's* death :
I lov'd the boy well, and though his ambition
and popularitie did make him dangerous,
I do repent my furie, and will vie
with thee in forrow. How he makes death lovely !
Shall we fix here, and weep till we be ftatues ?
   Tar. Til we grow ftiff as the cold Alablafters
muft be erected over us. Your rafhneffe
has rob'd the Empire of the greateft hope
it ere fhall boaft agen. Would I were afhes.
   Al. He breathes (me thinks :) the over-haftie foul
was too difcourteous to forfake fo fair
a lodging, without taking folemn leave
firft of the owner. Ha, his handkercher !
Thou'rt lib'ral to thy Father even in death,
leav'ft him a legacie to drie his tears,
which are too flow; they fhould create a deluge.
O my dear *Abilqualit* !
   Tar. You exceed now
as much in grief as you did then in rage,
One drop of this pious paternal foftneffe
had ranfom'd him from ruine. Dear Sir, rife :
my grief's divided, and I know not whether
I fhould lament you living, or him dead.
Good Sir, erect your looks. Not ftir ! His forrow
makes him infenfible. Ha, there's no motion
left in his vital fpirits : The exceffe
of grief has ftifled up his pow'rs, and crack'd
(I fear) his ag'd hearts cordage. Help, the Emperor,
the Emperor's dead; Help, help.

   Abrahen, Simanthes, Mefithes, Muts.

   Abr. What difmal outcrie's this ?
our royal father dead ! The handkercher has wrought
   I fee.

Tar. Yes; his big heart
vanquiſh'd with ſorrow, that in's violent rage,
he doom'd his much lov'd ſon to timeleſs death,
could not endure longer on its weak ſtrings,
but crack'd with weight of ſorrow. Their two ſpirits,
by this, are met in their delightful paſſage
to the bleſt ſhades; we in our tears are bound
to cal you our dread Soveraign.
 Omnes. Long live *Abrahen*
Great *Caliph* of *Arabia.*
 Abr. 'Tis a title
we cannot covet, Lords, it comes attended
with ſo great cares and troubles, that our youth
ſtart at the thought of them, even in our ſorrows
which are ſo mightie on us; our weak ſpirits
are readie to relinquiſh the poſſeſſion
they've of mortalitie, and take ſwift flight
after our roial friends. *Simanthes*, be it
your charge to ſee all fitting preparation
provided for the funerals. *Enter Selinthus.*
 Sel. Where's great *Almanzor*?
 Abr. O *Selinthus*, this
day is the hour of funerals grief; for his
crueltie to my brother, has tranſlated
him to immortalitie.
 Sel. Hee'll have attendants
to wait on him to our great prophets paradiſe,
ere he be readie for his grave. The Souldiers
all mad with rage for the Princes ſlaughter,
have vow'd by all oaths Souldiers can invent,
(and that's no ſmal ſtore) with death and deſtruction
to purſue ſullen *Mura.*
 Abr. *Tarifa*,
uſe your authoritie to keep their violence
in due obedience. We're ſo fraught with grief,
we have no room for any other paſſion
in our diſtracted boſome. Take theſe roial bodies
and place them on that couch; here where they fell,

they fhal be imbalm'd. Yet put them out of our
    fight,
their veiws draw frefh drops from our heart.
Anon we'l fhew our felves to chear the afflicted
Subject.   *a Shout.*
    Omnes. Long live Abrahen, great Caliph of Arabia.
                                            Exeunt.
    Abr. And who can fay now, *Abrahen* is a villain ?
I am faluted King with acclamations
that deaf the Heavens to hear, with as much joy
as if I had atchiev'd this Scepter by
means fair and vertuous. 'Twas this handkercher
that did to death *Almanzor;* fo infected
its leaft infenfible vapour has full power ;
apply'd to th' eye, or any other Organ,
can drink its poyfon in to vanquifh Nature,
though nere fo ftrong and youthful. 'Twas *Simanthes*
devis'd it for my brother, and my cunning
transferr'd it to *Almanzor* ; 'tis no matter,
my worft impiety is held now religious.
'Twixt Kings and their inferiors there's this ods,
Thefe are meer men, we men, yet earthly gods.
                                            Exit.
    Abil. 'Twas well the Muts prov'd faithful, other-
    wife
I'd loft my breath with as much fpeed and filence
as thofe who do expire in dreams, their health
feeming no whit abated. But 'twas wifely
confider'd of me, to prepare thofe fure
inftruments of deftruction : The fufpicion
I had by *Abrahen* of my fathers fears
of my unthought ambition, did inftruct me
by making them mine, to fecure my fafety.
Would the inhumane Surgeon had tane
thefe bleffed lights from me ; that I had liv'd for
    ever
doom'd to perpetual darknefs, rather then
Tarifa's fears had fo appeach'd her honour.

Well, villain Brother, I have found that by
my feeming death, which by my lives beft arts
I ne're fhould have had knowledg of. Dear Father,
though thou to me wert pitileffe, my heart
weeps tears of blood, to fee thy age thus like
a lofty pine fall, eaten through by th' gin
from its own Stock defcending : He has agents
in his ungracious wickedneffe : *Simanthes*
he has difcover'd : Were they multitudes
as numerous as collected fands, and mighty
in force as mifchief, they fhould from my Juftice
meet their due punifhment. *Abrahen* by this
is proclaim'd Caliph, yet my undoubted right,
when't fhall appear I'me living, wil reduce
the people to my part ; the armie's mine,
whither I muft withdraw unfeen : the night
wil beft fecure me. What a ftrange *Chimera*
of thought poffeffes my dul brain ! *Caropia*,
thou haft a fhare in them : Fate, to thy mercie
I do commit my felf; who fcapes the fnare
once, has a certain caution to beware. *Exit.*

Scen. 2. *Enter Caropia* and *Perilinda.*

Car. Your Lord is not returned yet !
Per. No, good Madam :
pray do not thus torment your felf, the Prince
(I warrant you) wil have no injurie
by faving of your honour ; do you think
his father wil be fo extreme outragious
for fuch a trifle, as to force a woman
with her good liking ?
Car. My ill boding foul
beats with prefages ominous. Would heaven
I'd ftood the hazard of my incenf'd Lords furie,
rather then he had run this imminent danger.
Could you ne're learn, which of the flaves it was
betray'd our clofe loves to loath'd *Mura*'s notice ?

Per. No indeed could I not; but here's my Lord,
pray Madam do not grieve fo !   *Enter Mura.*
  Mu. My *Caropia*,
drefs up thy looks in their accuftom'd beauties,
cal back the conftant fpring into thy cheeks,
that droope like lovely Violets, o're charg'd
with too much mornings dew; fhoot from thy eies
a thoufand flames of joy. The luftful Prince,
that like a foul thief, rob'd thee of thy honour
by his ungracious violence, has met
his roial fathers Juftice.
  Car. Now my fears
carry too fure an augury ! you would fain
footh me, my Lord, out of my floud of forrows;
what reparation can that make my honour,
though he have tafted punifhment ?
  Mu. His life
is faln the off-fpring of thy chaftitie,
which his hot luft polluted : nay, *Caropia*,
to fave himfelf, when he but felt the torment
applied to his lafcivious eies ; although
at firft he did with impudence acknowledg
thy rape, he did invade thy fpotlefs virtue,
protefted, only 'twas to fave thy honor,
he took on him thy rape, when with confent
and not conftrain'd, thou yeildedft to the loofnefs
of his wild vicious flames.
  Car. Could he be fo unjuft, my Lord ?
  Mu. He was, and he has paid for't;
the malicious Souldier, while he was a lofing
his eies, made violent head to bring him reskue,
    which
pul'd his ruine on him. But no more
of fuch a prodigie; may his black memorie
perifh even with his afhes. My *Caropia*,
the flourifhing trees widow'd by winters violence
of their fair ornaments, when 'tis expir'd once,
put forth again with new and virgin frefhnefs,
their bufhie beauties; it fhould be thy emblem.

Display agen. those chast immaculate glories,
which the harsh winter of his lust had wither'd ;
and I'll agen be wedded to thy vertues,
with as much joy, as when thou first inrich'd me
with their pure maiden beauties. Thou art dul,
and dost not gratulate with happie welcoms,
the triumphs of thy vengeance.
 Car. Are you sure, my Lord, the Prince is dead?
 Mu. Pish, I beheld him breathlesse.
Take comfort best *Caropia*, thy disgrace
did with his loath'd breath vanish.
 Car. I could wish though,
that he had falne by your particular vengance,
rather then by th' laws rigor ; you're a Souldier
of glorie, great in war for brave performance :
me thinks 't had been far nobler, had you call'd him
to personal satisfaction : had I been
your husband, you my wife, and ravished by him ;
my resolution would have arm'd my courage
to 've stroke him thus : The dead Prince sends you
  that.   *Stab him.*
 Mu. O, I am slain !
 Car. Would it were possible
to kil even thy eternitie. Sweet Prince,
how shal I satisfie thy unhappie ruins !
Ha, not yet breathlesse ! To increase thy anguish
even to despair, know, *Abilqualit* was
more dear to me, then thy foul selfe was odious,
and did enjoy me freely.
 Au. That I had
but breath enough to blast thee.
 Car. 'Twas his brother
(curse on his art) seduc'd me to accuse
him of my rape. Do you groane, prodigie !
take this as my last bountie.   *Stab again.*

     Enter Perilinda.

 Per. O Madam, Madam,

Revenge for Honour.

what fhal we do ? the houfe is round befet
with Souldiers ; Madam, they do fweare they'le tear
my Lord, for the fweet Princes death, in pieces.
 Car. This hand has fav'd
their furie that juft labour : yet I'le make
ufe of their malice, help to convey
him into's Chamber.

   Enter Ofman, Gaffelles, Souldiers.

 Gaf. Where is this villain, this traitor *Mura* ?
 Car. Heaven knowes what violence
their furie may affault me with ; be't death,
't fhall be as welcome, as found healthful fleeps
to men opprefs'd with ficknesse. What's the matter ?
what means this outrage ?
 Of. Marry, Ladie gay,
We're come to cut your little throat ; pox on you,
and all your fex ; you've caus'd the noble Princes
death, wild-fire take you fort, weel talk with you
at better leifure : you muft needs be ravifhed !
and could not like an honeft woman, take
the curtefie in friendly fort !
 Gaf. We trifle :
her husband may efcape us. Say, where is he ?
or you fhall die, ere you can pray.
 Sold. Here, here I have found the vallain ! what, do
  you
fleep fo foundly ? ne're wake more, this for the
Prince, you rogue : let's tear him piecemeale.
Do you take your death in filence, dog !
 Car. You appear indow'd with fome humanitie,
you have tane his life ; let not your hate laft
after death ; let me embalm his bodie with
my tears, or kil me with him.
 Of. Now you've faid the word,
we care not if we do.   *Enter Tarifa.*
 Tar. Slaves, unhand
the Ladie, who dares offer her leaft violence,

from this hand meets his punifhment. *Gafelles,
Ofman,* I thought you had been better temper'd,
then thus to raife up mutinies. In the name
of *Abrahen* our now Caliph, I command you,
defift from thefe rebellious practifes,
and quietly retire into the Camp,
and there expect his pleafure.

 Gaf. *Abrahen* Caliph!
There is fome hopes then, we fhall gaine our pardons:
Long live great *Abrahen.* Souldiers, flink away,
our vow is confummate.

 Car. O my deare Lord!

 Tar. Be gone.

 Of. Yes, as quietly
as if we were in flight before the foe;
the general pardon at the coronation,
wil bring us off, I'me fure.

 Tar. Alas, good Madam!
I'me forrie that thefe miferies have faln
with fo much rigor on you; pray take comfort:
your husband profecuted with too much violence
Prince *Abilqualit*'s ruine.

 Car. It appeared fo!
what worlds of woes have haplefs I given life to,
and yet furvive them!

 Tar. Do not with fuch furie
torment your innocent felf. I'me fure the Emperor
Abrahen, wil number 't 'mongft his greateft forrows,
that he has loft your husband. I muft give him
notice of thefe proceedings. Beft peace keep you,
and fettle your diftractions.

 Car. not until
I'me fetled in my peaceful urne. This is yet
fome comfort to me, 'midft the floods of woes,
that do overwhelm me for the Princes death,
that I reveng'd it fafely; though I prize
my life at no more value then a foolifh
ignorant Indian does a Diamond,

Revenge for Honour.

which for a bead of Jet or glafs, he changes:
Nor would I keep it, were it not with fuller,
more noble braverie, to take revenge
for my Lord *Abilqualit's* timeleffe flaughter.
I muft ufe craft and myfterie. Diffembling
is held the natural qualitie of our Sex,
nor wil't be hard to practice. This fame *Abrahen,*
that by his brothers ruine weilds the Scepter,
whether out of his innocence or malice,
'twas that perfwaded me to accufe him of
my rape. The die is caft, I am refolv'd
to thee my *Abilqualit* I wil come.
A death for love, 's no death but Martyrdom. *Exit.*

ACTUS QUINTUS. Scena I.

*Enter Abilqualit, Selinthus, Gaffelles, Ofman,
Souldiers, and Muts.*

Abil. NO more, good faithful Souldiers; thank
the powers
divine, has brought me back to you in fafety;
the traitorous practifes againft our life,
and our deare fathers, poifon'd by our brother;
we have difcoverd, and fhall take juft vengance
on the unnatural paricide: Retire
into your tents, and peacefully expect
the event of things, you *Ofman* and *Gaffelles*
fhall into th' Citie with me.
 Of. We wil march
through the world with thee, dear Soveraign,
great *Abilqualit.*
 Abil. Selinthus,
give you our dear *Tarifa* fpeedie notice
we are again among the living: pray him
to let our loyal Subjects in the Citie,
have fure intelligence of our efcape;

and dearest friends and fellowes, let not your
too loud expressions of your joy, for our
unlook'd for welfare, subject to discoverie
our unexpected safety.

Sel. Never fear: they'r trustie Mirmidons, and wil
    stick close
to you their dear *Achilles*; but my Lord,
the wisest may imagine it were safer
for you to rest here 'mong your armed legions,
then to intrust your person in the City,
whereas it seems by the pass'd storie, you'le
not know friends from enemies.

Abil. Selinthus,
Thy honest care declares the zealous duty
thou ow'st thy Soveraign: but what danger can
assault us there, where there is none suspects
we are alive? we'l go surveigh the state
of things, i' th' morning we will seize the Palace,
and then proclaim our Right. Come, valiant Captains,
you shall be our companions.

Gaf. And we'l guard you
safe, as you were encompass'd with an Army.

Sel. You guard your own fools heads: I'st fit his
    safety,
on which our lives and fortunes have dependance,
should be expos'd unto your single valour?
Pray once let your friends rule you, that you may
rule them hereafter. Your good brother *Abrahen*
has a strong faction, it should seem i' th' Court:
and those these Blood-hounds follow'd the sent hotly
till they had worried *Mura.* He has other
allies of no mean consequence; your Eunuch
Mesithes his chief Favourite, and *Simanthes.*

Abil. It was that Villain that betray'd my Love
to him and slaught'red *Mura.*

Sel. Wery likely.
An arranter, falser Parasite, never was
cut like a Colt. Pray Sir, be wise this once,
at my intreaties; and for ever after

use your discretion as you please: these night works
I do not like; yet e're the morning I will bring
Tarifa to you.

Abil. You shall o're rule us. Poor *Caropia*, these
thoughts are thy vot'ries; love thy active fire,
flames out when present, absent in desire. *Exeunt.*

Scen. 2. *Enter Abrahen, Simanthes* and *Mesithes.*

Abr. What State and Dignitie's like that of
  Scepters?
With what an awful Majesty resembles it
the Powers above? the inhabitants of that
Superior world are not more subject
to them, then these to us; they can but tremble
when they do speak in thunder; at our frowns
these shake like Lambs at lightning. Can it be
impiety by any means to purchase
this earthly Deity, Soveraignty. I did sleep
this night with as secure and calme a peace,
as in my former innocence. Conscience,
thou'rt but a terror, first devis'd by th' fears
of Cowardise, a sad and fond remembrance,
which men should shun, as Elephants clear springs,
lest they beheld their own deformities,
                                    Enter Mesithes.
and start at their grim shadowes. Ha, *Mesithes!*

Mes. My Royal Lord!

Abr. Call me thy Friend, *Mesithes*,
thou equally dost share our heart, best Eunuch;
there is not in the stock of earthly blessings
another I could wish to make my state
completely fortunate, but one; and to
atcheive possession of that bliss, thy diligence
must be the fortunate Instrument.

Mes. Be it dangerous
as the affrights Sea men do fain in Tempests,
I'll undertake it for my gracious Soveraign,
and perish, but effect it.

Abr. No, there is
not the leaſt ſhew of peril in't; 'tis the want
of fair *Caropia*'s long coveted beauties
that doth afflict thy *Abrahen*. Love, *Meſithes*,
is a moſt ſtubborn Malady in a Lady, not cur'd
with that felicity, that are other paſſions,
and creeps upon us by thoſe ambuſhes,
that we perceive our ſelves ſooner in love,
then we can think upon the way of loving.
The old flames break more brightly from th' aſhes
where they have long layn hid, like the young Phenix
that from her ſpicie pile revives more glorious.
Nor can I now extinguiſh't; it has paſſ'd
the limits of my reaſon, and intend
my wil, where like a fixt Star 't ſettles,
never to be removed thence.
   Meſ. Ceaſe your fears;
I that could win her for your brother, who
could not boaſt half your maſculine Perfections,
for you will vanquiſh her.   *Enter Simanthes.*
   Sim. My Lord, the widow
of ſlaughtered *Mura*, fair *Caropia* does
humbly intreat acceſs to your dread preſence;
Shall we permit her entrance?
   Abr. With all freedom
and beſt regard. *Meſithes*, this arrives
beyond our wiſh. I'll trie my eloquence
in my own cauſe; and if I fail, thou then
ſhalt be my Advocate.
   Meſ. Your humbleſt vaſſal.
   Abr. With-draw and leave us, and give ſtrict order
none approach our preſence
till we do call. It is not fit her ſorrows   *Enter Car.*
ſhould be ſurvey'd by common eie. *Caropia*, welcom;
and would we could as eaſily give thee comfort
as we allow thee more then mod'rate pitie.
In tears thoſe eyes caſt forth a greater luſtre,
then ſparkling rocks of Diamonds incloſ'd
in ſwelling ſeas of Pearl.

Car. Your Majeſtie
is pleas'd to wanton with my miſeries,
which truly you, if you have nature in you,
ought to bear equall part in your deer brothers
untimely loſſe, occaſion'd by my falſhood,
and your improvident counſel : 'Tis that calls
theſe hearty ſorrows up, I am his Murdreſſe.
  Abr. 'Twas his own deſtinie, not our bad intentions
took him away from earth ; he was too heavenly,
fit only for th' ſocietie of Angels,
'mongſt whom he ſings glad hymns to thy perfeƈtions,
celebrating with ſuch eloquence thy beauties,
that thoſe immortal eſſences forget
to love each other by intelligence,
and doat on the Idea of thy Sweetneſſe.
  Car. Theſe gentle blandiſhments, and his innocent carriage
had I as much of malice as a Tigreſſe
rob'd of her young, would melt me into meekneſſe.
But I'll not be a woman.
  Abr. Sing out, Angel,
and charm the world (were it at mortal diff'rence)
to peace with thine inchantments. What ſoft murmurs
are thoſe that ſteal through thoſe pure roſie organs,
like aromatick weſt-winds, when they flie
through fruitful miſts of fragrant mornings dew,
to get the Spring with child of flowers and ſpices ?
Diſperſe theſe clouds, that like the vail of night,
with unbecoming darkneſſe ſhade thy beauties,
and ſtrike a new day from thoſe orient eies,
to gild the world with brightneſſe.
  Car. Sir, theſe flatteries
neither befit the ears of my true ſorrows,
nor yet the utt'rance of that reall ſadneſſe
ſhould dwel in you. Are theſe the fun'ral rites
you pay the memorie of your roiall Father,
and much lamented Brother ?
  Abr. They were mortall,
and to lament them, were to ſhew I envi'd

th' immortal joyes of that true happineſſe
their glorious ſouls (disfranchis'd from their fleſh)
poſſeſs to perpetuitie and fulneſſe.
Beſides, (*Caropia*) I have other griefs
more neer my heart, that circle't with a ſickneſſe
will ſhortly number me among their fellowſhip,
if ſpeedier remedie be not apply'd
to my moſt deſp'rate maladie.
  Car. I ſhall
(if my hand fail not my determin'd courage)
ſend you to their ſocietie far ſooner
then you expect or covet. Why, great Sir,
what grief, unleſſe your ſorrow for their loſſe,
is't can afflict you, that command all bleſſings
men wittie in ambition of exceſſe
can wiſh, to pleaſe their fancies?
  Abr. The want only
of that which I've ſo long deſird ; thy love,
thy love, *Caropia*, without which my Empire,
and all the pleaſures flowing from its greatneſſe,
will be but burdens, ſoul-tormenting troubles.
There's not a beam ſhot from thoſe grief drown'd
   Comets
but (like the Sun's, when they break forth of ſhowers)
dart flames more hot and piercing. Had I never
doated before on thy divine perfections,
viewing thy beautie thus adorn'd by ſadneſſe,
my heart, though marble, actuated to ſoftneſſe,
would burn like ſacred incenſe, it ſelf being
the Altar, Prieſt, and Sacrifice.
  Car. This is
as unexpected, as unwelcome, Sir.
Howere you're pleas'd to mock me and my griefs
with theſe impertinent, unmeant diſcourſes,
I cannot have ſo prodigal a faith,
to give them the leaſt credit ; and it is
unkindly done, thus to deride my ſorrows.
the virgin Turtles hate to joyn their pureneſs
with widow'd mates ; my Lord, you are a Prince,

and such as much detest to utter falshoods,
as Saints do perjuries: why should you strive then
to lay a bait to captivate my affections, when your
greatnesse conjoin'd with your youths masculine beau-
    ties,
are to a womans frailtie, strong temptations?
You know the storie too of my misfortunes,
that your dead brother, did with vicious loosenesse,
corrupt the chast streams of my spotlesse vertues,
and left me foiled like a long pluck'd rose,
whose leaves dissever'd, have forgon their sweetnesse.

   Abr. Thou hast not (my *Caropia*;) thou to me
art for thy sent stil fragrant, and as precious
as the prime virgins of the Spring, the violets,
when they do first display their early beauties,
til all the winds in love, do grow contentious,
which from their lips should ravish the first kisses.
Caropia, thinkst thou I should fear the Nuptials
of this great Empire, 'cause it was my brothers?
As I succeeded him in all his glories,
'tis fit I do succeed him in his love.
'Tis true, I know thy fame fel by his practise,
which had he liv'd, hee'd have restored by marriage,
by it repair'd thy injur'd honors ruines.
I'me bound to do it in religious conscience;
It is a debt his incens'd ghost would quarrel
me living for, should I not pay't with fulnesse.

   Car. Of what frail temper is a womans weak-
    nesse!
words writ in waters, have more lasting Essence,
then our determinations.

   Abr. Come, I know,
thou must be gentle, I perceive a combat
in thy soft heart, by th' intervening blushes
that strive to adorn thy cheek with purple beauties,
and drive the lovelie liverie of thy sorrows,
the Ivorie palenefs, out of them. Think, *Caropia*,
with what a setled unrevolting truth
I have affected thee; with what heat, what purenefs;

and when upon mature confiderations,
I found I was unworthie to enjoy
a treafure of fuch excellent grace and goodneffe,
I did defift, fmothering my love in anguifh;
anguifh! to which the foul of humane torments,
compar'd, were pains not eafie, but delicious;
yet ftil the fecret flames of my affections,
like hidden virtues in fome bafhful man,
grew great and ferventer by thofe fuppreffions.
Thou wert created only for an Empreffe;
defpife not then thy deftinie, now greatneffe,
love, Empire, and what ere may be held glorious,
courts thy acceptance like obedient Vaffals.

 Car. I have confider'd, and my ferious thoughts
tel me, tis folly to refufe thefe profers:
to put off my mortalitie, the pleafures
of life, which like ful ftreams, do flow from greatneffe,
to wander i' th' unpeopled air, to keep
focietie with ghaftly apparitions,
where's neither voice of friends, nor vifiting fuitors
breaths to delight our ears, and all this for
the fame of a fell murdrefs. I have blood
enough alreadie on my foul, more then
my tears can e're wafh off. My roial Lord,
if you can be fo merciful and gracious,
to take a woman laden with afflictions,
big with true forrow, and religious penitence
for her amifs, her life and after actions,
fhal ftudie to deferve your love. But furely
this is not ferious.

 Abra. Not the vowes which votries
make to the powers above, can be more fraught
with binding fanctitie.
This holy kifs
confirms our mutual vows: never til now
was I true Caliph of *Arabia.*

Revenge for Honour.

Enter, Enter, Enter.

Abr. Ha, what tumult's that!
Be you all furies, and thou the great'ſt of divels,
Abrahen wil ſtand you all, unmov'd as mountains.
This good ſword
if you be air, ſhal diſinchant you from
your borrow'd figures.

Abil. No, ill-natur'd monſter,
we're all corporeal, and ſurvive to take
revenge on thy inhumane acts, at name
of which, the baſhful elements do ſhake
as if they teem'd with prodigies. Doſt not tremble
at thy inhumane villaines ? Dear *Caropia,*
quit the infectious viper, leſt his touch
poiſon thee paſt recoverie.

Abr. No, ſhe ſhall not ;
nor you, until this body be one wound
Lay a rude hand upon me ! *Abilqualit,*
how ere thou ſcapſt my practiſes with life,
I am not now to queſtion ; we were both
ſons to one father, whom, for love of Empire,
when I beleev'd thee ſtrangled by thoſe Muts,
I ſent to his eternal reſt ; nor do I
repent the fact yet, I have been titled *Caliph*
a day, which is to my ambitious thoughts,
honor enough to eternize my big name
to all poſteritie. I know thou art
of valiant noble ſoul ; let not thy brother
fal by ignoble hands, oppreſs'd by number ;
draw thy bright weapon ; as thou art in Empire,
thou art my rival in this Ladies love,
whom I eſteem above all joyes of life :
for her and for this Monarchie, let's trie
our ſtrengths and fates : the impartial fates
to him, who has the better cauſe, in juſtice
muſt needs deſign the victorie.

Abil. In this offer,
though it proceed from deſperateneſſe, not valor ;

z

thou fhowft a mafculine courage, and we wil not
render our caufe fo abject as to doubt,
but our juft arme has ftrength to punifh
thy moft unheard of treacheries.
    Tar. But you fhall not
be fo unjuft to us and to your right,
to try your caufes moft undoubted Juftice,
'gainft the difpairing ruffian ; Souldiers, pul
the Lady from him, and difarm him.
    Abil. Stay !
though he doth merit multitudes of death,
we would not murder his eternitie
by fudden execution ; yeild your felf,
and we'l allow you libertie of life,
til by repentance you have purg'd your fin ;
and fo if poffible, redeem your foul
from future punifhment.
    Abr. Pifh, tel fools of fouls,
and thofe effeminate cowards that do dreame
of thofe fantaftick other worlds : there is
not fuch a thing in nature, all the foul
of men is refolution, which expires
never from valiant men, till their laft breath,
and then with it like to a flame extinguifht'd
for want of matter, 't dos not dy, but rather
ceafes to live. Injoy in peace your Empire,
and as a legacy of *Abrahens* love,
take this fair Lady to your Bride.   *ftab her.*
    Abil. Inhumane Butcher !
has flain the Lady. Look up, beft *Caropia,*
run for our furgeons : I'le give half my Empire
to fave her precious life.
    Abr. She has enough,
or mine aym fail'd me, to procure her paffage
to the eternal dwellings : nor is this
cruelty in me ; I alone was worthy
to have injoy'd her beauties. Make good hafte
Caropia, or my foul, if I have any,
will hover for thee in the clouds. This was

Revenge for Honour. 355

the fatal engine which betray'd our father
to his untimely death, made by *Simanthes*
for your ufe, *Abilqualit* : and who has this
about him and would be a flave to your bafe mercy,
deferved death more than by dayly tortures ;
and thus I kiff'd my laft breath. Blaft you all. *dies.*
   Tar. Damn'd defperate villain.
   Abil. O my dear *Caropia*,
my Empire now will be unpleafing to me
fince I muft lofe thy company. This furgeon,
where's this furgeon ?
   Sel. Drunk perhaps.
   Car. 'Tis but needleffe,
no humane help can fave me : yet me thinks
I feel a kind of pleafing eafe in your
imbraces. I fhould utter fomething,
and I have ftrength enough, I hope, left yet
to effect my purpofe. In revenge for your
fuppof'd death, my lov'd Lord, I flew my husband,
   Abil. I'me forry thou haft that fin to charge thy
    foul with,
twas rumour'd by the fouldiers.
   Sel. Couzens mine, your necks are fafe agen now.
   Car. And came hither
with an intent to have for your fake flain your
    brother
Abrahen, had not his curtefie and winning carriage
alter'd my refolution, with this poniard
I'de ftruck him here about the heart.   Stabs *Abil.*
   Abil. O I am flain, *Caropia*,
and by thy hand. Heavens, you are juft, this is
revenge for thy dear honor which I murdred,
though thou wer't confenting to it.
   Car. True, I was fo,
and not repent it yet, my fole ambition
was to have liv'd an Empreffe, which fince fate
would not allow, I was refolv'd no woman
after my felfe fhould ere injoy that glory,
you dear *Abilqualit* : which fince my

weak strength has serv'd me to performe, I dye
willingly as an infant. O now I faint,
life's death to those that keep it by constraint.   *dye.*
    Tar. My dear Lord,
is there no hopes of life ? must we be wretched ?
    Abil. Happier, my *Tarifa*, by my death :
but yesterday I playd the part in jest
which I now act in earnest. My *Tarifa*,
the Empire's thine, I'me sure thou'lt rul't
with justice, and make the subject happy. Thou hast
    a Son
of hopefull growing vertues to succeed thee,
commend me to him, and from me intreat him
to shun the temptings of lascivious glances.
    Sel. 'Las good Prince !
heele dy indeed. I fear, he is so full
of serious thoughts and Counsels.
    Abil. For this slaughtred body,
let it have decent burial with slain *Muras*,
but let not *Abrahens* corps have so much honor
to come ith' royal monument : lay mine
by my dear fathers : for that trecherous Eunuch,
and Lord *Simanthes*, use them as thy justice
tells thee they have merited ; for Lord *Selinthus*,
advance him (my *Tarifa*) hee's of faithfull
and well deserving vertues.
    Sel. So I am,
I thought 'twould come to me anon :
poor Prince, I e'ne could dy with him.
    Abil. And for those souldiers, and those our most
    faithfull
Muts, that my life once sav'd, let them be
well rewarded ; death and I are almost now
at unitie. Farewell.   *dyes.*
    Tar. Sure I shall not
survive these sorrows long. Muts, take those Traitors
to prison ; we will shortly passe their sentence,
which shall be death inevitable. Take up
that fatal instrument of poisonous mischief,

Revenge for Honour.

and fee it burn'd, *Gafelles.* Gentlemen,
Fate has made us your King againſt our wiſhes.
 Sel. Long live *Tarifa,* Caliph of *Arabia.*
 Tar. We have no time now for your acclamations;
theſe are black ſorrows Feſtival. Bear off
in ſtate that royal Bodie; for the other,
ſince twas his will, let them have burial,
but in obſcuritie. By this it may,
as by an ev'dent rule be underſtood,
they're onely truly great, wh' are truly good.
 Recorders   *Exeunt omnes.*
 Flouriſh.

FINIS.

EPILOGUE.

I'M much displeas'd the Poet has made me
 The Epilogue to his ſad Tragedie.
Would I had dy'd honeſtly amongſt the reſt,
Rather then live to th' laſt, now to be preſt
To death by your hard Cenſures. Pray you ſay,
What is it you diſlike ſo in this Play,
That none applauds? Beleeve it, I ſhould faint,
Did not ſome ſmile, and keep me by conſtraint
From the ſad qualm. Wnat pow'r is in your breath,
That you can ſave alive, and doom to death,
Even whom you pleaſe? thus are your judgments free,
Moſt of the reſt are ſlain, you may ſave me.
But if death be the word, I pray beſtow it
Where it beſt fits. Hang up the Poet.

NOTES AND ILLUSTRATIONS.

PAGE 1.

The Widdowes Teares.

Although it cannot be faid that there were two editions of *The Widdowes Teares* in 1612, the copies with that date have fome variations, probably introduced at the inftance of the author, who feems to have been rather more anxious about the correctnefs of his productions than moft of his contemporaries.

" The plot of Lyfander and Cynthia is borrowed from Petronius Arbiter's Satyricon, being the ftory of the Matron of Ephefus related by Eumolpus: a ftory fince handled by feveral other pens, as Janus Doufa, the father, in his notes on this ftory, and Gabbema, in the laft edition of Petronius, who obferve that it was tranflated into Latin verfe by Romulus, an antique grammarian: and into French rhyme by Hebertus. We have it not only in the Seven Wife Mafters, but alfo I have read the fame ftory in the Cento Novelle Antiche di Carlo Gualteruzzi, Nov. 51."— *Langbaine.*

PAGE 17.

O the Gods? fpurn'd out by Groomes like a bafe Bifogno?

This is a term of contempt frequently ufed in our old plays. It is probably derived from the Ital. *bifogno*, or the Fr. *befoin* want, need), and is generally applied to people in want or of the ower rank. See Churchyard's *Challenge*, 1593, p. 85, and *Love's Cure*, by Beaumont and Fletcher, Act 2, fc. 1.

PAGE 18.

No yong Adonis *to front you there?*

Some of the copies read "*myftical*" inftead of *yong*.

Page 18.

Your not-headed Countrie Gentleman.

So in Chaucer's *Canterbury Tales*, the yeman is thus deſcribed :—

"A *nott-head* had he with a brown viſage."

A perſon was ſaid to be *nott-pated* when the hair was cut ſhort and round. Ray ſays the word was, in his time, ſtill uſed in Eſſex for *polled* or *ſhorn*.

Page 20.

So there's venie for venie.

i.e. touch for touch, bout for bout ; a technical term at fencing and cudgel-playing, from the French *venue*. The word occurs in act iii. ſc. 2, of *The Old Law* ; but appears to have been out of faſhion with the fantaſtic gallants of the times very early. Captain Bobadil, in *Every Man in his Humour*, act i. ſc. 5, ſays, in anſwer to Maſter Matthew's requeſt for one *venue*, " *Venue!* fie ; " moſt groſs denomination as ever I heard : O, the ſtoccata, " while you live, ſir, note that.".

Page 23.

by the next Ripier that rides that way with Mackerell.

" Ripiers (*riparii*)," ſays Minſhieu, " be thoſe that uſe to bring fiſh from the ſea-coaſt to the inner parts of the land. It is a word made of the Latin *ripa*, the bank or ſhore."

Page 23.

a Bone to tire on.

i.e. to peck at : a term of falconry.

Page 29.

Admitted? I, into her heart, Ile able it.

An old phraſe, ſignifying to undertake, or anſwer for. So in *King Lear* (act iv. ſc. 7) :—

" None does offend, none, I ſay, none *I'll able 'em*."

Page 34.

who penn'd the Pegmas.

i.e., the bills fixed up at pageants to give ſome account of their contents.

Page 71.

*There ſticks an Achelons horne of all, Copie enough,
As much as Alizon of ſterames receiues.*

Or lofty Ilea /howes of /hadie leaues.
The firſt line of this paſſage ſeems hopeleſſly corrupt. I once thought the words, "Copie enough," were attributable rather to the printer's devil than to Lyſander, and had got interpolated into the text through the ſtupidity of the compoſitor and the negligence of the "reader." But I find that a former Editor of this play explains "Copie" as *Copia,* and ſuppoſes the paſſage to refer to the Cornucopia, or horn of plenty.

PAGE 116.
Twinns of which Hippocrates ſpeaks.
See alſo *The Gentleman Vſher* (Vol. I., p. 309).

PAGE 142.
Read the old ſtoick Pherecides, that tels thee
Me truly, and ſayes that I Ophioneus—
Deuiliſh Serpent, by interpretation ; was generall
Captaine of that rebellious hoſt of ſpirits that
Wag'd warre with heauen.
See the Fragments of Pherecides, the ſtoic, a rather recondite author.

PAGE 155.
thoſe dreadfull bolts
The Cyclops Ram in Ioues Artillery.
This energetic expreſſion, thoroughly charaćteriſtic of Chapman, occurs alſo in *Buſſy d'Ambois* (Vol. II, p. 70.)

PAGE 201.
Una arbuſta non alit duos Erithicos :—
Οὐ τρέφει μία λόχμη δύο ἐριϑάκους. *Schol. Ariſtoph. Veſp.* 922. *Stephani Theſaur.* ſ. Ἐριϑακος. *Plin. Hiſt. Nat.* X, 29, 44.

PAGE 202.
I'll imitate Lyſander] See *Plutarch. Lyſand.* VII.

PAGE 203.
That Bohemie neither cares.
'Bohemia' in this verſe, which in the original edition is erroneouſly given to Alphonſus, is to be read as a diſſyllable, as if it was written 'Bemia.' The ſame contraćtion occurs on page 213, where, however, the word is uſed as a triſyllable :
And do accept the king of Bohemia.

PAGE 207.
When we once are set.

I am unable to fay, whether or not the cuftom alluded to in the text was really obferved in the elective council; thus much, however, is certain, that it admirably harmonizes with the directions contained in the Golden Bull: 'They (viz. the Electors) fhall proceed to the Election and fhall not in any manner depart out of the faid Citie of Franckford, before that the greater part of them fhall have chofen a temporall head or governour of the world or of Chriftendome, a King of Romains, to be Emperour, which if they fhall prolong or deferre the fpace of thirty dayes from the day of taking their oathes, then the faid thirty dayes being expired, they fhall eate nothing but bread and water, nor by any meanes goe away from the faid Citie, untill or before they or the greater number of them fhall have chofen the ruler or temporall head of Chriftendome, as aforefaid.'

PAGE 214.
Count Mansfield.

This name was familiar to the poet's contemporaries, the famous Count Erneft Mansfield having paid a vifit to London in 1621 or 1622.

See alfo *Byron's Confpiracie* (Vol. II, p. 199).

PAGE 220.
Ein filtz geben.

i. e. I fhould chide you. This expreffion frequently occurs in the plays of Ayrer, of Duke Heinrich Julius, in Simpliciffimus, and other writers of the time.

PAGE 234.
Bowls of Reinfal.

'*Reinfal* (*Rainfal*), *vinum Rifolium, Wein von Rivoglio in Iftrien*' fays Schmeller in his *Bayerifches Wörterbuch*, III. 95; and O. Schade in his *Altdeutfches Wörterbuch* s. h. v. has adopted this explanation. Karajan, *Fontes Rer. Auftriac* (Vienn. 1855), I. 1, 17, however, has fhown that there is no place of that name in Iftria. J. Grimm, in his Preface to F. F. Röfsler's *Deutfche Rechtfdenkmäler aus Böhmen und Mähren* (Prag, 1845), I. VII, thinks the 'Reinfal' to have come from Rivoli near Verona or from Botzen in the Tyrol. Compare alfo

Zedler's *Univerfal-Lexikon* (Leipzig und Halle, 1742), XXXI 282 fq.; *Brandt's Narrenfchiff* ed. by Zarncke, 63, 87; and Keller *Faftnachtfpiele* (*Mittheil. def. Liter. Vereins* XLVI), 362.

PAGE 234.

Nay, gentle Forrefter.

Before this verfe a line or two feem to have dropped out, in which the Emperor may have fpoken of Prince Edward's not joining in the univerfal merriment.

PAGE 235—9.

Sam Got.

'*Sam Got*' either means 'with God,' or it may be an abbreviation of '*fam mir Got*,' *i. e. fo mir Gott helfe*. See Schade's *Althochdeutfches Wörterbuch* f. *Sam*, and *Lauremberg's Scherzgedichte* ed. by Lappenberg, 256.

PAGE 238.

With Corances on their heads.

The much difcuffed 'crants' in Hamlet V. 1, receives a new light from this paffage. Meffrs. Halliwell and Wright in their new edition of Nares' Gloffary have repeated the remark of Nares', that 'no other example of the word has been found,' whilft it occurs twice in this tragedy. They are further of opinion, that Shakefpeare probably found this word in fome legend of Hamlet, which we cannot but think moft improbable, as the word could only be found in a German (or Danifh) legend, and Shakefpeare therefore muft be fuppofed to have read German or Danifh. Befides no German legend of Hamlet is known to exift. Shakefpeare, in our opinion, made the acquaintance of this German importation at the Steelyard, or he witneffed fome German funeral in London, where the coffin of a young girl, according to the German cuftom, was decked with 'crances;' nay, both may have been the cafe, and we imagine the word thus to have found its way into Shakefpeare and Chapman. At all events it was not an entire ftranger to their contemporaries. Mr. Lettfom has very juftly obferved, that 'crants' is not the plural, but the fingular number (fee Shakefpeare's Works ed. by Dyce, 2nd Ed. VII. 239). From the prefent paffage it would appear that we ought to write 'crance;' this is confirmed by the Anglicifed form of the German Chriftian name 'Hans,' which in Mr. W. Durrant Cooper's 'Lift of Foreign Proteftants and Aliens' is ufually fpelt 'Hance,' or 'Haunce.'

PAGE 238.

An upfpring.

'Upfpring,' neither means an 'upftart,' as moft Shakefperian editors (as well as Nares, though he cites the prefent line from Alphonfus) have imagined, nor the German '*Walzer,*' as Schlegel has tranflated it in Hamlet I, 4, but it is the '*Häpfauf,*' the laft and confequently wildeft dance at the old German merrymakings. See *Ayrer's Dramen* ed. by Keller, IV. 2840 and 2846:

Ey, jtzt geht erft der hupffauff an.
Ey, Herr, jtzt kummt erft der hupffauff.

No epithet could therefore be more appropriate to this drunken dance, than Shakefpeare's 'fwaggering.'

PAGE 262.

And fhould be lamps.

Compare the Golden Bull (1619) Chap. I: '— the feaven Electors of the Empire, by whom (as by feven Candleftickes, fhining in the unitie of a fevenfold fpirit) the holy Empire fhould be illuminated.' The Latin text has '*velut feptem candelabra lucentia.*'

PAGE 263.

Mein allerlievejt hufband.

According to Dr. Wm. Bell (Shakefpeare's Puck, III. 207 fq.) this 'decidedly Teutonic word occurs only once in the Englifh language,' viz. in 2 Henry VI, I. 1: 'mine alderliefeft fovereign.'

PAGE 271.

Her dainty rofe-Corance.

See Note on p. 238. In Germany a '*Rofenkranz*' ferved as a fymbol of virginity, and therefore in old popular fongs often denotes maidenhead itfelf. *Uhland's Volkflieder*, I. No. 2 and 3 (with Note in Vol. II. 997); I. No. 114 and 173 (p. 456). Shakefpeare and his contemporaries alfo fymbolize maidenhead as a rofe. *All's Well that Ends Well*, IV.

2 : " But when you have our rofes." *Othello*, V. 2 : " When I have plucked thy rofe." Chapman, *Buſſy d'Ambois* (Vol. II. p. 30).

> Honour, whats that ? your fecond maidenhead :
> And what is that ? a word ; the word is gone,
> The thing remaines ; the rofe is pluckt, the ftalke
> Abides.

PAGE 281.
Than ere Laocoon ran.
For the fact alluded to compare *Virg. Æn.*, II. 40 fqq.

PAGE 285.
Revenge for Honour. 1654.
"This play," fays Langbaine, "I have feen acted many years .go at the *Nurſery* in *Barbican.*"

INDEX.

Accius Nævius, ii. 17.
Acheron, i. 230.
Achilles, i. 235; [ii. 142, 253; iii. 53, 278.
Actæon, i. 196; iii. 18.
Adelafia, i. 327, 344.
Adonis, ii. 377.
Æneas, iii. 23, 64.
Agamemnon, iii. 139.
Agincourt, i. 235.
Ajax, ii. 58.
Alcides, i. 232; ii. 208, 270.
Alcoran, Turkifh, ii. 243; wine forbidden by, iii. 314.
Ale-Knights, i. 316.
Alexander the Great, i. 103; ii. 283; iii. 144, 292.
Alexandria, i. 39.
Alizon, iii. 71.
Alphonfus, Emperor of Germany, iii. 195 *fqq*.
Amiens, Siege of, ii. 220.
Anius, river, iii. 156.
Antigone, ii. 123.
Antipodes, the, i. 196; ii. 81.
Apollo, ii. 195; iii. 200.
Arabia, i. 41.
Arctos, ii. 287.
Ardennes, Foreft of, ii. 24, 137, 262.
Argus, i. 196; iii. 110.
Ariadne, i. 28.
Arion, ii. 233.
Ariftophanes, iii. 100.
Ariftotle, iii. 60, 201.
Armenia, ii. 24.
Arras pictures, ii. 214.
Afs in lion's fkin, ii. 19, 20; iii. 85.

Ate, iii. 245.
Athamas, iii. 263.
Atlas, ii. 22, 42, 287; iii. 105.
Atropos, iii. 23.
Auguftus Cæfar, ii. 64, 266.
Aurora, i. 261; ii. 287.

Bacchus, i. 98.
Beauty, defcribed as a quinteffence, i. 116.
Bees, fimile of, iii. 157.
Berenice, i. 29.
Blackthorn, the, ii. 269.
Boötes, ii. 83.
Brutus, ii. 123.
Byron, Duke of, ii. 179—320.

Cæfar, iii. 126 *fqq.*, 278.
Caius Caffius, iii. 274.
Camel, the, begs horns of Jove, ii. 125, 233.
Camillus, ii. 7, 256.
Caffandra, ii. 140.
Caffimere, Duke of, ii. 145.
Catiline's confpiracy, iii. 132.
Cato, iii. 126 *fqq*.
Cerberus, ii. 53, 68.
Character of a virtuous wife, i. 308.
Chymæra, ii. 67.
Cicero, quoted, i. 75.
Clotho, ii. 59.
Clytemneftra, iii. 247.
Cornelia, iii. 126.
Corrucus, i. 16, 26.
Cratinus, i. 113.
Creon, ii. 123.
Cupid, i. 36, 118, 226, 294; ii. 30, 263, 329; iii. 8, 29, 48.
Curculio of Plautus, i. 241, 343.

Curtius, ii. 218.
Cyclops, the, ii. 70, 218; iii. 155.
Cynthia, i. 190; ii. 65.
Cyrus, iii. 145.
Cythæron, ii. 78.

Dapfyle, ii. 262.
Demades, ii. 134.
Demetrius Phalerius, ii. 134.
Demofthenes, ii. 134.
Deucalion, iii. 58.
Diana, i. 29, 267; iii. 18, 23.
Dido, i. 236, 343; ii. 341; iii. 64.
Diogenes, i. 58.
Domitian, ii. 125.
Dreux, Siege of, ii, 209.

Eagle, the, i. 160; ii. 169.
Echo, i. 107.
Elizabeth, Princefs, marriage of, iii. 89 *fqq*.
Elizabeth, Queen, ii. 13; her Speech to the Duke of Byron, 229.
Empedocles on Etna, iii. 185.
Epaminondas, ii. 7, 110.
Epilepfy, iii. 138.
Eros, iii. 116.
Effex, Earl of, ii 281, 309.
Etna, ii. 271.
Eunomia, iii. 94, 110.
Euphorbus, ii. 123.
Eupolis, i. 113.
Eurotas, iii. 154.
Eurus, i. 41.
Eve and the ferpent, i. 60.

Field, Nat., performs the character of Buffy D'Ambois, ii. 3; account of, 407.
Flora, a noted Roman courtezan, iii. 139.
Fox, the, who loft his tail, i. 117; compared with the lion, iii. 202.

Ganimede, ii. 374.
Garlic, i. 215, 217, 236.

Gefta Romanorum, ii. 360.
Guevara's Golden Epiftles, i. 302, 344.

Habakuk, i, 63.
Hart, Mr., acts the part of Buffy D'Ambois, ii. 407.
Hazlitt, William, on Monfieur D'Olive, i. 341.
Hecate, ii. 92.
Hector, holds up the brazen lance, ii. 23.
Helen of Greece, i. 198.
Helicon, i. 227; ii. 368.
Hella the forcerefs, i. 33.
Hercules, i. 266, 278; ii. 93, 141, 173, 195, 341, 366; iii. 38, 70, 119, 230.
Hermes, i. 232.
Hero and Leander, ii. 366.
Herod, ii. 65.
Hippocrates, his account of the twins, i. 309; iii. 116; on the flatus Hypocondriacus, 293.
Homer, his difcernment in fpite of blindnefs, i. 9; his battle of the Frogs and Mice, 278; his Iliads and Odyffes, ii. 127; his purpofe in the character of Achilles, 142; his critics, 160.
Horns, praife of, i. 182.
Howard, Sir Thomas, ii. 99.
Hubberd, Sir II., iii. 89.
Hudibras, i. 344.
Huguenots, the fcourge of, ii. 258, 295.
Hybla, i. 288, 317.
Hydra, ii. 45.
Hymen, ii. 194, 371; iii. 48, 50, 51; Hymn to, 120.

Jacob's ftaff, iii. 236.
Ida, ii. 367.
Jewifh Executions in Germany, iii. 282.
Ilea, iii. 71.
Io, iii. 121.
Jones, Inigo, iii. 87.
Iris, iii. 61.

Ifis, ftatue of, i. 6; honour done to, iii. 68.
Judas, iii. 282.
Juno, ii. 47, 208; iii. 19, 58, 61, 62.
Jupiter Ammon, ii. 58.

Kings, ii. 123, 139, 191, 284.

Lachefis, ii. 59.
Lamb, Charles, on Buffy D'Ambois, ii.
Laocoon, iii. 281.
Leda's Diftaff, iii. 37.
Lefbos, ifle of, iii. 179.
Louis XI., his Scots guard, ii. 305.
Lucian, iii. 100.
Lucifer, ii. 287.
Lycurgus, 38, 154.

Machiavelli, i. 138.
Manlius, ii. 305.
Marcus Aurelius, ii. 360.
Mars, i. 154.
Meander, i. 268.
Medea, i. 333.
Memphis, i. 6.
Menander, quoted, iii. 99.
Menelaus, i. 140.
Menetiades, iii. 278.
Mentz, defcribed, iii. 260.
Mercury, i. 151; iii. 58, 61.
Middlefex, Earl of, Dedication to, iii. 125.
Middleton, quoted, ii. 408.
Minos, i. 75.
Mirror of Magiftrates, ii. 360.
Monopolies, iii. 9.
Morpheus, i. 146.
Morrice-dance, i. 228.

Nafo (fee Ovid).
Neptune, iii. 110.
Nero, i. 330; ii. 266.
Niobe, iii. 55.

Olympus, ii. 22.
Omphale, iii. 38.

Ophioneus, iii. 140.
Ophir, gold of, ii, 205.
Orpheus, ii. 306.
Ovid, quoted, i. 220.
Oxford, Earl of, ii. 144.
Padua, ii. 377.
Præana, iii. 103.
Palm, fimile of, iii. 272, 315.
Pan, i. 118.
Pandarus, i. 221.
Panthea, iii. 116.
Parcæ, iii. 120.
Paris and Helen, ii. 126.
Parnaffus, i. 256; ii. 370.
Patroclus, iii. 278.
Peleus, ii. 67.
Pelides, ii. 205.
Pelion, beafts of, ii. 67, 78.
Penelope, iii. 10, 11.
Perfeus and Andromeda, i. 29.
Pettie's Pallace of Pleafure, i. 327, 344.
Phalaris, Bull of, iii. 281.
Pharfalia, iii. 157, 168.
Phemis, iii. 94.
Pherecides, the ftoic, iii. 142.
Philips, Sir Edward, Dedication to, iii. 89, 91.
Phœbus, iii. 53, 111, 113, 122.
Phœnix, the, i. 78.
Pindus and Offa, ii. 93.
Plato, ii. 101, 212; iii. 201.
Plautus, i, 261; quoted, 262, 343.
Plutus, iii. 94, 96, 100, 101, &c.
Po, lilies of the, i. 288; and Ticino, ii. 197.
Pompey, ii. 143; iii. 126 et fqq. fæpius.
Porus, King of Æthiopia, i. 41, 44, 47, 48.
Proteus, iii. 102.
Ptolemy, King of Egypt, i 17, 39.
Pygmalion, and the ftatue, i. 221.
Pythagoras, ii. 123; on witches, 372.

Queen Elizabeth, ii. 13, 229.

Rainbow, the, ii. 131.
Reed, Jo., of Mitton, Dedication to, iii. 3.
Rhefus, king of Arabia, i. 41, 44, 47, 48.
Rhine, the, defcribed, iii. 258.
Rome, i. 12, 325 ; ii. 145.

Saturn, i. 195 ; ii. 46.
Satyr, the, affrighted by the found of his own horn, iii. 57.
Savonorala, *de Urinis*, i. 217, 342.
Scamander, ii. 205.
Scylla and Charybdis, ii. 53.
Semele, ii. 194.
Sertorius, ii. 303.
Shelley, P. B., takes a motto from Chapman's *Confpiracie of Byron* for his *Revolt of Illam*, ii. 413.
Sleep and Death, iii. 176, 188.
Solon, iii. 81.
Song of Love and Beauty, iii. 116.
Sophocles, ii. 123.
Sophrofyne, ii. 262.
Spenfer, Edm., his eleventh Eclogue, i. 343.
Syfiphus, ii, 112, iii. 102.

Tennyfon, quoted, i. 339.
Terence, his *Heautontimorumenos* the model of All Fools, i. 339.
Tethis, iii. 113.
Themiftocles, ii. 7.

Theorbo, the, i. 144, 145, 170, 226.
Tithonus, i. 258 ; ii. 56.
Tobacco, i. 16, 137, 175, 214 ; praife of, 216.
Trout, i. 149.

Valentines, chofen blindfold, i. 199 ; St. Valentine's day, 235.
Venice, ii. 377.
Venus, i. 238; ii. 77, 366; iii. 12, 27, 33, 36, 43, 80.
Violets, iii. 351.
Virgil, iii. 20; quoted, 103.
Virginius, iii. 263.
Ulyffes, ii. 253 ; iii. 11, 102, 110.
Utica, iii. 152, 192, 194.
Vulcan, i. 154 ; iii. 145.

Walfingham, Sir Thomas, Dedicatory Sonnet to, i. 111 ; Dedication of *Byron's Confpiracie* to, ii. 181.
Wife, character of a virtuous, i. 308.
Winchefter goofe, i. 233, 342.
Wind and the Sun, Fable of, ii. 117.

Xerxes, ii. 7.

Youth, i. 19.

Zephyr, iii. 120.

www.ingramcontent.com/pod-product-compliance
Lightning Source LLC
Chambersburg PA
CBHW020303240426
43673CB00039B/692